# TRAVEL AND TOURISM

# TRAVEL AND TOURISM

John Ward

**LONGMAN**

**Addison Wesley Longman Limited**
Edinburgh Gate, Harlow
Essex CM20 2JE, United Kingdom
*and Associated Companies throughout the world*

First published 1997

ISBN 0 582 31256 6

**British Library Cataloguing-in-Publication Data**
A catalogue record for this book is available from the British Library.

Printed in Great Britain by Henry Ling Ltd., at the Dorset Press, Dorchester, Dorset

# Contents

## Module 4  Employment in the tourist industry

# Preface

## The growing importance of Travel and Tourism

Travel and tourism has increased in popularity as a subject of study in schools and colleges at a tremendous rate over the past few years. Though often referred to as a single industry, travel and tourism is made up of a wide range of very different, but interdependent, activities and operations. These include accommodation, catering, transport, tourist attractions, tour operations, and retail and business travel. It also has a considerable degree of overlap with other leisure and recreation sectors such as sport, entertainment and the arts. Tourists are frequent users of the services and facilities provided by these sectors.

The importance of the travel, tourism and leisure industries in creating new employment is one factor in their growing popularity as subjects of study. They are also perceived as 'young' industries, in the sense that they employ a young work-force, offer a rapidly changing working environment and are part of a process whose main purpose is to provide enjoyment. However, any industrial activity that develops so rapidly on such a large scale is bound to have some impacts that are potentially harmful and that require careful planning and management. The case studies in this book look at both the benefits tourism can bring and at the harm tourists can do. Many of the activities challenge students to find ways of improving the travel and tourism industry's performance.

Government and industry reports frequently suggest that the future of the travel and tourism industry in Britain will depend very much on improving the quality of service and the value for money that visitors receive and that this can only be achieved by raising standards of training and professionalism. GCSE Travel and Tourism and GNVQ Leisure and Tourism have a part to play in raising an initial awareness of what is needed to sustain a thriving tourism industry.

## The purpose and structure of the book

This book is intended to provide background knowledge for students studying for GCSE Travel and Tourism. Because of the degree of content overlap between GCSE Travel and Tourism and GNVQ Leisure and Tourism, especially at Intermediate Level, the book should also provide a useful insight into current industry practice for GNVQ students.

The book is divided into four main sections, each one covering one of the four modules in the GCSE Travel and Tourism syllabus:

- Tourist destinations
- Leisure facilities
- The social, cultural and environmental impacts of tourism
- Employment in travel and tourism industry

Within each of these four sections there is a general introduction and four contrasting case studies. These case studies cover a range of different industry sectors and vary in scale from an international airline to an independent arts centre.

## A case study approach

Case study approaches are valuable in helping students to understand the operational practices of an industry. They help to demonstrate how organizations begin, develop and change. They also place subjects such as marketing, customer service, event management, health and safety, tourism impacts and conservation in contexts which make them more accessible to students. Many of the ideas and issues raised by the case studies will have applications to other companies, organizations, locations and facilities that students may have chosen to study.

The case studies are drawn from a variety of geographical locations. Some users of the book may feel their own towns or regions are under-represented, one of the drawbacks of using just 12 UK-based case studies! Many of the activities specifically require students to focus on a different local facility, destination or organization.

## Activities for students

The activities that appear regularly throughout the text are a vital part of the book. They are intended both to test the students' understanding of the material in the case studies and also to encourage them to apply their own knowledge, skills and understanding to issues and problems that have to be overcome by people working in or otherwise affected by tourism. They will certainly help to prepare students for the demands of the GCSE Travel and Tourism examination, the first part of which requires questions to be answered on case study material. However, they can also be used to develop skills that are valued in other areas of the curriculum, by potential employers and by Further and Higher Education.

Most of the activities have several different parts, requiring different responses. Among other things, students are required to discuss issues, carry out research, write plans, reports, letters, presentations and guidance notes. There are opportunities for both individual and group work. The tasks suggested frequently encourage discussion as a means of building understanding and identifying a range of possible conclusions. It is unlikely that there will be time to use all the activities in the book on a GCSE course. The number of activities offered within the text is intended to be sufficiently extensive to allow teachers and lecturers to offer choice and to direct students towards activities appropriate to their particular interests and abilities. In other words, it is not intended that all students should be expected or have the time to attempt all sections of the activities.

## Glossary

A glossary giving definitions and explanations of key words and phrases used in the case studies can be found on page 287.

## Packs for teachers and lecturers

This textbook will complement two packs of material developed for teachers and lecturers to help to define the scope of the syllabus content and the main concepts and principles that students should understand. These are available from:

The Travel & Tourism Programme
3 Redman Court
Bell Street
Princes Risborough            phone: 01844 344208
Bucks HP27 0AA                fax:  01844 274340

# Acknowledgements

We are grateful to the following individuals and organisations for permission to reproduce material:

Peak Tourism Partnership for figures 2.7, 2.8 and 2.9 (©Peak National Park)
Chester City Council for figures 3.1, 3.2, 3.3, 3.7, 3.8, 3.9, 3.10, 3.11, 3.12
The NEC Group for figures 4.1, 4.2, 4.3, 4.4, 4.5 and 4.6
Derngate Trust for figures 5.1, 5.2, 5.3, 5.4, 5.5 and 5.8
The Hull Arena for figures 6.1, 6.2 and 6.5
Oxford United Football Club for figures 7.1, 7.2, 7.3 and 7.4
Knebworth House for figures 8.1, 8.2, 8.3, 8.4, 8.5, 8.6 and 8.7
Uluru-Kata Tjuta Cultural Centre for figures 9.2, 9.3, 9.4, 9.5 and 9.6
David Young for figures 10.4, 10.5 and 10.6
Magic of the Orient for figure 12.5
Holiday Inn, Maidenhead for figures 13.1, 13.2, 13.3, 13.4, 13.5, 13.6 and 13.7
Lilleshall Sports and Conference Centre Ltd for figures 14.1, 14.2 and 14.3
British Airways plc for figures 15.1, 15.2, 15.3, 15.4, 15.5 and 15.6
Chessington World of Adventures for figures 16.2, 16.4, 16.5 and 16.6

Whilst every effort has been made to contact copyright holders, this has not always proved possible, and we would like to take this opportunity to apologise to anyone whose rights we may have inadvertently infringed.

# Grids showing how case studies relate to elements of the GCSE Travel and Tourism syllabus

| Module one | Intro | cs 1 | cs 2 | cs 3 | cs 4 | also in cs |
|---|---|---|---|---|---|---|
| *1.1  Components of a tourist destination* | * | | | | | |
| 1.1.1  Accommodation | | * | * | * | | |
| 1.1.2  Attractions | | * | * | * | | |
| 1.1.3  Transport systems | | * | | | * | |
| 1.1.4  Facilities and services | | * | | * | * | 5,6,7,8,13 |
| *1.2  Different types of destination* | * | | | | | |
| 1.2.1  Seaside Resort | | * | | | | |
| 1.2.2  Countryside | | | * | | | |
| 1.2.3  Historic Town | | | | * | | |
| 1.2.4  Major event or conference venue | | | | | * | |
| 1.2.5  Activity centre | | | * | | | |
| *1.3  Factors that affect destination choice* | * | | | | | 16 |
| 1.3.1  Climate | | * | | | | 10 |
| 1.3.2  Location | | * | * | * | * | 9 |
| 1.3.3  Accessibility | | * | * | * | * | |
| 1.3.4  Purpose of visits | * | | * | | | |
| 1.3.5  Price | | | | | | 5 |
| 1.3.6  Marketing and promotion | | | * | * | * | 11 |
| *1.4  Factors affecting tourism in different destinations* | | | | | | |
| 1.4.1  Economy | | * | | | * | |
| 1.4.2  Local and national politics | | * | | * | | 11 |
| 1.4.3  Regulation | | | * | | | 7 |
| 1.4.4  Visitor numbers and visitor spend | | * | | * | * | 16 |

| Module two | Intro | cs 5 | cs 6 | cs 7 | cs 8 | also in cs |
|---|---|---|---|---|---|---|
| *2.1 Factors determining the level/range of local leisure provision* | * | | | | | |
| 2.1.1  Demand | * | | | | | |
| 2.1.2  Funding | * | * | | * | | |
| 2.1.3  Location | | * | * | | * | 13 |
| *2.2 Operation of leisure facilities* | | | | | | |
| 2.2.1  Management structure | | | * | | | 16 |
| 2.2.2  Staffing | | * | * | * | | 16 |
| 2.2.3  Pricing policy | | | * | * | | |
| 2.2.4  Health and safety | | | * | | * | 2 |
| 2.2.5  Community relations | | * | | * | | |
| 2.2.6  Special interests | | | | | * | 2 |

| Module two | Intro | cs 5 | cs 6 | cs 7 | cs 8 | also in cs |
|---|---|---|---|---|---|---|
| 2.2.7  Programmes of events | | * | * | | * | |
| 2.2.8  Promotion | | | * | * | * | |
| *2.3  Staging events* | | | | | | 4 |
| 2.3.1  Planning process | | * | | | * | |
| 2.3.2  Resources | | * | | | * | |
| 2.3.3  Schedules | | * | | | * | |
| 2.3.4  Safety and security | | * | | * | * | |
| 2.3.5  Evaluation | | | | | * | |

| Module three | Intro | cs 9 | cs 10 | cs 11 | cs 12 | also in cs |
|---|---|---|---|---|---|---|
| *3.1  Impact of tourism on society* | * | | | | | |
| 3.1.1  Employment | | | * | | | 1 |
| 3.1.2  Wealth | | | * | | | |
| 3.1.3  Values and attitudes | * | * | * | | * | |
| *3.2  Impact of tourism on culture* | * | | | | | |
| 3.2.1  Cuisine | | | * | | | |
| 3.2.2  Dress | | | * | | | |
| 3.2.3  Performance | | | * | * | * | |
| 3.2.4  Arts and crafts | | * | * | * | * | |
| 3.2.5  Language | | * | | * | | 13 |
| 3.2.6  Religion | | * | * | | * | |
| *3.3  Impact of tourism on the environment* | * | | | | | |
| 3.3.1  Landscape | | * | * | * | * | |
| 3.3.2  Air and sea | * | | | | | |
| 3.3.3  Wildlife habitats | | * | * | | * | |
| 3.3.4  Building development | | * | * | | * | 3,4,7 |
| 3.3.5  Transport development | | * | * | | * | |
| 3.3.6  Noise | * | | | | | 8 |
| 3.3.7  Litter | | | | | | 1 |
| 3.3.8  Energy and water consumption | | * | | | | |
| 3.3.9  Congestion | | | | | * | 2,3 |
| 3.3.10  Conservation and preservation | | * | | | * | 2,3 |

| Module four | Intro | cs 13 | cs 14 | cs 15 | cs 16 | also in cs |
|---|---|---|---|---|---|---|
| *4.1 Nature and range of jobs in travel and tourism* | * | | | | | |
| 4.1.1 Catering | | * | | | | 8 |
| 4.1.2 Hospitality | | * | | * | | |
| 4.1.3 Transport | | | | * | | |
| 4.1.4 Tour operations | * | | | | | |
| 4.1.5 Retail travel | * | | | | | |
| 4.1.6 Attractions | | | | | * | |
| 4.1.7 Sport and leisure | | * | * | | | 6 |
| *4.2 Skills/ qualities valued in travel and tourism industry* | | | | | | |
| 4.2.1 Personal skills | * | * | * | * | * | |
| 4.2.2 Technological skills | * | * | * | * | | |
| 4.2.3 Job-specific skills | * | * | * | * | * | |
| *4.3 Working in a specific travel and tourism context* | | | | | | |
| 4.3.1 Company aims and objectives | | | * | * | * | 7 |
| 4.3.2 Structure of organizations | | | * | | * | |
| 4.3.3 Communications (including IT) | | | | * | | 7 |
| 4.3.4 Working conditions | * | * | | * | * | |
| 4.3.5 Duties | | * | * | * | * | |
| 4.3.6 Training | | * | | * | | 7 |
| 4.3.7 Career progression | * | * | | * | | |

# Module 1
# TOURIST DESTINATIONS

**Introduction**

**Case study 1**
   Skegness – a seaside resort

**Case study 2**
   The Peak District – a National Park

**Case study 3**
   Chester – a historic city

**Case study 4**
   The National Exhibition Centre, Birmingham

This module covers the following components of the syllabus:

1.1  Components of a tourist destination
1.2  Different types of destination
1.3  Factors which affect destination choice
1.4  Factors affecting tourism development in different destinations

# What is a tourist destination?

Think about what each of these two words means. A **destination** is a place you are going to. A good definition of **tourism** describes it as 'the temporary movement of people to destinations outside their normal places of work and residence, the activities undertaken during their stay in those destinations, and the facilities created in order to cater for their needs.'

So, people travel away from the area in which they live and work to go to a tourist destination, but they only mean to stay there for a limited time. While they are there they will make use of **facilities** and **services** in the destination. For example, they may stay in a hotel, use a local bus service, go on a guided tour or have a go at wind-surfing.

- A **service** provides actions on an organized commercial basis which meet someone else's needs, e.g. home delivery pizzas.
- A **facility** is something specially arranged or constructed in order to provide either recreation or a service, e.g. a restaurant.

A tourist destination is a place or region away from their own homes that people travel to for one of a number of reasons. They might go there:

- To enjoy themselves
- To visit family or friends
- To attend a conference, exhibition or business meeting
- To take part in an event or activity

A destination is made up of a number of **features**. These can be divided into **primary** features, the characteristics of the destination that were there before it attracted tourists, and **secondary** features, the things that were added as a result of tourists coming to the destination; see Table 1.

Primary features are an important factor in attracting tourists to a destination. However, tourism will not grow unless enough secondary features are made available. If the development of secondary features is too fast, especially if it threatens to spoil the attractions of some of the primary features, the destination will lose its popularity.

## Table 1

| Primary features | Secondary features |
|---|---|
| • **Climate**, e.g. average temperatures<br>• **Landscape**, e.g. the length and quality of beaches; the surrounding scenery<br>• **Culture**, e.g. the traditional clothes, language, music, art and dance, festivals<br>• **Ecology**, e.g. the plants, trees and animals found locally<br>• **Architecture**, e.g. churches, cathedrals, country houses | • **Accommodation**, e.g. hotels, apartments, campsites<br>• **Catering**, e.g. restaurants, cafés, bars<br>• **Transport**, e.g. airports, roads, railway, car hire, ferry services<br>• **Activities and amusements**, e.g. water sports, fairgrounds, night-clubs<br>• **Tourist services**, e.g information centres, currency exchange bureaux, tour guides, souvenir shops |

## Activities

1  List six places in Britain you have visited either for a holiday or on a day trip. For each one write down the main primary and secondary features of the destination.

2  Complete the following table for each of the destinations:

award marks in columns ii–viii as follows:

good (3 marks); average (2 marks); poor  (1 mark)

| i<br><br>Destination | ii<br><br>Food | iii<br><br>Accommo-dation | iv<br><br>Travel there and back | v<br>Activities and amusements | vi<br><br>Places of interest | vii<br><br>Weather | viii<br><br>Scenery |
|---|---|---|---|---|---|---|---|
| 1 | | | | | | | |
| 2 | | | | | | | |
| 3 | | | | | | | |
| 4 | | | | | | | |
| 5 | | | | | | | |
| 6 | | | | | | | |

Add up the totals and see which destination you have rated the highest and which one the lowest.

3 Compare your results with other students in the group. Write a paragraph explaining why some features of tourist destinations are more important to you than others, and why other people may think different features are important to them.

# Different types of tourist destination

Look at the photographs that follow. Each one is of a place that is visited by tourists. Yet these four places do not have the same features. They have different climates. Some have more activities and entertainments than others. The scenery varies. Some are easier to get to than others. Some have large hotels; others have only small hotels and campsites. Some are more expensive than others, both to get there and to live there.

*Mediterranean beach resort*

*London*

**National Park**

**Disneyworld**

There are a number of simple ways of dividing different types of tourist destination. For example they might be:

- Urban or rural areas
- In the United Kingdom or overseas
- Built by and for residents or developed specially for tourists
- Peaceful or lively

Table 2 shows some examples of different types of tourist destination in the UK.

**Table 2**

| Example | Type | Features attracting tourists |
| --- | --- | --- |
| York | Historic town | Architecture, museums, city walls, shops, courses |
| Windermere | Tour centre for Lake District | Scenery, boating, walking, climbing, centre for exploring surrounding countryside |
| Alton Towers | Purpose-built attraction | Rides, entertainments, activities, family atmosphere |

**Table 2 Continued**

| Example | Type | Features attracting tourists |
|---|---|---|
| Aviemore | Ski centre | Skiing, outdoor pursuits, centre for exploring surrounding countryside |
| Stratford-upon-Avon | Town with cultural associations | Shakespeare connections, theatre, shops |
| Ironbridge | Industrial heritage site | Re-creations of historic buildings, demonstrations of former industrial processes |
| Newquay | Seaside resort | Beach, surfing, shops, entertainments |

## Activities

1 Give one example of each of the following:

- A major city in the UK that attracts visitors

- An established UK seaside resort

- A town used as a base for touring the surrounding countryside

- A purpose-built tourist resort

2 Discuss the main similarities and differences in the four examples you have chosen.

3 What effects might the differences have on the types of people who would choose to visit each of your four selected destinations?

# Why do people choose to go to different destinations?

Tourists may visit a destination for a number of different reasons. Even when they have decided *why* they want or need to travel away from home they may still be able to choose from a number of different destinations. The conversation on page 8 shows some of the factors people take into account when they are making their decisions about where to go:

'So where do you fancy going, Ian?'

'I liked the look of some of the resorts in that Morocco brochure you brought home. I've never been to North Africa before and it looked as though there would be a lot of new things to see. Did it appeal to you?'

'Yes, but it might be a bit hot in August and the hotel I picked out was a bit more expensive than we'd budgeted for.'

'Julie, you're always so sensible! Well, how about Brittany then? If we use Eurotunnel it will be much quicker to get to and I'm sure we can find relatively inexpensive hotels while we're over there. If we take the car, it means we can get around and explore more easily.'

'That's not a bad idea. We could look in on Phil and Diana on the way. I'd love to see them again and they're always going on about how they'd like to show us round that cottage of theirs.'

'I've got to take some reading with me for that course I'm starting next September so I want to be somewhere we can get a bit of peace and quiet occasionally.'

'Well you should be OK. Remember all those quiet coves we found last time we went? Your only problem will be staying awake after a good French lunch!'

'What will you do while I'm catching up on my reading though?'

'As I remember there are some good walks along the coast and I can always go off and arrange a round of golf if I get bored. I'm sure I'll thoroughly enjoy it. We can start saving a bit of money to go somewhere a bit more exotic next summer.'

'That's agreed then. I'll pop down to the travel agency at lunchtime and see what they still have available. If there's nothing suitable we can book the travel and look for hotels over there.'

## Activities

1  List the factors that Ian and Julie took into account in deciding which destination they would choose for their summer holiday.

2  Suggest some other destinations which you think would meet all their needs.

3  Discuss how changes in Ian and Julie's circumstances, or changes in Morocco and Brittany as destinations, could make them change their minds about where to go.

**Skegness – a seaside resort**

# History

The town of Skegness is on the east coast, in the county of Lincolnshire. A hundred years ago it was no more than a hamlet. Its population in 1850 was just 150 people. The next 30 years saw the planned development of the town. The ninth Earl of Scarbrough produced a plan to develop the village into a watering place. £120,000 was borrowed to help build roads and a sea wall. The wall, constructed from local stone, was very important because the impact of the sea had shifted the coast some miles inland over previous centuries.

In 1872 the Great Northern Railway Company extended its Lincolnshire line to Skegness and this produced an immediate increase in the number of visitors to the town. The line linked Skegness to towns in the North and East Midlands, such as Nottingham, Derby, Sheffield and Leeds. On August Bank Holiday Monday in 1882 19,000 people visited the town by means of 24 rail excursions. A pier, complete with a concert hall for entertainment and refreshment rooms, was opened in 1881. In August 1889 20,000 people paid to go on the pier in a single day. It was finally destroyed by a combination of fire and storms in 1978. By 1880 five hotels had been opened in the town.

The belief that bathing in sea water was good for health became popular in the second half of the eighteenth century. Dr Russell's medical treatise, 'Concerning the Use of Seawater', published in 1752, encouraged people to visit the seaside. Advertisements for building plots in Skegness in 1877 described the town as 'one of the healthiest watering places in England, its water being remarkably pure and soft beneath the chalk and drainage being so efficient in the town that there seems to be no doubt that the place will be "a model watering place".'

So the railway and the pier were the most important features of Skegness's development as a seaside resort, but other additions followed. Queen Victoria celebrated her Diamond Jubilee in 1899 and a Clock Tower was constructed on the seafront to mark this occasion.

The coastline had traditionally belonged to the Crown but in 1923 the Council leased the foreshore area for an annual rent of £1. This gave it greater control over the foreshore's development as an area suitable for leisure and recreation.

Despite the popularity of the destination it was realized quite early that the season for visitors was short. As early as 1889, attempts were made to extend the programme of shows and entertainments into September. However, the railway company refused to run extra services and so the plan was not successful. By the 1920s entertainments were running in the resort from Whitsuntide through to the end of September and illuminations on the foreshore were introduced in the 1930s. Shows included music hall acts, musicals and comedians (Figure 1.1).

**Fig. 1.1 Joe Ramsden and his Players**

By 1936 the first Butlin's holiday camp had opened in Skegness. Increases in car ownership after the Second World War also enabled more families to take camping and caravan holidays. Camping and caravan sites developed in resorts close to Skegness, such as Ingoldmells.

Package holidays to the Mediterranean became increasingly popular during the 1960s and 1970s. They promised better weather than most traditional British resorts could expect. The use of charter flights also meant that the cost of continental holidays came down. The result of this change in holiday habits was that many British seaside resorts found it more difficult to attract summer visitors. As less money was spent each season, so there was less to spend on improving and maintaining facilities and the general appearance of the resorts. Skegness, like other UK seaside resorts, still has to compete with the Spanish 'Costas' in attracting British holiday-makers.

# Skegness now

Skegness has all the attractions of a modern seaside resort. The first Butlin's holiday camp opened there in 1936 and is now known as Funcoast World. The modern Butlin's is both a place to stay and an entertainments centre that can be visited for the day. It offers tennis courts, an adventure playground, a boating lake, roller skating, a monorail, films, live entertainment, bowling and a variety of pools.

A modern promotional leaflet describes Skegness like this:

Skegness, with its famous character The Jolly Fisherman, is renowned internationally as one of the top seaside resorts in Britain, and with good reason. If you
were asked to plan the ideal holiday resort, you could not better Skegness with
its acres of beautiful gardens, tree lined avenues, award winning beaches, clean
air and, of course, value for money. Amongst the 34 acres of formally laid out
sea front gardens, are the many foreshore attractions including excellent bowling
greens, boating lakes, a mile long waterway, crazy golf and putting greens, the
largest outdoor heated swimming pool on the east coast and an indoor pool.

Butlin's Funcoast World, Fantasy Island, Natureland Seal Sanctuary, Church
Farm Museum, Hardy's Animal Farm, Pier Superbowl, Model Village,
Fairgrounds, Pandas Palace Indoor Children's Playground and Gibraltar Point
Nature Reserve are amongst the attractions of Skegness.

## Activities

1. List as many reasons as you can think of for choosing to visit Skegness.

2. Discuss which features of Skegness might put some people off visiting the town.

# Accommodation

The rate at which tourist resorts develop depends on how well and how quickly they
can provide for the needs of visitors. If there are fewer places to stay than there are
people wishing to visit, those who cannot find anywhere will go somewhere else.

A large percentage of the visitors who stay in the Skegness area stay in either holiday
camps, camping and caravan sites or self-catering accommodation. Caravans form the
largest accommodation sector on the Lincolnshire coast, representing more than 70% of
bedspaces. If tourism is going to help the economy of a town such as Skegness, accommodation is very important. Research has shown that payments for accommodation
account for 36% of all the money earned from holidays taken in the United Kingdom.

**Occupancy rates** are used to measure how well hotels and guest houses are performing. These rates can measure either the percentage of rooms occupied or the
percentage of beds slept in over a given period. What these figures show on the
Lincolnshire coast is that tourism is very seasonal. Hotels and guest-houses may
have occupancy rates of around 80% in the summer but this is likely to fall to about
20% for most of the autumn and winter. Many close entirely for the winter period.

## Activity

Look carefully at the graphs in Figure 1.2, showing bed and room occupancy rates
on the Lincolnshire coast from July 1993 to June 1994:

1 Which are the highest and lowest occupancy points in the year?

2 Why are room occupancy figures higher than bed occupancy figures?

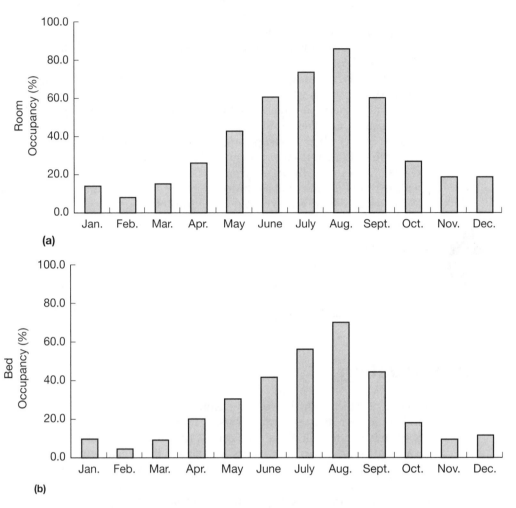

**Fig. 1.2 Lincolnshire Coast accommodation occupancy rates for serviced accommodation: (a) typical room occupancy pattern; (b) typical bed occupancy pattern**

(*Source*: East Midlands Tourist Board)

3 What can hotels and guest-houses do to improve their occupancy figures between October and March?

4 Use computer software in order to display this data in different formats, e.g. pie charts, line graphs.

# Deciding where to stay

Most resorts try to provide plenty of information about the types of accommodation they have available (Figure 1.3). Visitors also want to know what facilities and services they can get in a hotel or campsite they are thinking of staying in. Accommodation guide books often use a set of symbols like the one in Figure 1.4 to show what is on offer in each establishment.

There is a **Tourist Information Centre** in Skegness's Embassy Centre, next to the foreshore area. Details of all accommodation in the area are provided here and advance bookings are made by post or telephone and for personal callers from here.

To help visitors to get a better idea of the standard of accommodation they are booking, there are several schemes that classify hotels, guest-houses, self-catering apartments and campsites. The AA and the RAC award stars to inspected hotels belonging to their schemes. The English Tourist Board runs schemes to classify a range of types of accommodation. These show what facilities guests should expect to find and may also show the quality of the accommodation. An outline of the schemes, 'Sure Signs of Where to Stay', is shown in Figure 1.5.

*Fig. 1.3 Hotel on Skegness sea front*

### HOTELS, GUEST HOUSES, FARMHOUSES, INNS AND BED & BREAKFAST

P Off-street parking

Dogs accepted by arrangement

Central heating throughout

Television in all bedrooms

Totally non-smoking establishment

Children welcome (a number following gives minimum age)

£ Accepts major credit cards

Evening meals available

Tea/coffee making facilities available in all bedrooms

Licensed for the sale of alcohol

### SELF-CATERING COTTAGES, FLATS AND CARAVAN HOLIDAY HOMES

P Off-street parking

Dogs accepted by arrangement

M Gas/electricity by coin meter or meter reading

Linen provided free or on hire

Children welcome (a number following gives minimum age)

Clothes washing machine and drying facilities

Television in all units

Totally non-smoking establishment

### TOURING CARAVANS AND CAMPING SITES

Electricity hook-up

WC Flush toilets on site

Children's play area

Lighting throughout park

Shop

Hot showers

Chemical closet disposal point

Gas cylinder exchange/refill

P Car parking beside caravan or tent

Dogs accepted by arrangement

*Fig. 1.4 Some symbols used in accommodation guide books*

**THE CROWN**
Looking for a hotel, guesthouse, inn, B&B or farmhouse? Look for the CROWN. The classifications: 'Listed', and then ONE to FIVE CROWN, tell you the range of facilities/services you can expect. The more Crowns, the wider the range.

**THE LODGES**
Looking for somewhere convenient to stop overnight on a motorway or major road route? Look out for the 'Lodge' MOON. The classifications: ONE to THREE MOON tell you the range of facilities you can expect. The more Moons, the wider the range.

**THE KEY**
Looking for a self-catering holiday home? Look for the KEY. The classifications: ONE to FIVE KEY, tell you the range of facilities and equipment you can expect. The more Keys, the wider the range.

**THE GRADES:** APPROVED, COMMENDED, HIGHLY COMMENDED and DE LUXE, whether alongside the CROWNS, KEYS or MOONS, indicate the quality standard of what is provided.

**THE QUALITY Q**
Looking for a holiday caravan, chalet or camping park? Look for the Q symbol. The more ✓'s in the Q (from one to five), the higher the quality standard of what is provided.

**ACCESSIBLE**
All places displaying their symbol are annually inspected to ensure they meet the criteria that reflects the practical needs of wheelchair users. There are three categories of accessibility shown by the number of bars in the circle.

Throughout Britain, the tourist boards now inspect over 30,000 places to stay, every year, to help you find the ones that suit you best.

More detailed information on the CROWNS, the KEYS and the Q is given in free *SURE SIGN* leaflets, available at any Tourist Information Centre.

**English Tourist Board**

We've checked them out before you check in!

*Fig. 1.5 English Tourist Board schemes*

## Activities

1 Which scheme would help you to decide which caravan site to choose? How could you tell which ones offered the most facilities?

2 What do the grades awarded to a hotel or guest house show?

3 Explain how a hotel with only *one* crown for its facilities/services might be given a *highly commended* grade.

# Transport

## Getting to Skegness by road

Road access to Skegness is very important because a large number of visitors either bring their own caravans or else drive to caravan sites at nearby coastal resorts such as Ingoldmells. The main roads into Skegness (Figure 1.6) are as follows:

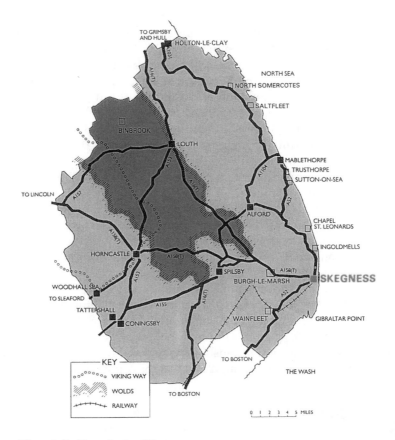

*Fig. 1.6  Roads to Skegness*

- A52 from the south – bringing traffic that has come from or through Peterborough, Derby, Nottingham or Grantham
- A158 from the west – bringing traffic that has come from or through Louth or Lincoln
- A52 from the north – bringing traffic that has come down the coast from the direction of Mablethorpe or Grimsby

The main disadvantage of all of these routes is that none of them is a dual carriageway. This means that the traffic on them sometimes moves very slowly, especially at the height of summer and on bank holidays.

## Skegness by train

The railway line into Skegness comes through Grantham. There are regular services to Grantham from cities like Nottingham, Derby and Sheffield. In 1995 a brochure encouraging people to come to Skegness described rail services to the town like this:

Regional Railways will be upgrading its services to and from Skegness with the introduction of the summer timetable in May 1995.

The weekday service will be increased to an hourly frequency with all day-time trains running through Crewe, giving one change connections from the North West of England and a regular through service from The Potteries and East Midlands Conurbations.

We will be improving journey times to and from Nottingham and will continue to run through trains from and to the West Midlands on summer Saturdays along with the shuttle service to Grantham to provide connections for visitors travelling from the North East of England, South Yorkshire and the South of England.

All weekday services on the route will be operated by modern 153 and 156 class units which start to go through their refurbishment programme this year, giving an even better quality product in which customers will be able to take advantage of seat reservations, and we are currently discussing the prospects of supplying on-train trolley catering facilities.

For the day-trip market, we are introducing special day return fares to relaunch a Sunday 'Jolly Fisherman' facility between Nottingham and Skegness and will be looking to offer discounts on a wide range of facilities along the coast. We will also be introducing a Lincolnshire Day Ranger Ticket which will be available for travel to all stations in Lincolnshire by Regional Railways services giving ample opportunity for visitors to sample all that the county has to offer

## Activities

1　Refer to a road map of Great Britain and plan *two* different routes for driving to Skegness from each of the following towns: Cheltenham, Chester, Middlesbrough, Bolton. In each case discuss the factors which would help you to decide which one would be the better route to take.

2　All of the following groups are planning to visit Skegness:

(a)　The Chapman family live in Stoke-on-Trent: Mr and Mrs Chapman have four children, aged between 3 and 10. Mr Chapman is unemployed and Mrs Chapman works as a nurse. They recently sold their car. They are planning a week's holiday in Skegness in June.

(b)　Tina, Gary and Michelle live in Bradford: they have just completed their 'A' levels and think a week in Skegness might be a fun way to celebrate. Michelle's mother has offered to lend her her car for a week in June if they want it.

(c)　Mr and Mrs Wellings, now in their mid-70s, have lived in America for 40 years. In June they will be visiting England for the first time since they left in 1956. They will fly into Heathrow and have booked accommodation in Stratford, York, Chester and the Cotswolds. Mrs Wellings is keen to re-visit Skegness, the town in which she was born and spent her childhood.

Describe the choices of means of transport and routes which are available for each of these groups. Which option would you advise them to take and why?

# Attractions

Figure 1.7 shows some of the attractions that can be found in Skegness.

Attractions are the things that draw people towards a particular place. Attractions can be divided into those that are part of the natural environment and those that have been constructed as a result of human activity.

## SKEGNESS PIER & SUPERBOWL

Skegness Pier, Grand Parade, Skegness.
Open 9.00 a.m. – midnight.

P L

Skeggy's No. 1 all weather fun centre, spend the day here – there is something for everyone. A.M.F. Ten pin bowling, Laser Quest, shops and side stalls, licensed bar, variety of food bars, bingo, kiddies and toddler play areas, amusements.

*Free Admission*
Tel: (01754) 761341

## BOTTONS PLEASURE BEACH
### SKEGNESS
For a great family day out
Open 11am to 10pm. Every weekend from 19th March
Daily – May 28th to end September

- One of Europe's most modern Pleasure Parks
- Great new rides for Children and Adults
- Arcades
- Restaurants and Snack Bars

## NATURELAND
### SEAL SANCTUARY
North Parade, Skegness. Tel: Skegness 764345
Open daily from 10am

A

- Seals & Penguins
- Aquarium & Reptile House
- Tropical Butterflies (May-Oct)
- Seal Hospital
- Pets Corner etc.
- Gift shop, brass rubbings
- Party bookings welcome

Admission charged

MIDDLE ENGLAND
*Visitor Attraction of the Year 1994*

## RICHMOND LEISURE COMPLEX
Richmond Holiday Centre, Richmond Drive,
Skegness, Lincolnshire.
Open 8am-10pm daily

- 25m x 10m Heated Indoor Swimming Pool
- Swimming in Sessions - telephone for details
- Whirlpool Spa
- Sauna
- Sunbeds
- Newly extended excellent gymnasium
- Free Parking

P A L

Swimming Admission Charges
Adults £1.10. OAPs/Children 70p
Tel (01754) 769265

## CHURCH FARM MUSEUM
Church Road South, Skegness
Open Daily: April-October 10.30am-5.30pm

- Thatched Cottage & Garden
- Lincoln Longwool Sheep
- 19th Century Farmhouse displays
- Special events & exhibitions
- Refreshments & gift shop
- Free coach & Car Parking

Admission Charged

P L

Tel (01754) 766658

LINCOLNSHIRE COUNTY COUNCIL

## THE EMBASSY CENTRE
Grand Parade, Skegness, Lincs.
Open: All Year

A superb Theatre and Entertainment complex
- Top Name Stars
- Shows for all ages
- Free Colour 'Whats On'
- Souvenir Shop/Tourist Information Centre.

P A L

Tel (01754) 768333

***Fig. 1.7 Skegness attractions***

Skegness, like most seaside resorts, has both natural and built attractions. The natural attractions are the traditional three S's – sun, sand and sea. The built attractions include all of those shown on the previous page. The main built attractions also include sea defence walkways which run for six miles along the edge of the beaches and the landscaped foreshore area which includes waterways and a boating lake.

---

The five main visitor attractions in Skegness are:

- Natureland Seal Sanctuary
- Skegness Pier
- Embassy Centre
- Botton's Pleasure Beach
- Panda's Palace

Each of these attractions receives more than 100,000 visitors a year.

---

## Activities

Research has suggested that the foreshore area of Skegness would benefit from the development of at least two new attractions. Three groups have been identified as the most likely users of any new attractions:

- Families with children – the largest group of visitors
- People over 55 years of age – a smaller group but with more to spend per person
- Visitors with special activity interests e.g, watersports

1 Write a brief outline of ideas for three new attractions for the foreshore area, each one intended to appeal mainly to one of the three groups listed above.

2 Discuss the advantages and disadvantages of each of your three proposals, including things such as:

- amount of use that might be expected throughout the year
- whether it would be expensive to build, staff and maintain
- how much income it might bring
- whether it would create employment
- whether other similar attractions exist elsewhere

3 Discuss which three proposals suggested by your group as a whole you think would best meet the needs of the three groups of most likely users identified above.

4 Assuming that money is available for only one new development, prepare a short presentation to be made to the rest of your teaching group, making out a case for going ahead with one particular proposal.

# Climate

Seaside resorts traditionally attracted people because the combination of sea bathing and fresh air were thought to be good for your health. The most famous poster advertising Skegness used the slogan 'Skegness is so bracing.' The poster (Figure 1.8), showing the Jolly Fisherman, was created by John Hassall and sold to the Great Northern Railway in 1908 for just £12.

**Fig. 1.8 The 'Jolly Fisherman' poster**

Nowadays seaside visitors expect more than just sea air and a good, fresh breeze. The idea of a 'bracing' resort is no longer popular. It suggests that there is always a cold wind about! However, hours of sunshine are still important. Fine weather allows more time for sunbathing, sitting on the beach or strolling along the sea front. Rain makes it more difficult to keep children amused and means the holiday becomes more costly as more indoor entertainment is needed and more drinks and snacks are consumed.

Many resorts list the hours of sunshine and millimetres of rainfall in their brochures. Research carried out on the Lincolnshire Coast in 1992 also tested what holidaymakers thought of the weather in Skegness during July, August and September. Table 1.1 shows the results.

**Table 1.1**

|  | July | August | September | Total |
|---|---|---|---|---|
| Very good | 39% | 14% | 2% | 20% |
| Good | 46% | 41% | 47% | 44% |
| Just okay | 9% | 32% | 43% | 27% |
| Poor | – | 5% | 8% | 4% |
| Very poor | – | 2% | – | 1% |
| Only arrived today | 6% | 6% | – | 4% |
| Mean score* | 1.32 | 0.63 | 0.43 | 0.81 |

\* Marks scored: Very good = +2;  Good = +1;  Poor = –1;  Very poor = –2

## Activities

1  Which month appeared to have the best weather and which month the worst?

2  If 613 people answered the survey altogether, how many people overall said that they had enjoyed 'very good' weather?

3  Would you expect the Total results of this survey to have been different if it had also included the months of May, June and October? Why?

4  Discuss with other members of your teaching group how important the weather is to you when you go on holiday.

5  Create your own survey to find out in more detail the extent to which the weather is a factor in people's enjoyment of their holidays.

6  Carry out the survey with a combined sample of at least 100 respondents and write a brief report about what conclusions can be drawn from the results.

# Visitor numbers and visitor spend

## The importance of information

It is important for those planning the future of tourist destinations to have some factual information about their visitors. They need to know:

● How many people visit and at what times of year
● What the ages and interests of their visitors are
● Where most of their visitors come from
● What transport they use to get to their destination
● Where they stay when they are at their destination
● How long they stay
● What activities they do while they are there
● What aspects of the destination they like and dislike

Accurate answers to these questions mean that changes can be made to accommodation, transport and entertainments so that they are more likely to be exactly what visitors want.

This information can also be compared with results of surveys of the population as a whole. For example, if the average age of the population of Britain goes up over a ten year period but the average age of visitors to Skegness remains the same, this might show that the resort was failing to attract as many older visitors as it could. It might be that its advertising methods were not reaching older people or else were giving them the impression that it was not a suitable resort for them to visit.

## Information about visitors to the Lincolnshire coast

It is not surprising to find that a large number of visitors to the Lincolnshire coast come from the regions closest to the county. It is far easier to get to Skegness from Nottingham than it is from, say, Aberdeen! Figure 1.9 shows where the majority of visitors come from.

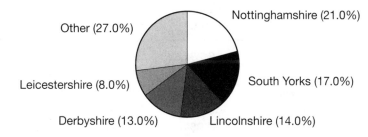

Nottinghamshire (21.0%)

Other (27.0%)

Leicestershire (8.0%)

South Yorks (17.0%)

Derbyshire (13.0%)

Lincolnshire (14.0%)

**Fig. 1.9 *Where visitors to Skegness come from***

## Activities

1 Many of the towns and cities in West Yorkshire are only two hours' drive from the Lincolnshire coast. Why do you think only a small proportion of the people who live there choose to visit Skegness?

2 Set out in Tables 1.2–1.4 there is some information about the populations of the areas sending most visitors to Skegness. If Skegness wishes to attract more tourists and encourage them to spend more money in the town, what might be learnt about potential visitors from these figures?

## Employment and seasonality

It is estimated that tourists spend £214 million a year in the district of East Lindsey, which includes Skegness. Tourism in the region accounts for 21,500 jobs. Accommodation provides many jobs, through the 550 accommodation establishments and the caravan sector. There are over 24,000 static caravans and nearly 3,000 touring pitches in the area.

**Table 1.2 Population changes in areas sending the most visitors to the Lincolnshire Coast**

| Area | Population | % change 1981 – 1991 |
|---|---|---|
| UK as a whole | | +1.9 |
| Humberside | 859,200 | +0.2 |
| South Yorkshire | 1,296,200 | -1.6 |
| Derbyshire | 933,000 | +2.1 |
| Leicestershire | 897,700 | +4.5 |
| Lincolnshire | 591,300 | +7.0 |
| Northamptonshire | 580,100 | +8.9 |
| Nottinghamshire | 1,016,600 | +2.2 |

**Table 1.3 Age distribution in areas sending the most visitors to the Lincolnshire coast**

| Area | Under 5 years | 5 – 14 years | 15 – 24 years | 25 – 74 years | Over 75 years |
|---|---|---|---|---|---|
| UK as a whole | 6.7% | 12.3% | 62.7% | 18.3% | 6.9% |
| Humberside | 6.8% | 12.7% | 61.9% | 18.6% | 6.8% |
| South Yorkshire | 6.5% | 12.0% | 63.1% | 18.4% | 6.8% |
| Derbyshire | 6.4% | 12.2% | 63.1% | 18.4% | 6.8% |
| Leicestershire | 6.9% | 12.8% | 63.4% | 16.9% | 6.4% |
| Lincolnshire | 6.0% | 11.8% | 62.8% | 19.4% | 7.1% |
| Northamptonshire | 7.0% | 13.0% | 63.1% | 16.9% | 6.3% |
| Nottinghamshire | 6.6% | 12.1% | 63.5% | 17.8% | 6.6% |

**Table 1.4 Income and employment in areas sending the most visitors to the Lincolnshire Coast**

| Area | Disposable income compared with national average 1986 | Disposable income compared with national average 1991 | % unemployed 1992 | % unemployed 1994 |
|---|---|---|---|---|
| UK as a whole | 100 | 100 | 9.4% | 10.3% |
| Humberside | 91.4% | 91.4% | 10.3% | 11.1% |
| South Yorkshire | 93% | 90.1% | 12.6% | 13.1% |
| Derbyshire | 89.6% | 91% | 9.1% | 9.8% |
| Leicestershire | 99.5% | 96.9% | 7.7% | 8.0% |
| Lincolnshire | 96.7% | 101.5% | 8.6% | 9.7% |
| Northamptonshire | 98.8% | 96.2% | 7.6% | 8.2% |
| Nottinghamshire | 97.2% | 94.3% | 10% | 11.6% |

The largest single employer in the area is Butlin's Funcoast World holiday centre. It has a permanent staff of 300 and over 700 annual seasonal vacancies. The centre now stays open for 10 months of the year.

The tourism season in Skegness lasts for 20 weeks, with a high season of 8 weeks in July and August. The 1993 unemployment figures in the town show the effects of the seasonal nature of tourism. The unemployment rate rose to 18.4% in January and fell to 9.7% in June.

## Ways of extending the tourism season in Skegness

All of the following ideas were suggested in the Strategic Tourism Development Plan for Skegness Foreshore as ways of encouraging more people to visit outside the main tourist season:

- Developing more undercover attractions for wet days
- Encouraging more existing attractions to open out of season
- Encouraging the use of caravans for weekend breaks
- Encouraging pubs to make families with children more welcome
- Establishing festivals or special events
- Encouraging the growth of watersports

## Activities

1 List some of the types of employment that you think would be available in Skegness and the surrounding coastal area during the 20 weeks of the tourism season.

2 Discuss what you think might be the possible effects of having so much seasonal employment in the town. You might consider:

- How this affects different age groups

- What people do in the winter months

- What impact it has on family incomes in the region

- Whether it is likely to affect population migration

Study Table 1.5.

3 Which industry sector showed the fastest rate of decline in employment between 1981 and 1989? What reasons can you suggest for this?

4 Which other industry sectors are affected by whether tourism in the region is increasing or decreasing? Suggest some examples of how tourism can affect employment levels in other industry sectors.

5 What conclusions can be drawn from the national employment figures for different industry sectors shown in Table 1.6?

**Table 1.5  Trends in employment by sector – Skegness travel-to-work area**

| Sector | 1981 % | 1984 % | 1987 % | 1989 % | % change 1981–1989 |
|---|---|---|---|---|---|
| Services | 26.5 | 22.8 | 31.7 | 26.7 | +0.4 |
| Tourism/leisure | 24.4 | 24.3 | 22.7 | 27.2 | +1.8 |
| Distribution | 16.0 | 16.0 | 17.3 | 15.5 | −0.5 |
| Agriculture | 10.0 | 11.3 | 8.7 | 7.1 | −3.8 |
| Mechanical/ Engineering | 6.0 | 6.8 | 5.1 | 5.1 | −1.6 |
| Manufacturing | 4.8 | 4.6 | 4.9 | 6.9 | +5.0 |
| Construction | 2.9 | 3.6 | 2.9 | 1.9 | −2.0 |
| Food processing | 2.1 | 2.0 | 2.9 | 1.9 | −0.8 |
| Other | 7.3 | 8.6 | 3.8 | 7.7 | 0.0 |
| **Totals** | **9,314** | **8,759** | **9,113** | **9,599** | **+0.4** |

**Table 1.6**

| | Males (%) | | | Females (%) | | |
|---|---|---|---|---|---|---|
| | 1981 | 1991 | 1994 | 1981 | 1991 | 1994 |
| Agriculture | 2 | 2 | 2 | 1 | 1 | 1 |
| Energy and water supply | 5 | 3 | 2 | 1 | 1 | 1 |
| Manufacturing | 35 | 29 | 28 | 19 | 13 | 12 |
| Construction | 8 | 7 | 6 | 1 | 1 | 1 |
| Distribution, hotels, catering and repairs | 15 | 19 | 20 | 24 | 25 | 24 |
| Transport and communication | 9 | 9 | 9 | 3 | 3 | 3 |
| Financial and business services | 7 | 11 | 13 | 9 | 13 | 13 |
| Other services | 18 | 20 | 21 | 41 | 44 | 45 |
| **All employees (thousands)** | **12,277** | **11,254** | **10,539** | **9,107** | **10,467** | **10,363** |

*Source*: Employment Department.

# Local and national politics

## The local community

Tourism affects the people who live in Skegness. The local council, East Lindsey District Council, is elected to represent the interests of the local community. It is up to it to ensure that developments are acceptable to the majority of local people. When the Council was preparing to develop the Skegness foreshore it carried out extensive research to find out the feelings and attitudes of local residents. Local groups were invited to meetings to express their views, and the plans for the development were put on public display for six months. Local people were invited to comment on them.

Within any local community there are various interest or pressure groups. These groups may have been formed for a variety of reasons:

- To protect the environment
- To represent the interests of people with disabilities
- To help with the conservation of wildlife
- To stimulate interest in local history and heritage

These groups will also have to be consulted over major tourism developments. The developers, often in partnership with the local council, will have to persuade them of the benefits. They will need to show how the quality of life of local people can be improved, for example through job creation or through better local services.

## Politics and planning

Tourism is often influenced by politics. This is particularly true where planning decisions have to be made. If anyone was allowed to develop a tourism facility in any way that they wanted, it would be very difficult to control the overall appearance and quality of the destination. One way of trying to make sure that all tourist developments are contributing towards the overall improvement of the destination is to develop regional tourism strategies and policies. These are often produced by Regional Tourist Boards who will work closely with local authorities and local businesses to agree the best recommendations for the region. There are four main purposes behind tourism planning:

- To enhance visitor satisfaction
- To improve the national or regional economy
- To protect tourism resources, both natural and built
- To integrate tourism into the pattern of local community life

## Regional tourism planning in the East Midlands

In 1990 visitors to the East Midlands spent about £1.1 billion and an estimated 100,000 people were employed in tourism in the region. Because tourism is so important to the regional economy, there needs to be some planning for the future to ensure that this continues to be the case.

In order to achieve this the East Midlands Tourist Board prepared a tourism strategy for the period 1992-1997, 'Raising the Standard'. As the title suggests, the main idea of this strategy was to make the region's tourism destinations and facilities so good that people would think they were excellent value for money.

The strategy reviews the present state of tourism in the East Midlands. It shows how many people visit, how much they spend, and where they come from. It also looks at how much money has been invested in tourism facilities and how many jobs have been created in tourism in the region. An important part of a planning strategy is to try and forecast future trends. For example, Table 1.7 shows the forecast of the number of tourist trips to the region. Making this kind of estimate is important in deciding what new facilities, such as accommodation or parking spaces, might be needed if future tourists are still going to enjoy their experience of visiting the region.

**Table 1.7**

|  | Trips 1989 (m) | Trips 1997 (m) | % change 1989/1997 | % yearly growth |
|---|---|---|---|---|
| **Staying visitors** | | | | |
| UK residents | 7.0 | 7.8 | +11.4 | +1.3 |
| Overseas visitors | 0.6 | 0.9 | +47.7 | +5.0 |
| Total staying visitors | 7.6 | 8.7 | +18.4 | +1.6 |
| **UK residents' day trips** | 51.0 | 57.5 | +12.7 | +1.5 |

A very important part of any strategy is its **objectives**. These explain what the plan is trying to achieve. 'Raising the Standard' had five objectives:

- **Objective one: Driving for quality.** Ensuring satisfied customers, improved business performance and an assured future, through high-quality products and services.
- **Objective two: Boosting business growth.** Creating an environment in which tourism businesses can grow and prosper.
- **Objective three: Building an image.** Heightening awareness both at home and abroad of the region and its constituent products and destinations.
- **Objective four: Developing the product.** Continuing investment in existing operations and new product development to retain the competitive edge.
- **Objective five: Sustaining growth.** Protecting the future by continuous care of the environment and improved visitor management.

The next stage in the planning process is to decide what needs to be done to make sure that these objectives can be achieved. Some of the actions which were recommended in the tourism strategy for the East Midlands were:

- Spending more money on staff training
- Increasing the number of establishments joining national accommodation classification schemes
- Improving the availability of tourist information in the region
- Improving the way the region was marketed, especially in off-peak seasons
- Encouraging the development of new attractions in the region
- Seeking more government funds for new projects
- Developing green tourism products such as cycling holidays and forest tourism
- Promoting less visited areas where there is capacity, opportunity and local support

# Activities

Study Figures 1.10–1.14 of the Skegness foreshore area.

1 Discuss the general appearance of these views and the ways in which they might be improved.

2 List the people and organizations whose opinions could be asked for about any new development of these areas.

3 Suggest four developments (one for each picture) that might be appropriate in these areas and four that you think would not be suitable. What main arguments would you use in trying to persuade a planning authority to approve or turn down these ideas?

**Fig. 1.10  Sea front road and clock tower**

**Fig. 1.11  Beach**

**Fig. 1.12  Pier end**

**Fig. 1.13 Formal flower beds and statue of the Jolly Fisherman**

# The development of National Parks

In 1929 the National Park Committee suggested the establishment of a series of parks in areas that had been identified as having outstanding natural beauty. Such places were already becoming popular with visitors. There were three main objectives behind this proposal:

- To protect the areas from damage and unattractive development
- To make it easier for pedestrians to get access to these areas
- To find new ways of protecting the flora and fauna found in these areas

The Dower Report, published in 1945, described the kind of National Park that was needed in Britain. It talked about areas of natural beauty, the need for more footpaths, the protection of wildlife, and the preservation of traditional styles of architecture. The recommendations contained in this report, including some about how National Parks should be administered, eventually became national policy.

The 1949 National Parks and Access to the Countryside Act created the **National Parks Commission**. This group had the task of deciding which areas in Britain should become National Parks. The Act also defined the two main objectives of National Parks. These were:

- Preserving and enhancing the natural beauty of the parks
- Promoting their enjoyment by the public

The Act also recognized that there might be some conflicts of interest in areas that became National Parks. All of them were used for agriculture and forestry. Farmers and forestry workers did not always welcome an increase in the number of visitors and ways of taking the interests of both visitors and people who worked on the land into account would need to be found. Because the Parks were not nationally owned, visitors had no legal rights to cross farm and forestry land except where public rights of way were well established.

The Countryside Act of 1968 gave the National Parks Commission wider responsibilities and renamed it the **Countryside Commission**. It became responsible both for conservation of the countryside and also for providing recreation opportunities for visitors.

There are now ten National Parks in the UK and two other areas, the New Forest and the Norfolk Broads, which do not have National Park status but which are considered to share the same tourism development issues. Some areas of the coastline have been named the **Heritage Coast** in an attempt to encourage the kind of tourist use that will preserve rather than destroy their appeal.

## Activities

1  Study Figure 2.1 which shows the location of National Parks, Areas of Outstanding Natural Beauty and Heritage Coast.

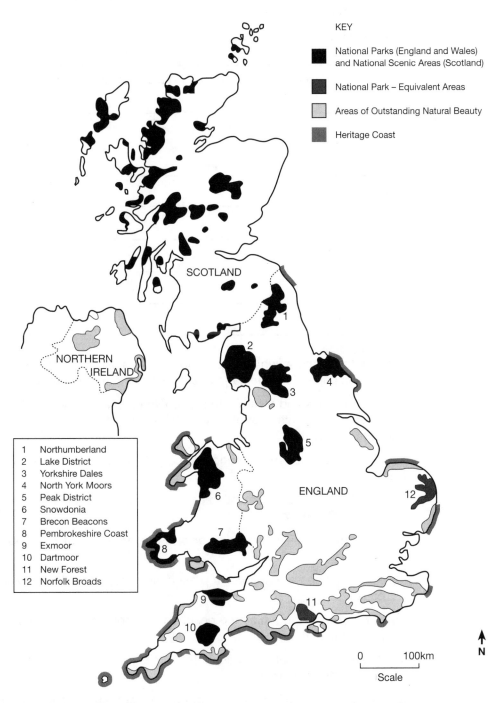

**KEY**

■ National Parks (England and Wales) and National Scenic Areas (Scotland)

■ National Park – Equivalent Areas

▨ Areas of Outstanding Natural Beauty

▨ Heritage Coast

SCOTLAND

NORTHERN IRELAND

ENGLAND

1 Northumberland
2 Lake District
3 Yorkshire Dales
4 North York Moors
5 Peak District
6 Snowdonia
7 Brecon Beacons
8 Pembrokeshire Coast
9 Exmoor
10 Dartmoor
11 New Forest
12 Norfolk Broads

0    100km
Scale

N

*Fig. 2.1 The location of National Parks, Areas of Outstanding Natural Beauty and the Heritage Coast*

(*Source*: Rosemary Burton, *Travel Geography*, Pitman)

2 Use an atlas to find out the location of each of the following cities: Exeter, Sheffield, Norwich, Chester, York, Preston, Southampton.

3 Complete the following table:

| City | Nearest National Park, Area of Outstanding Beauty or Heritage Coast |
|---|---|
| Exeter | |
| Sheffield | |
| Norwich | |
| Chester | |
| York | |
| Preston | |
| Southampton | |

4 Discuss the reasons why some National Parks, Areas of Outstanding Natural Beauty and parts of the Heritage Coast receive more visitors than others.

What advantages and disadvantages can you think of in living in (a) an attractive rural area that attracts a lot of visitors; (b) an attractive but remote rural area that attracts fewer visitors?

5 List three examples of recreational activities that people might want to do in National Parks.

How might these activities cause conflict between visitors and people who live within the National Parks?

6 What arguments can you think of *for* and *against* each of the following points of view:

(a) 'Old buildings are not worth preserving. They should be replaced by new ones...'

(b) 'If people want to enjoy the beauty of the countryside, they should have to pay for their enjoyment...'

(c) 'Most people wouldn't notice if the occasional wild flower, rare small animal or butterfly became extinct...'

(d) 'Beautiful countryside is part of our heritage and should not be in private ownership. People should be free to walk where they want...'

# The Peak District

The Peak District National Park covers 555 square miles (1440 square kilometres), including parts of Staffordshire, Cheshire and Derbyshire. It is ideally positioned for day visitors, since there are over 18 million people living within 60 miles (96 km) of the Park (Figure 2.2). It is within easy reach of Manchester, Sheffield, Derby, Nottingham and Stoke. It is not surprising then, to find that it is the busiest National Park in Europe, attracting 22 million visits a year. Since the majority arrive by car the Park has suffered from severe traffic congestion in recent times, especially in the summer months. The local resident population numbers 38,000.

The closeness of the Peak National Park to so many cities means that the great majority, between 90 and 95%, of the people who take trips there are day visitors. For example, people living in Sheffield can be in the Park in 20 minutes. Since many of these people drive their own cars and bring their own food with them, they do not spend very much while they are inside the Park. This means that the economic benefits of tourism to the people who live inside the Park are not great.

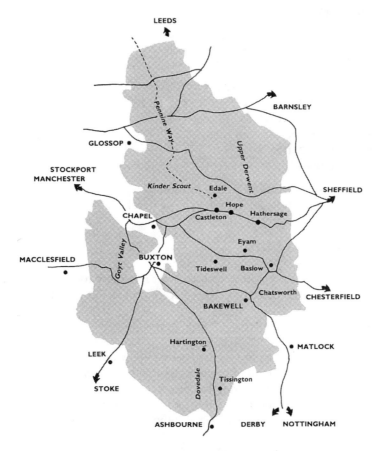

*Fig. 2.2 The Peak District National Park*

There are a number of other pressures on the Park. Because of its location there is a substantial amount of commercial traffic which crosses it daily. So far any suggestions that a cross-Park motorway should be built have been resisted but the existing roads were not built to allow for large, heavy vehicles. The boundaries of the Park include 15 different local authorities and so gaining agreement for policies throughout the Park is not always easy. The landownership and land management for the Park are given in Table 2.1.

**Table 2.1  Landownership and land management in the Peak District National Park**

| National Park Authority | National Trust | Forestry Commission | Nature Conservancy Council | Water Authorities | Private |
|---|---|---|---|---|---|
| 4.2% | 9.7% | 0.5% | 0.1% | 13.0% | 72.5% |

# Accommodation

There is a wide range of accommodation available in the Peak District. It includes:

- Hotels
- Family run guest-houses
- Farm holidays
- Self-catering cottages
- Camping and caravan sites
- Camping barns
- Youth hostels

A high proportion of the accommodation available is either bed and breakfast or self-catering. There are very few large hotels in the region.

## Choosing where to stay

If you decide to visit the Peak District for a few days there are a number of factors that might influence what kind of accommodation you choose to stay in.

### Category

You might already have a fixed idea that you want to stay in a hotel, or on a farm, or at a camping site. This kind of preference probably depends on your past experience. If you had a good camping holiday last year you might want to do it again; if it rained all the time you might choose something different. Some of the other factors below will also probably influence your views about the category of accommodation you prefer.

### Location

If one of the purposes of your visit is to meet up with friends in Ashbourne, you will probably not choose to stay in Castleton. However Castleton would be a much better choice if you intend to spend some time walking on the Pennine Way. Most people will choose accommodation that is convenient for what they want to do or that is reasonably easy to get to from where they live. Those arriving by car may look for somewhere with convenient and secure car-parking facilities.

### Cost

People looking for an inexpensive holiday are more likely to choose bed and breakfast or self-catering accommodation than a luxury hotel. Hotels with attractive settings, carefully designed interiors and quality restaurants will generally cost more than those offering just basic facilities.

### Family size and age

There are many personal factors involved in choosing the best kind of accommodation. Families with small children may look for places that welcome children and provide special menus and activities for them.

### Atmosphere and appearance

Hotels, especially those in the country, often advertise themselves on the basis of their good service and their period authenticity. In other words they say that visitors will be made to feel very welcome, will be well looked after, and can enjoy themselves in a comfortable, attractive environment. Hotels often use antique furniture, paintings and decoration to emphasize aspects of the period in which they were built.

### Facilities

These may vary from hotels that have televisions and tea/coffee-making facilities in each room to campsites that have a social and recreation centre. People tend to expect more expensive accommodation to provide a wider range of facilities.

## Advertising different types of accommodation in the Peak District

### The Queen's Head Hotel and Public House

The Queen's Head is advertised as a 'family run business' (Figure 2.3). This suggests that it is more intimate and friendly than a large hotel owned by a national chain. The advertisement describes Buxton as being in 'the heart of the Peak District'. This suggests it has a central position and is therefore a good base for exploring the whole area.

Some potential customers might think that, because the hotel is attached to a pub, it might be a bit noisy. The advertisement stresses that the bedrooms are far enough away at the rear of the pub to be quiet. The advertisement emphasizes the facilities available in guest rooms and also shows that, despite being in the centre of Buxton, the hotel is able to offer private parking.

## THE QUEEN'S HEAD
### HOTEL & PUBLIC HOUSE

*The Queen's Head is a family run business situated in the centre of Buxton, in the heart of the Peak District.*

*The bedrooms are quietly situated at the rear of the pub in converted stables and cottage, and are reached by separate entrances. Each room has en-suite facilities, which include bath and shower, and is comfortably furnished and equipped with colour television, tea making facilities and central heating. There is private free parking for residents.*

High Street · Buxton ·Derbyshire
Tel: 01298 23841 · Mobile: 0831 899530
Fax: 01298 71238

---

"THE" HOTEL IN DERBYSHIRE
## Ye Olde Nags Head
### CASTLETON, DERBYSHIRE
### FREEHOUSE
"FOR THOSE WHO APPRECIATE THE BEST OF THE PAST AND THE BENEFITS OF MODERN HOSPITALITY"

Ye Olde Nags Head Hotel is a 17th century Coaching House situated in the picturesque village of Castleton, right at the heart of the beautiful Peak District National Park.

Privately owned and personally run by Mr. & Mrs. Graham Walker with the help of efficient and friendly staff, your stay will be a gloriously pleasant and comfortable one, with fresh flower arrangements in abundance, 4 poster beds, old paintings, antique furniture.

Individually designed to a very high standard, each bedroom has private bathroom or shower, direct dial telephones, trouser presses, hairdryers and tea-making facilities. Three rooms have 4 poster beds, one with whirlpool bathroom.

Open log fires blaze in winter in the public bar which serves Traditional Ales and a selection of beers and lagers, together with an extensive menu of delicious hot and cold bar food.

Beautiful china and cut glass adorn the tables in the elegant dining room, renowned for its first class cuisine, which is open to residents and non-residents for breakfasts, luncheons and dinners.

Brochure on request – Also details of our 2, 3 or 7 day break prices.

Castleton, Derbyshire S30 2WH
Tel: (01433) 620248

---

# NORTHFIELD FARM

**The Old Stables**

Three self-contained centrally heated flats fully equipped for two to six people. Situated in Flash, the highest village in England, on a working farm. Ground floor flat available for the less able. Laundry and recreation room.

3 Key up to Commended.

THE BRITISH HORSE SOCIETY

APPROVED RIDING ESTABLISHMENT

**Riding and Trekking Centre**
BHS Approved.

**For further details
fax/phone 01298 22543
Mrs Elizabeth Andrews,
Northfield Farm,
Flash, Nr Buxton,
Derbyshire SK17 0SW**

---

## PRIORY LEA HOLIDAY FLATS
### 50 White Knowle Road, Buxton SK17 9NH

APPROVED

• **Enhanced by beautiful situation adjoining own farm and riding stables**

• **Walks start from car park**

• **Comfortably furnished, equipped to Tourist Board standards**

• **Cleanliness assured. Colour TV**

• **Children and pets welcome**

• **Open all year. Sleeps 2-8**

S.A.E for colour brochure to resident proprietors Gill and Paul Taylor.
Phone 01298 23737 or 71661

Established 25 years

**MEMBER OF BDTA – BUXTON DISTRICT TOURIST ASSOCIATION**

---

## BRAEMAR BED & BREAKFAST
10 Compton Road, Buxton, Derbyshire SK17 9DN. Tel: 01298 78050

Offering a warm welcome with quality accommodation at a fair price from March to October. We are situated in a quiet but central part of this historic spa town renowned for its scenic beauty, having all the Peak District's famous attractions near at hand also. Guests are accommodated in newly refurbished and very comfortable double and twin bedded rooms all with colour TV, hospitality trays and all facilities etc.
Non-smokers are welcome. All diets catered for.

*Enjoy a restful break in this beautiful spa town.*

**Reservations 'phone Maria or Roger on
01298 78050.**

**Bed and full English breakfast £15.95 inclusive.
Weekly terms available. Registered with English Tourist Board. Member Buxton Tourist Association.**

*Special off-peak breaks available.*

Listed

---

*Fig. 2.3 Different types of accommodation in the Peak District*

### Northfield Farm

The farm is situated at Flash, 'the highest village in England', and will probably appeal more to those who want a quiet, rural location than those who prefer the bustle and activity of a town.

The Old Stables at Northfield Farm are advertised in a way that is intended to appeal to people with an interest in horse-riding. The fact that it is an established riding stable is shown both in the text of the advertisement and by the British Horse Society logo.

The description of the flats available is brief and relies on people having checked the meaning of the key classification system for self-catering flats. In addition to seeking to appeal to horse riders as a potential market, the advertisement also indicates that one of the flats is suitable for 'the less able'.

### Priory Lea Holiday Flats

The advertisement for Priory Lea Holiday Flats contains some detail intended to appeal to families. It mentions that children and pets are welcome and points out the accommodation can sleep any number from 2 to 8.

It attempts to catch the attention of people seeking active holidays by references both to walks and to the adjacent riding stables.

Several methods are used to stress the quality of this accommodation. It has been established for 25 years, it is 'equipped to Tourist Board standards', and the owners live on the site and so are available to deal with any problems or enquiries.

### Ye Olde Nags Head

Ye Olde Nags Head makes use of its seventeenth century origins in describing its appeal. It contains '4 poster beds, old paintings, antique furniture'. Reference is also made to log fires and beautiful china and cut glass. All of these features are intended to create an image in the reader's mind of an attractive interior with many reminders of the past.

The advertisement emphasizes the quality of hotel in a number of ways. Use of the heading, "THE" HOTEL IN DERBYSHIRE, implies that it is better than the others. The staff are 'efficient and friendly' and the restaurant menu is 'extensive' and 'delicious'. The hotel's ETB classification is given, four crowns representing a full range of facilities and 'highly commended' confirming the quality of the service it offers.

### Braemar Bed & Breakfast

Bed and breakfast properties often appeal to people on a tight budget and so it is not surprising to find that the first sentence of the advertisement for Braemar Bed & Breakfast mentions 'a fair price'. In order to convince people of this the actual price, £15.95, is listed. It also refers to the possibility of special off-peak breaks, implying that these will be cheaper.

The owners have attempted to appeal to a wide variety of people by mentioning both the attractions of Buxton as a town and also its closeness to other Peak District attractions. Details such as the fact that 'all diets are catered for' are also intended to widen the appeal.

## Activities

1 Allocate each of the five potential visitors to the Peak District listed below to one of the five accommodation choices given in the advertisements.

  (a) Mr and Mrs Johnson and their three children, aged 9, 6 and three months – seeking a healthy, active short break in February, preferably somewhere where they can take their spaniel, Patch, with them.

  (b) Mr and Mrs Gianelli, American tourists in their 50s – seeking a comfortable place for a June stay in what they describe as 'a typical English village'. They intend to tour the region by car.

  (c) Mrs Andrews, aged 65, a widow – seeking a quiet, inexpensive holiday at Easter. Would like a town centre location, preferably somewhere warm, comfortable and friendly.

  (d) Three university students, Dave, Alison and Zara – seeking inexpensive accommodation in August, reasonably close to a cycle hire centre in Buxton.

  (e) Mr Martin, aged 36, his sister Ms Harris, aged 33, and her two daughters, aged 11 and 8 – seeking an inexpensive summer holiday. The children are very fond of animals.

2 Write a letter from *one* of the visitors to the owners/managers of the accommodation you have allocated to them, in which they attempt to find out further specific details about exactly how suitable the accommodation will be to meet their needs.

3 Write a letter making a reservation at the accommodation. Make sure you have included all the important details.

## Camping barns

An inexpensive way of staying in the Peak District is to use one of the camping barns found in the National Park. These are stone barns that have been converted to provide basic overnight shelter. Visitors bring their own sleeping bags and mats. Toilets and cooking facilities are provided. Figure 2.4 shows a plan of the typical layout of a camping barn and Figure 2.5 gives descriptions of the location and size of two of the barns.

As there are over 4,000 (6,500 km) miles of public footpaths in the Peak National Park, it is not surprising to find that the main users of camping barns are walkers. Unless a group is large enough to book the whole barn in advance, the accommodation will probably be shared with other people. This means that while it does not cost too much, this kind of accommodation would probably not suit people who like a lot of privacy.

# Popular activities in the Peak District

The majority of the people who visit the Peak District take part in some kind of activity while they are there. Some will tour the area by car, but many choose to do something involving rather more exercise. Walking is the most popular activity, with over 4000 miles (6,500 km) of public footpaths in the area. Other outdoor activities are shown on page 38.

# PLAN OF TYPICAL BARN

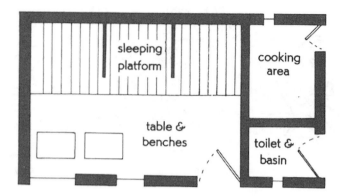

**Fig. 2.4  The typical layout of a camping barn**

## 4 ABNEY

Mr and Mrs Chadwick
Ivy House Farm
Abney
Derbyshire

**Location**
The small village of Abney is nearly 1,000 ft. up on the gritstone hills at the head of Abney Clough. The moors round about are notable for their archeological remains and fine viewpoints.

**Grid Reference**
198798

**Accommodation**
The barn sleeps a maximum of 8 people on two separate sleeping platforms. There is a stone bench in the porch and a separate toilet.

**Telephone**
Book through Losehill Hall
01433 620373
(to confirm arrival time)
Hope Valley
(01433) 650481

## 6 ONE ASH GRANGE

Mr and Mrs Wells
One Ash Grange
Monyash
Near Bakewell
Derbyshire

**Location**
Perched high above Lathkill Dale, One Ash Grange was once owned by the monks of Roche Abbey in Yorkshire. The area is limestone country, with a wealth of plants and wildlife. Lathkill Dale is a National Nature Reserve.

**Grid Reference**
169652

**Accommodation**
The barn sleeps a maximum of 12. The living and sleeping areas are at first floor level. Toilet in smaller building behind the barn.

**Telephone**
Book through Losehill Hall
01433 620373
(to confirm arrival time)
Youlgreave
(01629) 636291

**Fig. 2.5  Description of camping barns**

**cycling**

**caving**

**canoeing**

**climbing**

**fishing**

**horse riding**

**hang-gliding**

**sailing**

## Cycling

The Peak National Park has produced a booklet describing over 20 Peak Park Cycle Routes. All of these routes have been specially selected for their sustainability. They use surfaces where cycling will cause the least damage – such as bridleways, minor roads, abandoned railway routes and green lanes. Cycling on footpaths or across land where access has been agreed is discouraged. The booklet reminds cyclists of the erosion and damage their activities can cause, especially on steep slopes and peat moorland.

# Activity centres

The Peak District is an ideal environment for activity holidays. There are mountains, footpaths, caves and fast-flowing rivers which offer plenty of opportunities for walking, climbing, pot-holing, canoeing, rafting, mountain biking and orienteering.

The Youth Hostels Association Activity Centre at Edale is a good example of a holiday venue specialising in outdoor activities. The Centre's brochure says:

Edale YHA Activity Centre nestles below the edge of Kinder Scout plateau in the heart of the Peak District National Park. Built as a large country house in land-scaped grounds with a stable block and separate cottage, the Centre enjoys unrivalled views across the beautiful Edale valley.

The location is superb for a wide range of activities. To the south, the natural cave systems of the limestone area are suitable for exploring by beginners and experienced cavers. Gritstone rock fringes the Peak District – offering 'edges' for climbing and abseiling tuition. For hillwalking, orienteering and mountain biking the opportunities are endless.

The majority of visitors to the centre come as members of an organized group. This kind of residential holiday is particularly popular with schools. Groups are offered a range of activity programmes. Some, like the example in the box, are designed to give visitors a sample of a wide range of activities.

---

Sample five-day activity programme

*Day 1*
Arrive at Activity Centre early afternoon
Welcome and settle in
Activity/ice-breaking session
Dinner
Night hike/navigation exercise

*Day 2*
Breakfast
Canoeing
Lunch
Orienteering
Dinner
Problem solving/group development exercise

*Day 3*
Breakfast
Rock climbing
Lunch
Adventure course/archery
Dinner
Treasure hunt

*Day 4*
Breakfast
Caving
Lunch
Stream/gorge walk
Dinner
Action games or disco

*Day 5*
Breakfast
Abseiling
Lunch
Depart

---

# Safety at outdoor activity centres

Many of the activities available at outdoor centres involve some risk to those taking part. For example climbers may fall, mountain walkers lose their way in bad weather, and canoes may overturn in rough water. Activity centres have a responsibility to make sure that all reasonable precautions have been taken to minimize the risks. Activities have to be carefully supervised and instructors need training and qualifications that show that their knowledge and expertise is sufficient.

The following letter, from an activity centre manager, seeks to reassure potential customers that safety standards at the centre are high:

---

Dear Group Leader,

Recent events such as the Lyme Bay tragedy have drawn much media attention to outdoor adventure activities and the centres that offer them. I would like to take this opportunity to stress the high standards of quality and safety maintained by all the staff here at Uphill & Downdales Centre.

We have developed our own Outdoor Activity Safety Manual, copies of which are available for visitors to look at while they are here. The Centre has also gained approval from the British Canoe Union, the Mountain Leader Training Board, and the British Orienteering Federation. We are also affiliated to the National Caving Association and a member of the British Activity Holiday Association.

Two experienced instructors are provided for groups of up to 12 people. One will always have a current first aid certificate and a specialist qualification from one of the National Governing Bodies of outdoor sports.

All the mini-buses used by the Centre are modern, and have forward facing seats and seat belts.

We invite all group leaders to make an advance visit to the Centre. All the needs of their individual group can be discussed and the range of facilities can be fully inspected.

If you have any questions about the levels of safety here, or about any other aspect of our operation, please do not hesitate to contact us or, even better, pay us a visit.

Honour Ledge
Centre Manager

---

## Activities

1 Write to Ms Ledge, raising a particular safety issue that you think group leaders might be concerned about.

2 Write her reply, in which she explains what particular measures are taken to minimize the risks in the circumstance you described in your letter.

# Stately homes and gardens

The Peak District contains a number of notable examples of stately homes and gardens open to the public, including Eyam Hall, Haddon Hall and the restored gardens at Alton Towers. However, the best known of these historic houses is the home of the Duke and Duchess of Devonshire, Chatsworth.

## Chatsworth

The original house at Chatsworth was Elizabethan, built in 1555 by Bess of Hardwick. The first Duke of Devonshire, William Cavendish, made considerable alterations to the house between 1686 and 1707 and further extensive additions were made in the 1820s.

It is not just the house itself that attracts people. It has a very attractive setting on the River Derwent. The garden and the landscaped park attract people with an interest in plants, as well as providing a pleasant environment for walking. Inside the house is a collection of paintings, drawings, sculpture, silver and porcelain. The furniture and decor provide striking examples of how the wealthy lived in former times.

Tours of the house take about an hour. The route is marked by signs so that visitors can follow it at their own pace.

**Fig. 2.6  Chatsworth House**

## Activities

Study the information in Figure 2.6 about the house, garden and park at Chatsworth.

1 Outline some of the problems the owners are likely to face in opening the house to the public.

2 Discuss some of the ways in which they might try to solve some of these problems.

3 Look carefully at the picture of the library. What kind of questions do you think visitors would ask about it and its contents? What different ways of answering these questions can you suggest, apart from having a member of staff permanently on duty in the room?

4 What impact on the garden and the park will the regular presence of large numbers of visitors have? What things could be done to limit any harmful effects?

5 Chatsworth also has a farmyard and an adventure playground. Why do you think these extra attractions were developed?

# Congestion and visitor management

Regular users of several of the most popular of the 50 car parks managed by the Peak National Park can buy an annual season ticket.

The annual parking permits, to be displayed on the car dashboards, will apply at all National Park car parks where there are either pay-and-display machines or honesty boxes.

Visitors' permits are available at £15 per annum. Permits are also available on proof of identity for local residents at £5 per annum or coaches at £30 per annum.

*Source: Peakland Post 1996*

## Coping with traffic congestion

Traffic is the most serious problem faced in the more popular parts of the Peak District National Park. It has increased by 20% over five years, and it is still increasing. Peak District roads were not built to take so many cars. Congestion, damage to the roadside verges and pollution from exhaust fumes were, and still are, considered serious problems requiring some practical solutions.

Finding the best solutions is not easy. The first task is to gather accurate information about the actual traffic use in places where the problem is acute. A survey was carried out in the village of Castleton on an August Sunday. It was intended to find out how far motorists had travelled, which different sites in the area they stopped at, and how long they stayed in each place. Tables 2.2 and 2.3 summarize some of the survey's findings:

**Table 2.2  Length of stay per vehicle at different sites on an August Sunday**

|  | Main car park | Peak Cavern plus A625 | Pub car parks plus Centre | A625 to Odin plus Speedwell | Mam Nick car park | Blue John car park |
|---|---|---|---|---|---|---|
| Up to 1 hour | 6% | 4% | 0% | 10% | 16% | 7% |
| 1 – 2 hours | 23% | 28% | 30% | 28% | 28% | 45% |
| 2 – 4 hours | 46% | 48% | 55% | 38% | 28% | 35% |
| 4 – 8 hours | 23% | 20% | 9% | 23% | 26% | 13% |
| Over 8 hours | 3% | 0% | 6% | 2% | 2% | 0% |
| Sample | 565 | 356 | 178 | 355 | 239 | 141 |

No answer = 42 vehicles all sites

**Table 2.3 Time spent in total journey compared to time spent on site (August Sunday)**

| Journey time | Length of stay | | | | | |
|---|---|---|---|---|---|---|
|  | up to 1 hour | 1 – 2 hours | 2 – 4 hours | 4 – 6 hours | 6 – 8 hours | over 8 hours |
| Up to 1 hour | 0% | 25% | 6% | 3% | 24% | 0% |
| 1 – 2 hours | 29% | 15% | 34% | 25% | 36% | 28% |
| 2 – 4 hours | 48% | 31% | 37% | 65% | 32% | 72% |
| 4 – 6 hours | 0% | 7% | 17% | 7% | 8% | 0% |
| 6 – 8 hours | 0% | 10% | 3% | 0% | 0% | 0% |
| Over 8 hours | 23% | 7% | 2% | 0% | 0% | 0% |
| Sample | 19 | 152 | 299 | 143 | 68 | 19 |

No answer = 53 in total

## Activities

From Table 2.2:

1 Work out how many vehicles were left for more than two hours in Castleton's main car park.

2 Discuss ways of estimating the average time spent at each car-parking site by visiting motorists. At which site would you estimate that vehicles were left longest?

3 Suggest some of the possible consequences of imposing a two hour parking limit on some or all of the listed car-parking sites.

From Table 2.3:

4 Why do you think the samples questioned in the first and last columns of this table were considerably smaller than the others?

5 Discuss ways of working out how many motorists travelled more than four hours and left their vehicles at their chosen parking site for more than four hours.

6 Of the group that spent the least time on their journey to the Peak National Park (less than an hour) suggest possible reasons why they are well represented both in groups that stay for 1–2 hours and those who stay for 6-8 hours.

General questions:

7 Suggest some further information you think might help in future traffic planning for these sites and describe what you think would be the most accurate way of collecting this information.

8 Write a short paragraph explaining how the data in these two tables could be used to support some practical proposals for easing summer traffic congestion in featured sites within the Peak District National Park.

## A practical proposal in the Upper Derwent Valley

One practical idea was the introduction of a new traffic control scheme in the Upper Derwent Valley. The road was closed at weekends and Bank Holidays and all roadside parking was banned. In place of cars, park-and-ride minibus and cycle hire services (Figure 2.7) were provided, along with car parks, a visitor centre and a ranger service.

Some experts predicted that tourists would not walk more than 400 metres from their cars but this has not proved to be the case in this part of the Peak District. Comments

*Fig. 2.7  Cycling in the Derwent Valley*

about the scheme from visitors expressed their approval. They said such things as: 'This is how the country should be; peaceful, safe for children, and no traffic fumes.'

# Regulation of tourism development in the Park

The Board of the Peak District National Park was formed in 1951. It was created by an Order of the Secretary of State for the Environment made under the Town and Country Planning Acts. Its members are appointed either by the relevant local authorities or by the Secretary of State for the Environment. The only other National Park Board that acts as a planning authority is the Lake District. The other National Parks are administered by committees of the County Councils, with a separate authority for the Broads.

The Board has wide responsibilities. It develops strategic planning policies and controls development within the Park. Just like a local authority, the Board has to act in line with national and local laws and regulations. For example the Environment Act (1995) changed some of the functions of the Board, which became known as a National Park Authority. This Act sets out the duties of a National Park Authority which include:

- The conservation of natural beauty, wildlife and cultural heritage
- The promotion of opportunities for the public to enjoy the area
- The support of the economic and social well being of local communities

Table 2.4 sets out some of the ways in which a National Park Authority can use controls and regulations in order to carry out its statutory duties.

## Table 2.4

| Issue | Regulation and control |
|---|---|
| Proposal to modernize historic building in an inappropriate style | Planning Control Committee can refuse planning permission |
| Plans to establish limestone quarrying at a new site | Areas can be zoned with industrial use only allowed within limited areas and banned in areas designated as Natural Zones |
| Large increases in road traffic causing severe congestion in some areas | Park Management Committee can recommend selected road closures |
| Development work threatens to alter attractive views or landscapes | Planning Control Committee can use control processes such as Tree Preservation Orders |

## Activities

A farmer wishes to use a large field on the edge of a small Peak District Village as a caravan site.

1 What objections might the villagers have to this plan?

2 What restrictions and controls do you think the Peak District Authority might impose before considering whether or not to approve this plan?

3 What arguments do you think the farmer might put forward in defence of his proposal?

# Conservation and preservation of buildings and landscape

There are 45 sites within the Peak District National Park that have a special Conservation Area status. Many of them are villages such as Kettlehulme in Cheshire and Little Longstone and Sheldon in Derbyshire.

They have been given this special status because of the character and history of their buildings. It enables them to qualify for grants to help to restore historic buildings and paves the way for the Parish Council or others to carry out improvement work. Improvements might include schemes like the one at Hartington, where more than 4,000 metres (2.5 miles) of overhead phone and power lines were relaid underground. The removal of wires and telegraph poles considerably improved the appearance of the village.

Some 2,777 buildings within the Park come within the category of 'listed buildings'. This protects them from any kind of development that would spoil their original appearance and also means that their condition is regularly monitored. It means, for example that the owner of a listed sixteenth century cottage would be discouraged from replacing traditional leaded windows with modern, plastic framed window units (Figure 2.8).

*Fig. 2.8 Different window frames in a row of cottages*

Landscape needs to be developed in an appropriate way too. Industrial activity, such as quarrying, has left some derelict sites. However, many industrial sites are still active. Twenty million tonnes of limestone are quarried in the area each year. This creates conflict within the Park. While the planning authorities often wish to reduce quarrying on the grounds of the environmental damage it causes, local people may well support it because it provides employment.

A number of woodland sites are in need of improved management. Some trees need to be felled and others planted if the woodlands are to thrive and retain their original character.

# The Council for the Protection of Rural England

Organizations such as the Council for the Protection of Rural England (CPRE) campaign to protect the countryside, including National Parks. In the past they have helped to prevent four major proposals from being approved in the Peak District:

- A motorway across the Woodhead Pass
- A grand prix motor racing circuit north of Dove Dale
- A 400 KV power line between Dunford and Woodhead
- Reservoirs in Alport Dale, the Manifold Valley and Hassop

The CPRE summarises the main threats to the Peak District National Park at the present time as:

- Major road-building schemes
- Limestone quarrying
- Noisy, mechanized sports
- Large-scale tourist developments

# The National Trust

The National Trust, which owns over 3,600 acres (1,450 hectares)of land in the Peak District carries out various kinds of conservation work, including drystone walling, woodland management, moorland restoration and footpath repairs. The most obvious sign of the damage caused to the landscape by excessive numbers of visitors is soil erosion. In the area around Mam Tor, which receives an estimated 150,000 visitors a year, the Trust has spent £75,000 recently on footpath and erosion repairs. Yet erosion is not the only problem. Wild plants, some of them quite rare, are also disappearing from some sites as a result of being trampled on.

# Educating visitors

One way of attempting to limit the damage caused by visitors is to try to educate them. Visiting school groups are particularly encouraged to make themselves familiar with the Country Code before they come to the Peak District. A Teachers' Information Pack puts it like this:

WHEREVER YOU GO, FOLLOW THE COUNTRY CODE

Enjoy the countryside and respect its life and work;
Guard against all risk of fire;
Fasten all gates;
Keep your dogs under close control;
Keep to public paths across farmland;
Use gates and stiles to cross fences, hedges and walls;

Leave livestock, crops and machinery alone;
Take your litter home;
Help to keep all water clean;
Protect wildlife, plants and trees;
Take special care on country roads;
Make no unnecessary noise.

## Activities

A proposal is put forward by a member of the Peak National Park Authority to commission the design of some posters encouraging visitors to act in a way that will help to conserve the Park's natural beauty.

Some members of the Authority argue that this would help to encourage sensible behaviour by visitors. Others argue that the appearance of the posters themselves would be contributing to the sort of visual appearance that the Park Authority is trying to avoid.

1 Working in small groups, agree the type of message that the posters should be trying to put across.

2 Each member of the group should produce a rough sketch for the design of a poster.

3 The group should then meet to evaluate each of the sketches on the basis of:

   (a) whether it gets across a good message;

   (b) whether it would look out of place in an attractive rural setting.

4 Each group should agree which of the sketches best meets the two criteria listed in 3 and should then suggest ways of displaying it that might reduce its negative impact on a picturesque landscape.

5 Write out the text which you think should appear on the poster. Use desktop publishing software to produce three different ways of displaying the text and discuss which version would have the greatest impact.

# Case study 3   Chester – a historic city

## Origins and development of the city

Much of the appeal of Chester to visitors lies in its history, so it is worth a brief look at how the city developed.

Chester was sited at an important crossing point on the River Dee. It was settled by the Romans in the first century AD. They called the settlement Deva, and turned it into a fortified garrison. Its natural harbour and border position made it an important strategic outpost of the Roman Empire.

After the Romans left Britain the city experienced Viking raids but in the tenth century Alfred the Great's daughter, Aethelflaeda, helped to drive the Norsemen out. The city walls were extended and strengthened. After the Norman invasion the city was put in the hands of William the Conqueror's nephew, Hugh. He became the first Earl of Chester and oversaw the building of Chester Castle.

By the Middle Ages Chester had become the most important port in northern England. City merchants became wealthy as a result of the trade which the port allowed to flourish. However, the Civil War saw a setback as the city stayed loyal to King Charles, who watched from the walls as his troops were defeated by Cromwell's forces at nearby Rowton Moor. Chester was besieged for two years before it was forced to surrender.

By the eighteenth century the need for the city walls as a form of defence had passed. The River Dee had changed its course, so that the harbour had silted up. This led to a decline in trade and Liverpool eventually took over as the major port in the North West. As the county town of Cheshire, Chester was still a focal point for wealthy farmers, landowners and merchants and many elegant Georgian houses were erected in this period.

Canals, railways and roads were developed in the nineteenth century increasing the city's accessibility. A number of important buildings in the city were restored, including the Rows and the Cathedral. Eastgate Clock was put up in honour of Queen Victoria's diamond jubilee.

## The city today

The centre of present-day Chester is very compact. Many of its important historic buildings and monuments, such as the Rows, the Walls, the Cathedral and Grosvenor Bridge, are within walking distance of the centre. In addition to its architectural features, Chester is also a major shopping centre, drawing many visitors from other parts of the north west.

Nowadays 120,000 people live in the district of Chester. Under 1,000 of these actually live inside the original city walls.

With an estimated 5-6 million visitors each year, the centre of the city is under some pressure. While tourists spend a lot of money in the city, preserving the historic character of the city centre is costly. For example in early 1995 extensive repairs were needed to the city walls which had, in some places, begun to bend outwards.

Despite the disruptive nature of tourism on a large scale, the local community benefits economically. As one senior Council employee put it:

> This is a small city. Cestrians, as the inhabitants are known, are proud of their city. Also, they are friendly and welcoming by nature. The extent to which the local people find tourism acceptable is crucial. If there was not a warm welcome here it would be very difficult to market the place as an attractive destination. No one would want to come here...

## Activity

Study Figure 3.1, showing the centre of Chester.

1  Bithells Boats
2  Canal Trips & Cruises
3  Chester Candall Shop
4  Chester Cathedrall
5  Chester Heritage Centre
6  Chester Military Museum
7  Chester Visitor Centre
8  Dewa Roman Experience
9  Grosvenor Museum
10  Guided Tours
11  On the Air
12  Grosvenor Precinct
13  Toy Museum
14  Guide Friday Tour Bus Stops ●
15  Chester Town Crier

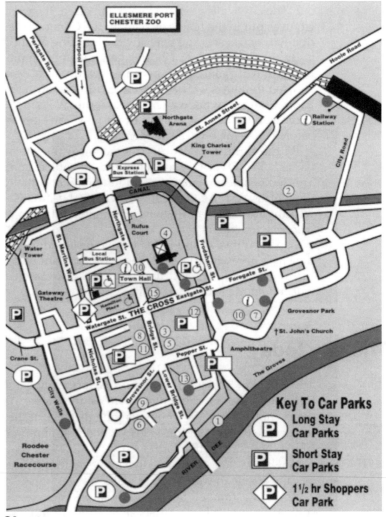

*Fig. 3.1  The centre of Chester*

1 Identify three different kinds of car park and suggest what the purpose of each kind was meant to be.

2 Guide Friday operates fully guided open-top bus sightseeing tours around Chester. Tours last 55 minutes and tickets are valid all day, so people can get on and off the buses whenever they choose.

Use the map to plan a whole day's itinerary, taking in a range of the attractions in Chester, using the Guide Friday buses. Show which places you would choose to get on and off at.

3 What do you think would be the main advantages and disadvantages of using Guide Friday buses as a means of exploring Chester?

# Accommodation

Chester has everything from deluxe hotels in the city centre and in the surrounding countryside to traditional farmhouses in rural communities. Many establishments are members of the Chester and District Hotels and Caterers Association. This is a local organization whose purpose is to help all its members to raise and maintain the standards of service which they offer. In order to achieve this a Code of Conduct, developed by the English Tourist Board, is used. The details of this Code are shown in Figure 3.2.

## Accommodation data

It is very important for tourism planning to have good sources of information. Data about the types of accommodation available and the amount of use it gets across the whole year can be helpful in a number of ways:

- It may reveal a shortage of a particular type of accommodation, e.g. luxury hotels, and so suggest whether future proposed developments would be appropriate or not.
- It should show the seasonal patterns of overnight visitors and so suggest at what times of year promotions featuring the city would be appropriate.
- It will help individual establishments to compare their performance with the average performance of similar establishments in the city.
- It will help establishments to determine whether their existing price structures are in need of revision.

Two of the most common types of accommodation data are **Bed Occupancy Rates** and **Room Occupancy Rates**.

All hotels will aim to increase their occupancy rates. Room occupancy rates may be broken down further into single and double occupancy rates. A hotel could be in a position where every room is occupied but it is not using its full capacity because some double rooms are occupied by single guests. Measuring these rates separately would show how much more the hotel could earn if all the rooms were double occupancy.

Larger hotels also need accommodation data so that they can plan their staffing rosters. At some times of the year they may employ fewer staff or part-time employees. If they know in advance what sort of occupancy rate they can expect, they can save money in employment costs.

## CHESTER AND DISTRICT HOTELS AND CATERERS ASSOCIATION †

The Association endeavours to ensure that standards of service from members are maintained to all levels and encourages the raising of establishments to a high standard commensurate with prices charged.

Membership is open only to Hotels and Guest Houses who have planning permission, are commercially rated, have a current Fire Certificate and Public Liability Insurance.

All members are expected to carry out business in accordance with ETB's Code of Conduct laid down as follows:

**CODE OF CONDUCT**

For establishments providing tourist accommodation and designed to ensure a fair deal for guests.

In addition to fulfilling its statutory obligations including the requirements of the Fire Precautions Act 1971 (if applicable), the Price Display Order (if applicable) and ensuring that the building and its fixtures and furnishings are] maintained in sound condition, the Management undertake to observe the following Code of Conduct:

1. To ensure high standards of courtesy, cleanliness, catering and service appropriate to the type of establishment.
2. To describe fairly to all visitors and prospective visitors the amenities, facilities and services provided by the establishment, whether by advertisement, brochure, word of mouth or any other means, and to allow visitors to see accommodation, if requested, before booking.
3. To make clear to visitors exactly what is included in all prices quoted for accommodation, meals and refreshments, including service charges, taxes and other surcharges. Details of charges for additional services or facilities should also be made clear. In the case of establishments with four bedrooms or more, to adhere to the Hotel Industry Voluntary Code of Booking Practice.
4. To adhere to, and not to exceed, prices current at time of occupation, for accommodation and other services.
5. To advise visitors at the time of booking, and subsequent to any change, if the accommodation offered is in an unconnected annexe, or similar, or by boarding out, and to indicate the location of such accommodation and any difference in comfort and amenities from accommodation in the main establishment.
6. To give each visitor, on request, details of payments due, and a receipt, if required
7. To deal promptly and courteously with all enquiries, requests, reservations, correspondence and complaints from visitors.

***Fig. 3.2 Chester and District Hotels and Caterers Association Code of Conduct***

The Chester Tourism Survey (1993) identified the type of accommodation used by visitors to the city. It also emphasized the point that only 38.5% of all visitors stayed. In other words, more than 60% were day visitors. Of those who did choose to stay, the average length of their visit was 2.4 nights, compared with 1.6 nights in 1983. Attempts to work out the most popular times of the year for overnight visitors proved hard to judge from the available statistics. Some weeks, only a quarter of all visitors asked stayed overnight; other weeks it was as many as half.

The survey also compared the number of overseas visitors using accommodation with those who had travelled from within the UK. As Table 3.2 shows, almost half of the 900 surveyed were from overseas. This kind of information is useful in deciding how and where to market the destination.

***Table 3.1 Accommodation establishments in Chester***

| Types of accommodation | Number | Capacity |
|---|---|---|
| Hotels, motels, inns and guesthouses | 78 | 3,819 bedspaces |
| Bed and breakfast establishments | 88 | 734 bedspaces |
| Farmhouse accommodation | 9 | 52 bedspaces |
| Group accommodation in hostels, educational establishments, etc | 7 | 780 bedspaces |
| Self-catering cottages, flats, chalets | 34 | N/A |
| Caravan and Camping Sites | 7 | 249 pitches |
| Hotels with 50 – 100 bedrooms | 9 | |
| Hotels with 100 – 200 bedrooms | 3 | |
| Hotels with more than 200 bedrooms | 0 | |
| Estimated total of service bed spaces in district of Chester | | 4,605 bedspaces |

**Table 3.2  Type of accommodation used by visitors to Chester**

|  | British | Overseas | Total | % |
|---|---|---|---|---|
| Large hotel | 109 | 63 | 172 | 19.1 |
| Small hotel, guest-house, B & B | 218 | 226 | 444 | 49.3 |
| Self-catering accommodation | 13 | 6 | 19 | 2.1 |
| Staying with friends or relatives | 58 | 72 | 130 | 14.4 |
| Caravan, motor caravan, camping | 40 | 17 | 57 | 6.3 |
| Youth hostel | 8 | 26 | 34 | 3.8 |
| Other (e.g. narrow boat, college) | 17 | 17 | 34 | 3.8 |
| Don't know yet/ not stated |  |  | 10 | 1.1 |
| **Totals** | **463** | **427** | **900** |  |

## Activities

Table 3.1 suggests that roughly 17% of the available bedspaces in Chester are in hostels and educational establishments.

Table 3.2 suggests that, at most, 7.6% of visitors who stay overnight use youth hostels or other accommodation such as colleges.

1  What possible reasons can you suggest to explain the 'gap' between the apparent number of bedspaces available in this type of accommodation and the proportion of visitors to the city who actually choose to stay in it?

2  Draw up a list of the types of visitor who might have good reasons for choosing youth hostels or educational establishments as a suitable place to stay.

3  Discuss the following proposals for accommodation development in Chester, listing arguments in favour of and against each one:

 (a)  provide small grants to encourage more owners of large houses to convert them into guest houses or bed and breakfast establishments;

 (b)  offer incentives for an international hotel group to develop a 5-star luxury hotel on a city centre site;

 (c)  provide free marketing advice for hostels and educational establishments and offer them discounted advertising rates in City Guides and brochures.

4  Which of these three proposals do you think would be in the best long term interests of the residents of Chester?

# Attractions

The presence of a range of attractions in and around Chester is important. It is a means of encouraging visitors using Chester as a base to stay longer. Research suggests attractions within a two hour drive of Chester are visited by people staying there. This means that in advertising the city's advantages as a place to stay reference can be made to locations as diverse as Manchester and Snowdonia.

The development of new attractions is not always easy to build into a strategy. For example the proposal to develop a Deep Sea World Centre raised concerns from Chester Zoo. The new attraction could be seen as direct competition because it would appeal to the same groups – families, children, animal lovers for example. The established attraction would wish to ensure that it could maintain or improve its current level of visitor numbers and might see the new attraction as diverting some of these elsewhere.

## The Rows

The Rows are perhaps Chester's most famous landmark. They are a series of black and white half-timbered buildings above street level with covered walkways. They provide access to shops and the occasional pub or museum. The Stalls are the areas next to the Rows on the street side (Figure 3.3). They are often at a slightly higher level and are open to the street. The Stall areas are enclosed by walls, pillars, ceilings and railings.

## Other attractions in Chester

Attractions are an important part of a tourist destination's development. For Chester, its most popular attractions – the Rows, the City Walls and the Cathedral – were not designed and built to attract visitors. They have become the main reason why many people visit.

However, in more recent times attractions have been developed with the prime intention of providing entertainment. The main reason for doing this is to try to persuade visitors to stay longer and to spend more money. An additional benefit for the city may be that more attractions can help to disperse the visitors a bit more and so reduce the effects of crowding in the most popular places. One unintended result may be that the city attracts different types of visitor, including those less interested in its history.

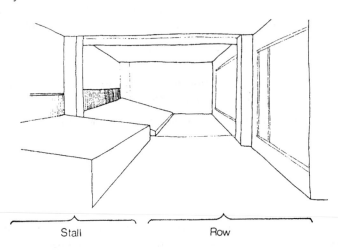

Stall          Row

*Fig. 3.3  Basic design of the Rows and Stalls*

In attempting to attract more visitors Chester also emphasizes the *range* of its attractions. They include organized tours, shopping opportunities, history and museums (Figure 3.4).

## Outside the city

Many tourist destinations stress the attractions that, though not actually found in the town or city itself, are within easy reach. Research suggests that staying visitors in a destination are willing to travel up to two hours each way to visit places of interest. Any further presents a problem. For those people who like a holiday 'base', more than four hours' travelling may seem too stressful for a holiday activity. For those on a touring holiday, it will probably seem more sensible to move on to an accommodation base nearer the attraction.

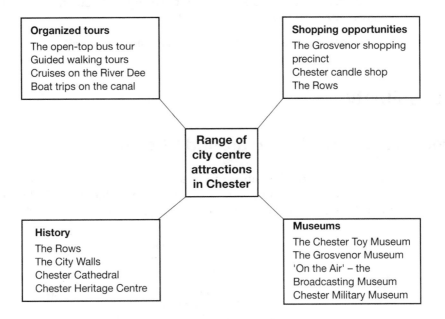

**Fig. 3.4 Range of attractions in Chester**

## Activities

When the Romans settled in Chester in the first century AD. they called it Deva. Suppose an entrepreneur plans to recreate a Roman fortress on a site some 10 or 15 miles (16 or 24 km) outside the city. It will be called Deva Fever, and will include replicas of the walls and the city as they were believed to be in Roman times. There will be a monorail carrying people around the site and a number of indoor entertainments, such as a virtual reality war game based on the Roman defence of the garrison.

1 Who do you think this kind of attraction would mainly appeal to?

**Table 3.3 Main methods of travel to Chester**

| Method of travel | British | Overseas | Total | 1993 | 1983 |
|---|---|---|---|---|---|
| Private car or van | 1,057 | 232 | 1,289 | 55.2% | 56% |
| Coach, excursion, organized group | 192 | 175 | 367 | 15.7% | 16% |
| Bus or coach, scheduled service | 122 | 75 | 197 | 8.4% | 6% |
| Hired car or taxi | 7 | 169 | 176 | 7.5% | 6% |
| Train | 126 | 118 | 244 | 10.4% | 12% |
| Other (e.g. foot, motorbike, bike, boat) | 36 | 26 | 62 | 2.7% | |
| **Totals** | **1,540** | **795** | **2,335** | | |

2 What reasons can you suggest for believing that such a development would have some effect on tourism in Chester?

3 Are there reasons why it might have little impact at all?

# Accessibility

## Transport routes into and around Chester

More than half of all visitors to Chester arrive by car. Many others come by coach, hired car or taxi, leaving only 12% who come on the train. Table 3.3 shows how the methods of travel to Chester have changed between 1983 and 1993.

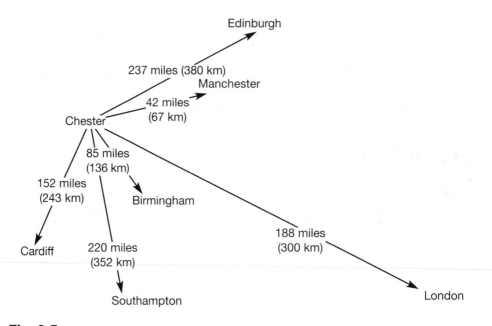

*Fig. 3.5*

Few major changes seem to have happened in the ten year period, although other figures show that the proportion of coach tour visitors who are from overseas has risen from 29% to 48%. The transport systems that link Chester to other parts of the UK all involve road or rail use first. However, airports and ports are not far away.

A simple method of deciding how accessible Chester might be by road is to consider how far it is from other main towns and cities, as shown in Figure 3.5. However, this would not be very useful information if it did not take the route into account. Fifty miles (80 km) on a motorway is generally a much quicker journey than 50 miles in suburban traffic. It is not always possible to tell how long a journey will take by road. Density of traffic, road works, accidents and weather conditions can cause delays. Travel by air or rail can also be subject to delays but the publication of timetables means people expect to arrive at or close to a specific time.

Figure 3.6 shows how Chester is linked to national and international travel networks.

## Activities

Table 3.4 shows the results of a 1993 survey question asking visitors to Chester where they had arrived from. It is based on answers from 2,335 visitors – 900 of whom were planning to stay overnight in the city.

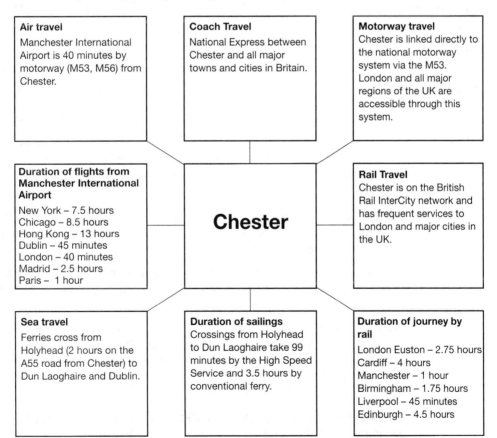

**Air travel**

Manchester International Airport is 40 minutes by motorway (M53, M56) from Chester.

**Coach Travel**

National Express between Chester and all major towns and cities in Britain.

**Motorway travel**

Chester is linked directly to the national motorway system via the M53. London and all major regions of the UK are accessible through this system.

**Duration of flights from Manchester International Airport**

New York – 7.5 hours
Chicago – 8.5 hours
Hong Kong – 13 hours
Dublin – 45 minutes
London – 40 minutes
Madrid – 2.5 hours
Paris – 1 hour

**Chester**

**Rail Travel**

Chester is on the British Rail InterCity network and has frequent services to London and major cities in the UK.

**Sea travel**

Ferries cross from Holyhead (2 hours on the A55 road from Chester) to Dun Laoghaire and Dublin.

**Duration of sailings**

Crossings from Holyhead to Dun Laoghaire take 99 minutes by the High Speed Service and 3.5 hours by conventional ferry.

**Duration of journey by rail**

London Euston – 2.75 hours
Cardiff – 4 hours
Manchester – 1 hour
Birmingham – 1.75 hours
Liverpool – 45 minutes
Edinburgh – 4.5 hours

*Fig. 3.6 Links from Chester to national and international travel networks*

**Table 3.4**

| Departure point | Day visitors | % of day | Staying visitors | % of staying | Total visitors | % of total |
|---|---|---|---|---|---|---|
| Scotland | 33 | 2.3 | 64 | 7.1 | 97 | 4.2 |
| North England/Cumbria | 23 | 1.6 | 38 | 4.2 | 61 | 2.6 |
| North East England | 5 | 0.3 | 28 | 3.1 | 33 | 1.4 |
| Yorks/Humberside | 49 | 3.4 | 48 | 5.3 | 97 | 4.2 |
| North West England | 689 | 48.0 | 144 | 16.0 | 833 | 35.7 |
| Wales | 311 | 21.7 | 96 | 10.7 | 407 | 17.4 |
| Midlands | 136 | 9.5 | 89 | 9.9 | 225 | 9.6 |
| Central/Eastern | 35 | 2.4 | 31 | 3.4 | 66 | 2.8 |
| East Anglia | 12 | 0.8 | 31 | 3.4 | 43 | 1.8 |
| Home Counties | 15 | 1.0 | 27 | 3.0 | 42 | 1.8 |
| London | 43 | 3.0 | 70 | 7.8 | 113 | 4.8 |
| South East England | 9 | 0.6 | 44 | 4.9 | 53 | 2.3 |
| Southern England | 6 | 0.4 | 28 | 3.1 | 34 | 1.5 |
| South West England | 14 | 1.0 | 46 | 5.1 | 60 | 2.6 |
| Northern Ireland | 0 | 0 | 5 | 0.6 | 5 | 0.2 |
| Ireland | 17 | 1.2 | 23 | 2.6 | 40 | 1.7 |
| Other countries | 15 | 1.0 | 53 | 5.9 | 68 | 2.9 |
| Not stated | 23 | 1.6 | 35 | 3.9 | 58 | 2.5 |
| **Totals** | **1435** | | **900** | | **2335** | |

1 How would you explain the fact that a high proportion of Chester's day visitors, nearly 22%, come from Wales?

2 London is further away than the Central/Eastern region listed in the table yet more people from London visit Chester than do from Central/Eastern. What two reasons might account for this?

3 Almost twice as many Scottish visitors to Chester are staying rather than day visitors, yet on average over 60% of Chester's visitors are day visitors. How would you explain this?

4 Draw an outline map of the UK and mark Chester on it. Draw a circle with a radius of approximately 50 miles (80 km) from the city. Now draw circles at 100, 150 and 200 miles' distance (160, 240, 320 km). Mark the areas on the map covered by the following departure points listed in the table: Yorks/Humberside, East Anglia, South West England, Ireland.

Is it possible to draw conclusions about the relationship between distance to a destination and the numbers of people who go there?

Fig. 3.7 Pedestrians in a crowded street in centre of Chester

Fig. 3.9 Pedestrianized area in Chester

Fig. 3.8 Chester city centre

# Congestion

Parking is the major cause of complaint among visitors to Chester. A Park and Ride scheme has been introduced to ease the situation in the city centre. Approximately 6% of visitors make use of this. Given the fact that more than half of the visitors to the city arrive by car, there is potential to encourage greater use of this service. There are plans to extend the number of sites on the outskirts of the city where Park and Ride services can operate from (Figures 3.7 – 3.9).

City centre streets become very busy during the summer and over bank holiday weekends. Nearly everyone visiting attractions in the centre of the city is likely to be walking. This increases the arguments in favour of pedestrianizing some of the main streets.

An environmental capacity study of Chester raised the following proposals:

● Make people aware of other parts of the city (e.g. the Tower, the Wharf, the Port of Chester, the River Dee, the Racecourse, Chester Castle), so that pressure is reduced at honeypots like Eastgate Street
● Use marketing to encourage off-peak visits to Chester

- Improve the quality of sign-posting and interpretation
- Encourage use of rail systems such as MERSEYLINK
- Run free courtesy buses from the station to the city centre
- Encourage consortia of attractions and restaurants to support public transport use schemes
- Develop 'park and ride' sites
- Develop 'Winter Shopping in Chester' promotion

## Mobility

The compactness of the city centre means that the main attractions are easy to get to, but it also means that some are not very accessible for people with mobility problems. For example the City Walls are most frequently reached by steps from the main street. Wheelchair users can gain access to them by means of special routes using ramps.

The City Council has an Access Officer whose main responsibility is to encourage private sector businesses to acknowledge the importance of making premises accessible to wheelchair users and those with limited mobility. Where a hotel or a tourist attraction has secured an 'Accessible' grading this fact is included in marketing materials such as visitors' guides.

## Activities

The Chester Action Programme has a £25,000 annual budget to support 'Access for All'. Its purpose is to help businesses and groups to provide accessible services, particularly where there are financial problems in doing this.

Among the groups that the Council has identified as being disadvantaged in terms of access are: the profoundly deaf, the blind and partially sighted, wheelchair users, people with severe walking difficulties, and people with mental handicaps.

1 Can you suggest any other groups for whom access, especially in a busy city centre, may present difficulties?

2 List examples of improvements which you think would benefit each of the disadvantaged groups identified by the Council.

3 Choose a specific tourist attraction that you have visited and devise a method of assessing how accessible it is for each of these groups.

4 What problems might the attraction's owners face in making it more accessible?

5 Some of the 'Access for All' budget could be spent on trying to convince businesses that they should invest their own money in improving accessibility.
Design a single page leaflet setting out the arguments in favour of their doing this.

# Conservation and preservation

Some of the important historic buildings in Chester are in poor condition and are considered unfit for use. This makes restoration expensive, especially if they have been empty for a long time. Older buildings often have small windows which means they let in little light and do not have good ventilation. This makes them not very suitable for use as either offices or residential dwellings.

## Listed buildings

Important historic buildings are now protected by law. A 'listed' building is one that is included in the Statutory List of Buildings of Special Architectural or Historic Interest prepared by the Department of the Environment. All kinds of buildings can be listed: cathedrals, churches, houses, cottages, garden walls, gates and barns. In any area the Local Planning Authority will keep a record of all listed buildings, grouping them as Grade I, Grade II or Grade III according to the level of their importance.

Any application to demolish or alter a listed building also has to take account of local opinion. The proposal is publicly advertised and, in some cases, may be referred to national organizations for comment. For Grade I and Grade II listed buildings, the consent of the Secretary of State for the Environment may be required.

## Conservation areas

A conservation area is one that has distinctive historic or architectural character. This often means that the buildings have a local style, dating back to the time when all building materials came from within the region. The black and white timber-framed buildings in Chester used wood from the oak woodlands of Cheshire. Church buildings and boundary walls made use of local red sandstone. From the eighteenth century onwards red and orange bricks made from the local clays were used to build.

The wide availability of modern building materials – concrete, steel, glass and plastics for example – poses a threat to conservation areas. These materials may be lighter, more flexible, cheaper or more efficient but their use would affect the character of a conservation area. The practice of listing important buildings means that the use of modern materials can be controlled.

## Grants

The terms of the Local Authorities (Historic Buildings) Act (1962) allow the Council of the City of Chester to offer grants for the repair and restoration of important buildings. These grants cannot be used for normal house maintenance, such as rewiring or central heating installation. They are intended to be used for work on more visible features such as retiling roofs, repairing external walls, or replacing doors and windows. They may also be used for treating parts of an existing building in order to protect it. For example, timber may be treated against insect and fungal attack.

## Churches and chapels

In and around Chester there is a great variety of churches and chapels. Some of these date back to medieval times and many are listed buildings. They often contribute to the overall visual appeal of an area.

Churches are often large buildings (Figure 3.9), especially when their actual use is considered. They were generally built from local stone and were often designed in great detail. All these factors mean that they are very expensive to repair. Where they no longer attract large congregations they are sometimes sold for other uses. However, their design makes them unsuitable for most working or residential purposes. The best way of ensuring their preservation is by maintaining their religious use. Churches in Chester have received grants from both the Council and from central government to assist with necessary repairs.

## Preserving the appearance of the Rows

Many premises along the Rows are shops. Chester City Council offers guidance to occupiers of the Rows. This guidance covers a number of design issues and tries to encourage the use of colours, materials and shapes that do not look out of place. For example, a bright red burglar alarm on a timbered wall would be discouraged.

**Fig. 3.10  St Oswald's Church, Malpas, near Chester**

Because shop fronts in the Rows cannot be easily seen by pedestrians in the street below and because the Rows themselves are too narrow to give passers by a clear view of a window display, other methods of advertising goods for sale have been developed, including show cases of shop goods, signs applied to overhead beams, goods displayed on Row stalls, and hanging signs.

Figure 3.11 shows some of the alternative ways shops have found of advertising their products and services.

## Activities

1 List what you would say were the three most important guidelines which Chester Council should set out for the design of signs applied to beams in the Rows.

2 The occupier of a shop in the Rows proposes to have a wood and glass show-case erected. What conditions do you think Chester Council should lay down before approving the proposal?

3 Suggest some of the possible advantages and disadvantages to a shop occupier of being allowed to display goods on Row stalls.

4 What factors do you think Chester City Council should take into account before deciding whether a particular hanging sign in the Rows is acceptable or not?

# Local and national politics

In a city where tourism is of such economic importance, the city council has a responsibility to take an active role both in promoting tourism and ensuring that its impact on the city is controlled. Much of the control comes as a result of national

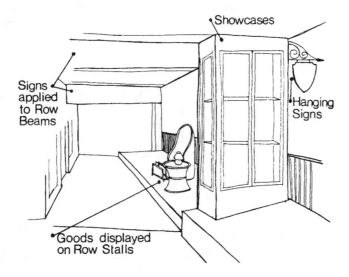

**Fig. 3.11  How shops advertise their wares in the Rows**

laws which enable the council to exercise planning controls. Some of these are mentioned in the section on Conservation and Preservation.

The support for tourism development comes through a series of partnerships, where the council works with industry and other interested organizations to make sure there is an overall strategy and that the interests of Chester are given a higher priority than the interests of one particular company or group.

The Chester Action Programme is a partnership between the private, public and voluntary sectors. Its main purpose is to identify Chester's main social, economic and environmental problems accurately and to find ways of solving them. The partnership includes Chester City Council, Cheshire County Council, the Chamber of Commerce, the Training and Enterprise Council, local MPs and MEPs, Hoteliers' Associations, the Rural Development Commission, and the Chester Economic Development and Environmental Forums (Figure 3.12).

Chester Council has a Tourism Promotion and Development Unit. This Unit works in partnership with the public and the private sectors of the local tourism industry. It has developed a five year Tourism Marketing Strategy and works with representatives of tourism businesses to develop a series of promotional campaigns.

Table 3.5 shows some of the activities and projects that the Chester Action Programme is or has been involved in:

## Activities

1 Discuss which of the activities and projects shown would benefit both tourists and the local community in Chester.

2 Issues such as tourism development, city centre congestion and employment opportunities are likely to be raised in the run up to local elections. Write a speech to be made by a candidate in an election for Chester City Council, setting out his or her views about the role local politicians should be taking in stimulating or controlling future tourism expansion in the city.

3 List the arguments for and against a national tourism tax on all visitors entering the UK from overseas, in order to raise funds for new tourism development.

**Fig. 3.12 Sign advertising redevelopment projects in and around Chester**

**Table 3.5**

| | |
|---|---|
| ● **Access for All** | Improving transport and access in Chester for people with all kinds of disability. |
| ● **Rural enterprise** | Providing advice and financial assistance to help diversify and expand the local rural economy. |
| ● **Strategic planning** | Developing an Action Plan covering issues like city centre management and cultural development. |
| ● **Marketing** | Working with partners to plan and coordinate promotional campaigns such as 'Winter Shopping in Chester'. |
| ● **Events** | Contributing to the funding and promotion of the Network Q RAC Rally which brings off-peak trade to the City. |
| ● **European Cities and Towns towards Sustainability** | Active membership of a Europe-wide group exchanging experience and ideas on how to integrate development, employment and transportation in the future. |
| ● **City centre management** | Funding projects to make the City centre cleaner, safer and more attractive. |
| ● **Walled Towns of Europe** | 123 walled towns and cities across Europe developing joint promotions, regional links, and exchanging ideas about conservation and visitor management. |
| ● **Funding applications** | Putting together bids for funds for city regeneration from national government through the Department of Employment, the Department of Trade and Industry and the European Commission. |

# Visitor numbers and visitor spend

Each year more than 5 million visitors come to Chester. They spend an estimated £45 million and support somewhere in the region of 16,000 jobs. This represents a quarter of the total local workforce. Chester's success as a shopping centre is supported by a national survey which placed two of its shopping streets 7th and 12th in the ranks of British retail centres.

## Problems in providing accurate data

However, it is not easy to arrive at exact numbers when trying to work out how many people visit a city and how much they spend. It is clearly impossible to count or interview everyone who visits, particularly since so many arrive by car. So in order to estimate the total numbers a representative **sample** of all visitors is questioned through a visitor survey. The answers to these questions produce data that is used to calculate probable figures for all visitors. For example, if the average spending of a sample of day visitors to Chester was £35 a head, in order to work out the total spending by day visitors to the city it would be assumed that they all spent the same amount on average.

There are additional problems involved in calculating people's spending. Usually their visit will not be over when they answer survey questions and so they may have to guess. People on organized tours tend not to count the cost of the tour, although a certain proportion of the total cost will bring money directly to Chester.

## Different ways of presenting data on visitor numbers and visitor spend

Data about visitor numbers and visitor spending in Chester may be put to a number of uses. It will be very important for those involved in future tourism planning and development. It will be used to monitor the continuing impact of tourism on the city. This kind of data often supports bids for funding and attempts to attract private sector investment. Nor should its use in educational assignments and projects be forgotten!

Because the data has so many potential uses, it is important to be able to present it in different ways. The use of simple formats like bar graphs or pie charts can both make the data look more attractive and present it in a way that makes it easier to understand and interpret.

The data on reasons for visiting Chester given below could be presented in several ways:

| | | | |
|---|---|---|---|
| Sightseeing, leisure, holiday | 78% | Visit a particular attraction | 1% |
| Shopping (special trip) | 9% | Conference, meeting | 0.5% |
| Visiting friends and relatives | 6% | Visiting a restaurant | 0.5% |
| Business | 2% | Other | 2% |
| Attending an event | 1% | | |

Figure 3.13 shows the data in three-dimensional pie charts and bar graphs.

It is often important to break down the data about visitors so that it provides information about specific groups. Visitors can be divided by any of the following:

- Where they began their journey
- Where their usual place of residence is
- What gender and age group they belong to
- What size of party they are travelling in

Each of these different ways of dividing the information may be helpful to people trying to decide on the most appropriate planning, marketing and development for Chester.

## Activity

Study the pie chart and bar graph shown in Figure 3.14.

1 Compare the way the data is presented in the two examples and suggest some general ways in which it could have been improved.

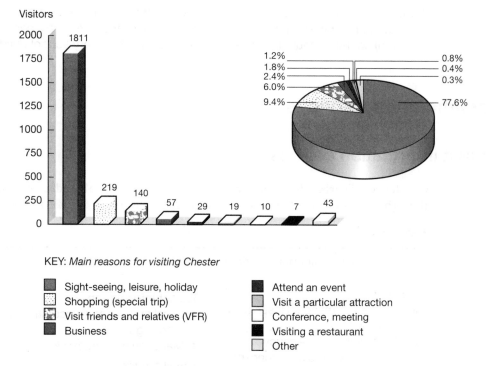

KEY: *Main reasons for visiting Chester*

| | | | |
|---|---|---|---|
| ▨ | Sight-seeing, leisure, holiday | ▉ | Attend an event |
| ▨ | Shopping (special trip) | ▨ | Visit a particular attraction |
| ▨ | Visit friends and relatives (VFR) | ☐ | Conference, meeting |
| ▨ | Business | ■ | Visiting a restaurant |
| | | ☐ | Other |

**Fig. 3.13  Reasons for visiting Chester**

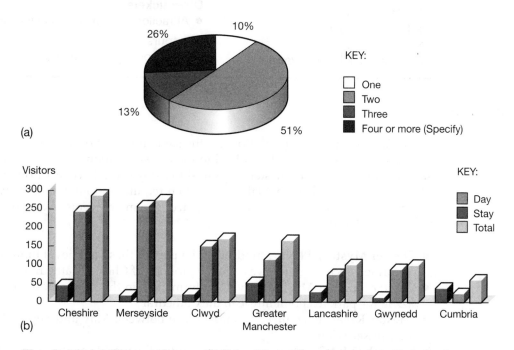

(a)

KEY:
☐ One
▨ Two
▨ Three
■ Four or more (Specify)

(b)

KEY:
▨ Day
■ Stay
☐ Total

**Fig. 3.14  (a) Group sizes and (b) where the groups have come from to visit Chester**

2 Suggest some alternative ways of presenting this data (a) so that it would make a good impression on a company planning a major tourism investment in Chester and (b) so that it could be understood by a class of primary school children.

# Facilities and services

## Tourist information centres

Chester has Tourism Information Centres in the Town Hall and at the railway station. There is also a Chester Visitor Centre. Table 3.6 shows the services offered.

**Table 3.6**

| Town Hall Tourist Information Centre | Chester Visitor Centre |
|---|---|
| **Services**<br>● National Roomfinder Reservation Scheme<br>● YHA Membership Agency<br>● Tickets for excursions, concerts, events, theatres, National Express coach services<br><br>**Guided walks**<br>● Pastfinder Tours<br>● Ghosthunter<br>● Roman Soldier Wall Patrol | **Tourist information**<br>● Local and national accommodation bookings<br>● Maps, guides and books<br><br>**Travel tickets**<br>● Sealink, Irish Ferries<br><br>**Other tickets**<br>● Attractions, excursions and theatre tickets<br><br>**City tours**<br>● Daily from April to October |

## Events

Some kinds of tourist information are the same for most of the year. For example giving directions from the Town Hall to the railway station will always require the same answer. However, Chester plays host to many special events during the course of the year. Potential and actual visitors often require up-to-date information about when and where such events will take place. The main events taking place in and around Chester in 1997 are:

● **Chester Mystery Plays**: Hundreds take part in these medieval biblical dramas performed once every five years in the grounds of Chester Cathedral.
● **Chester Summer Music Festival**: Performances in this annual festival vary from jazz in the park to choral music in the Cathedral.
● **Chester Races**: Race meetings take place between May and September at the Roodee Race Course.
● **Network Q RAC Rally**: Drivers from all over the world compete each year in this major motor rallying event.

# Language

Not all visitors to Chester are English language speakers. In an attempt to provide better access to information for such groups a wider range of city plans, maps and mini guides has been produced in foreign languages. The recruitment of Blue Badge guides places emphasis on the importance of speaking a second language. Apart from the expected languages like French, German and Spanish, there are currently guides in Chester speaking Japanese, Cantonese and Swedish.

## Activities

Consider the following comments, all made by individual visitors to a historic city:

(i) 'I think all information should be free...You shouldn't have to pay for a map...'

(ii) 'The guide maps for the city centre don't have enough information for motorists...'

(iii) 'None of the information I was sent in the post told me how much I'd have to pay for a meal in a restaurant...'

(iv) 'The Tourist Information Centre was closed on Sunday...'

(v) 'There were not enough seats around the city to take a rest on...'

(vi) 'The video at the Visitor Centre was too long...'

(vii) 'There weren't enough things for young children to do...'

1 Discuss which of these complaints you think tourism planners in the city should regard as serious and which you would treat as less important.

2 List the complaints in order of priority, with the one you think most urgently requires attention at the top and the one that is a more long-term concern at the bottom.

3 For each complaint suggest some possible means of putting it right. For each method you suggest indicate whether it would be easy or difficult to carry out and why.

4 Assume that each of these comments arrived in the form of a written complaint. Select three and write letters of reply from the appropriate council officer that are intended, as far as possible, to maintain good public relations.

# Case study 4 The National Exhibition Centre, Birmingham

## History

Throughout the early 1960s it was generally agreed that there was a need for an exhibition centre large enough to host major international trade exhibitions. These were seen as vital in improving the British export trade. The facilities offered by such a centre would also have to be of a very high standard if major international companies were to be persuaded to use it.

Various sites were proposed, including one at Northolt in West London. Farmland on the edge of Birmingham was purchased and plans for siting the national exhibition centre were started. The scheme was expected to boost the economy of the region. The only opposition came from some exhibition organizers who would have preferred a London site and some local voices who thought the centre might in time become a 'white elephant'.

Birmingham Chamber of Commerce and Birmingham City Corporation produced a feasibility study for an exhibition centre on a 300-acre (1,214,000 square metres or 121 hectares) site eight miles (13km) from the city centre. At the start of the 1970s a company, National Exhibition Centre Limited, was formed to take the plan forward. Government funding helped to market the scheme and in November 1971 the Secretary of State for the Environment granted outline planning approval for the scheme.

The National Exhibition Centre was opened by the Queen in February 1976. It contained 89,000 square metres of exhibition space. Three further exhibition halls were added in 1989 and another three in 1993, increasing the total exhibition space to 158,000 square metres. Some idea of its size can be gained by comparing it with Earl's Court, the next largest exhibition centre in the UK. It is two and a half times larger.

Table 4.1 shows how the NEC's activities have grown since its opening. The number of exhibitions held each year at the NEC has risen to 140, 70% of which are trade shows and the remaining 30% of which are open to the general public.

*Table 4.1*

|                             | 1976/7                                      | 1995/6                                        |
| --------------------------- | ------------------------------------------- | --------------------------------------------- |
| No. of exhibitions          | 36                                          | 140                                           |
| No. of exhibiting companies | 9,706                                       | 37,852                                        |
| Exhibition visitors         | 1.185 million                               | 2.6 million                                   |
| Total visitors              | 1.3 million                                 | up to 4 million                               |
| Share of the UK market      | 25%                                         | 40%                                           |
| Hall capacity               | 89,000 square metres (106,000 sq. yards)    | 158,000 square metres (189,000 sq. yards)     |
| Site area                   | 310 acres (1,255,000 sq. m)                 | 580 acres (2,347,000 sq.m)                    |
| Parking spaces              | 12,000                                      | 24,000                                        |

Three different business operations take place in the National Exhibition Centre:

- Exhibitions
- Conferences and events
- Sport and entertainment

# NEC Limited

NEC Limited looks after the sales, marketing and operation of a number of venues. Table 4.2 shows what each one is mainly used for.

*Table 4.2*

| Venue | Main uses |
|---|---|
| National Exhibition Centre | International, national and regional trade, and consumer exhibitions, conferences, product launches, sports events and animal shows |
| NEC Arena | Concerts and other entertainments |
| International Convention Centre | International and national association conferences; corporate conferences |
| Symphony Hall | Classical concerts and other entertainments |
| National Indoor Arena | International, national, and regional sports events; entertainment events |

The land on which these five facilities stand is owned by Birmingham City Council. NEC Limited is also half owned by the City Council, with Birmingham Chamber of Commerce owning the other half. The company was originally set up to run the exhibition centre opened in 1976. However, it now has the responsibility of managing all five facilities.

# Accessibility by different transport systems

Unlike exhibition centres in London, such as Earls Court, the NEC is located at an out-of-town site. This is both an advantage and a disadvantage. It does not have the same range of leisure and entertainment facilities as a major city centre. However, there is a range of entertainments available on the site and the centre of Birmingham is only 15 minutes away by train.

The main advantage is that the NEC is easily accessible from most directions and has road, rail and air transport links nearby.

# By road

Birmingham is easily reached from the UK motorway network. The M6, M42 and M40 provide connections to the M1, M5 and M4. New slip roads have been built, giving better access to the NEC site from the M42.

To travel by road from the NEC to the centre of Birmingham takes approximately 30 minutes.

There are 18,000 car-parking spaces at the NEC for concert-goers, exhibition visitors and organizers and the general public. A multi-storey car park at the National Indoor Arena provides 2,300 spaces for visitors to the International Convention Centre, the National Indoor Arena and the Symphony Hall.

A new shuttle bus service was introduced in 1996, linking the NEC halls with car parks. Ten buses carry up to 72 passengers and operate rather like the airport buses that run between terminals and car parks. Destination information is carried on the front of the buses which carry the NEC livery (Figure 4.1).

# By rail

Birmingham New Street station is part of the British Rail InterCity network. It is 90 minutes away from London Euston, from where trains run every half hour during the day and every hour during evenings and weekends. Eventually there will be a connection to the Eurostar service to provide a quick rail route into Europe.

# The InterCity rail network

Birmingham International station (Figure 4.2), which is close to both the NEC and Birmingham International Airport, is ten minutes away from Birmingham New Street, which is close to the International Convention Centre, the National Indoor Arena and the Symphony Hall.

**Fig. 4.1  NEC shuttle bus service**

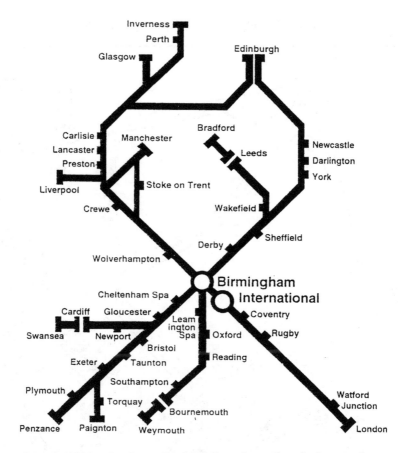

**Fig. 4.2  Birmingham International station is located at the heart of the NEC and is connected to the exhibition halls and conference facilities by a covered walkway**

## By air

Over 4 million passengers a year use Birmingham International Airport. There are currently scheduled flights direct from Birmingham to 35 different destinations. Many of these services are to major business destinations such as Paris (eight flights daily to and from), Amsterdam (seven flights daily to and from) and Frankfurt (five flights daily to and from).

British Airways is the largest airline operator at Birmingham International Airport, offering over 500 flights a week to and from 23 European, UK and intercontinental destinations. This includes a daily Birmingham/New York service. Four flights a week arrive and depart from Los Angeles, via Manchester.

## Activities

Study Figure 4.3 showing the location of the International Convention Centre, the National Indoor Arena and the Symphony Hall. Note the specific locations of Birmingham New Street Station, of the access routes to different motorways, and of

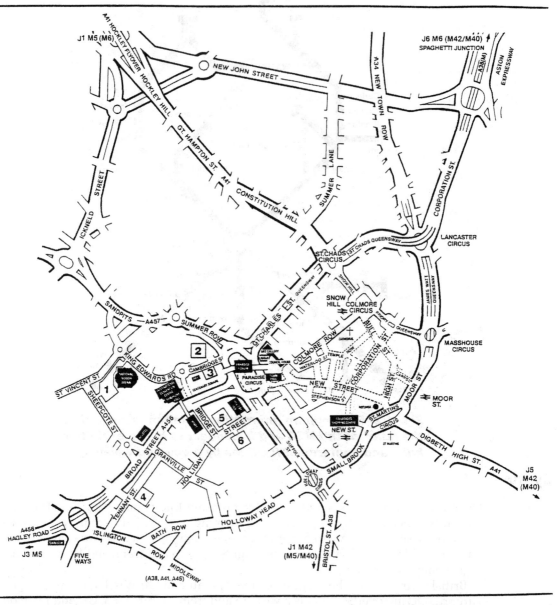

## KEY TO CAR PARKS

1. **National Indoor Arena.***
   Access off King Edwards Road
   and Sheepcote Street.

2. **Brindley Drive.***

3. **Civic Centre.**

4. **Tennant Street.**

5. **Central.***

6. **Holliday Street.**

Certain streets in the city have been pedestrianised
as part of a development programme.

*Multi-storey Car Park.
Please check car parking opening times before entering.
Subject to change.

Birmingham
*Europe's meeting place*

**Fig. 4.3 The location of the International Convention Centre, the National Indoor
Arena and Symphony Hall**

the car parks in the city. Note also the location of the streets with dotted lines, indicating that they have been pedestrianized and are therefore closed to motor traffic.

Work in pairs, with one person acting as someone ringing a facility's reception on a mobile phone and the other giving oral directions in response to the enquiries given below.

After each activity, swap roles.

1 'Hello...is that National Indoor Arena?...I've just come over Hockley Flyover...Someone has reserved me a parking space in the Holliday Street Car Park...I'm walking to the Arena from there...Can you direct me from where I am?'

2 'Hello...I've just arrived at New Street Station...I have to pick up a music score from a shop in Colmore Row before coming to the Symphony Hall for this afternoon's rehearsal...Can you help me with some directions?'

3 'Hi...I'm on the Aston Expressway heading into Birmingham and I need to get to the International Conference Centre fairly quickly...Can you tell me the best route and the most suitable place to park my car?'

4 'Hello...I'm coming into Birmingham on the A41...I'm due to visit the International Conference Centre this morning and the National Indoor Arena and the Symphony Hall this afternoon...Can you suggest the most central place to leave my car and how I get to the three facilities from there?'

# Facilities and services

The facilities available will have a considerable effect on the kind of events the NEC is able to put on. The NEC has the advantage of being purpose-built. This means it was designed specifically for exhibitions. Its out-of-town location meant that there was plenty of land available. This was important in creating halls large enough to accommodate major international exhibitions. It also meant there was enough room to build all the halls on one level. This makes the transport and delivery of large structures and heavy materials required in assembling exhibitions much easier.

The design of all the halls provides for all services, such as electricity, water and drainage, to be under the floor. This makes them much more accessible for any service and maintenance work.

The original halls were fairly functional in appearance but the more recent ones have exterior silver cladding. The interior design includes some important features. The newer halls do not have pillars, so that views in all directions are unobstructed. Ceiling windows allow things to be seen in natural daylight, but automatic blinds can be used whenever artificial lighting effects are required.

## NEC

The NEC can host events involving anything from 5 people to over 12,000. The 16 halls make it ideal for international trade fairs and exhibitions. Often five or six smaller exhibitions will run simultaneously.

The NEC Arena (Figure 4.4) seats 12,600. The design means that the roof is supported from outside the building so that no one inside has an obstructed view of events.

The seating can be arranged in many different formats. Special features of the NEC Arena include controlled lighting effects, TV standard lighting, extensive dressing-room areas, staging and demountable seating.

The Piazza houses visitor services such as shops, banks, information and business services and food outlets.

## International Convention Centre

The ICC is used for four main types of event:

- Association conferences
- Company conferences and product launches
- Banqueting and entertainment events
- Small exhibitions

The ICC consists of 11 halls and 10 smaller executive rooms. Access to all of these is possible from the Mall which runs through the middle of the Centre. The main visitor services in the ICC are found in the Mall, including an information desk, a visitor reception desk, a bank, shops, a travel agency, a business centre, a cloakroom and public catering areas. There is also a Box Office selling tickets for performances and events at the Symphony Hall, the National Indoor Arena and the NEC Arena.

The main conference hall contains 1,500 fixed tiered seats. There are 12 simultaneous translation booths. The stage is large enough for major presentation displays and has enough floor space to turn an articulated lorry (Figure 4.5).

The largest hall in the Centre can seat up to 3,000 for meetings and up to 2,500 for banquets. The smaller halls can be adapted for a variety of different uses for groups of varying sizes.

**Fig. 4.4  NEC Arena hosts European Gymnastics Championships for Women**

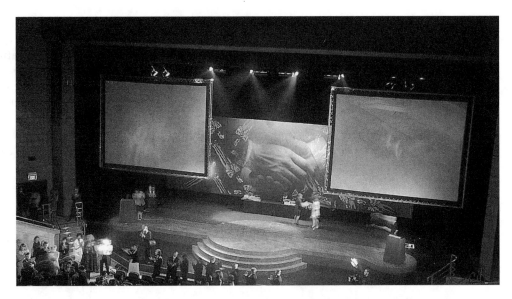

*Fig. 4.5  How the ICC's creative production services may be used*

## Symphony Hall

The most interesting aspect of the Symphony Hall is the way it was designed to provide the best sounds regardless of the type of music being played. Computer models
were used to add devices to the basic shape of the hall. These enable the sound of
different types of music to be modified. The sound heard within the hall is the same
from each of the 2,261 seats.

An acoustic canopy weighing 35 tonnes is suspended above the stage. It can be
raised or lowered to any height between the stage and ceiling to suit the acoustic
needs of the individual performance. For example, for a solo recital it would be lowered to about 10 metres (32 feet) above the stage. For an orchestral concert it would
be raised to 14 metres (46 feet)  above it.

The walls, floors and other surfaces are made of hard materials which reflect
sound waves. However, a more muted sound effect can be created by soft covered
panels which can be moved out to cover the hard wall surfaces.

The Symphony Hall is completely isolated from any sounds outside. It has even
been designed to sit on rubber bearings so that no sound comes through the ground.

## National Indoor Arena

The NIA is used primarily for international and national sporting events. However
it is also used for rock and classical concerts, family entertainment events, conferences and exhibitions.

Up to 8,000 people can be seated for sports events and up to 12,000 for concerts
and presentations.

The NIA is built on four levels. The Arena floor houses the UK's first indoor, demountable 200 metre six-lane athletics track. There is also a 60 metre sprint track, a sunken long jump pit and a pole vault box with run ups. A portable ice mat enables the staging of ice events.

When the athletics track is demounted the floor area can be used for sports such as Basketball – the Birmingham Bullets play there – and events such as the TV series *Gladiators*.

The Academy is a smaller venue within the NIA, seating up to 4,000. It includes facilities for people with disabilities. It is mainly used for popular music concerts.

## Activities

1 Choose a city in the UK, other than London or Birmingham, and *one* new facility from the following list:

- An exhibition centre

- A concert hall

- An indoor sports arena

2 List the arguments that might be used in *favour* of building the new facility.

3 List the arguments that might be used *against* building it.

4 If agreement was reached to go ahead with building the facility, what sort of conditions might be imposed before the plan went ahead?

5 What factors do you think should be taken into account in deciding the capacity of the new facility?

6 Suggest some ways of ensuring that the use of the facility was maximized.

# Visitor numbers and visitor spend

Data for the year 1994/5 (Table 4.3) relating to the International Conference Centre, The Symphony Hall and the National Indoor Arena suggest that they have had a major impact in terms of attracting visitors to Birmingham.

## Activities

A study to assess the economic impact of the four NEC venues, conducted over a 12 month period between 1992 and 1993, showed that there were 4.5 million visitors, of which 3.9 million were daytrippers. They attended 728 events. Nearly half a million visitors were from Birmingham itself and the city provided the Symphony Hall with 44% of its visitors.

Tables 4.4–4.6 provide data about the number of events and visitors, the total expenditure at the four venues, and the employment created by them. Table 4.4

shows the number of events and visitors to the NEC group of venues. Table 4.5 shows how much was spent by visitors, organizers, promoters and exhibitors. Table 4.6 shows the full-time employment resulting from this expenditure.

*Table 4.3*

| Venue | Attendance 1994/5 | Attendance 1991–95 | Number of events 1994–95 | Number of events 1991–95 | Visitor expenditure* |
|---|---|---|---|---|---|
| International Conference Centre | 116,000 delegates | Making a total of over 470,000 since 1991 | 380 conferences, exhibitions, banquets, and business meetings | Making a total of 1,500 events since 1991 | £66 million* |
| Symphony Hall | 326,000 concert-goers | Making a total of 1.3 million since 1991 | Over 200 concerts | Making a total of nearly 900 since 1991 | |
| National Indoor Arena | 700,000 attenders | Making a total of 2.5 million since 1991 | 67 different sporting and entertainment events | Making a total of nearly 200 since 1991 | £43 million * |

*These figure are based on an independent study carried out over a 12 month period in 1992–93

**Table 4.4  Events and visitors to the NEC group of venues from 1 September 1992 to 31 August 1993**

| | ICC | Symphony Hall | NIA | NEC | Total |
|---|---|---|---|---|---|
| Number of events | 263 | 242 | 40 | 183 | 728 |
| Number of visitors* | 114,000 | 409,000 | 584,000 | 3,375,000 | 4,482,000 |

*Visitors include event spectators, exhibition visitors, conference delegates, exhibitors, performers, conference speakers, technical support staff, competitors.

**Table 4.5  Total direct expenditure in Birmingham and the rest of the West Midlands (ROWM) from 1 September 1992 to 31 August 1993**

| | ICC & SH | NIA | NEC | Total |
|---|---|---|---|---|
| Expenditure in Birmingham | £59 million | £31 million | £55 million | £145 million |
| Expenditure in ROWM | £7 million | £12 million | £274 million | £293 million |
| **Total expenditure in West Midlands region** | **£66 million** | **£43 million** | **£329 million** | **£438 million** |

**Table 4.6 Full-time equivalent (FTE) employment in Birmingham and the rest of the West Midlands from 1 September 1992 to 31 August 1993**

|  | ICC & SH | NIA | NEC | Total |
| --- | --- | --- | --- | --- |
| FTE employment in B'ham | 1,100 | 700 | 4,000 | 5,800 |
| FTE employment in ROWM | 1,600 | 1,200 | 8,200 | 11,000 |
| **Total FTE employment** | **2,700** | **1,900** | **12,200** | **16,800** |

Use a calculator for activities 1–4.

1 Which venue attracts the highest number of visitors per event? What reasons can you suggest for this?

2 Which venue creates the smallest expenditure per visitor? What factors would account for this?

3 Compare the employment figures for the NEC venues with the number of visitors they receive and the amount of expenditure at them. What conclusions can you draw?

4 What other kinds of financial information about the NEC venues would you need in order to be able to make a fair assessment of their economic impact on the region?

5 Write a brief report outlining what the data provided suggests about the main economic impacts of the NEC venues on Birmingham and the West Midlands.

# Running events at the NEC

## Roles of NEC Limited and the client

The first task for NEC management is to attract exhibitions in the first place. There are a number of other competing venues in the UK: Earls Court for larger exhibitions and the Scottish Exhibition and Conference Centre in Glasgow, the Harrogate International Centre and the Manchester G-Mex Centre for medium sized exhibitions. In addition there are many venues in mainland European cities also seeking to host international exhibitions.

Once the NEC has agreed with a client to host an exhibition, each side in the arrangement will be responsible for a number of different areas. The main responsibilities are shown in Table 4.7.

The timing of individual exhibitions has to be agreed between NEC Limited and the client. The period from September to the end of November is generally busy since this is a traditional buying time in many industries. January to July is also a popular period for exhibitions but August, as a traditional holiday period, is very quiet and is used by the NEC for major maintenance work.

**Table 4.7**

| NEC Limited is responsible for | The client is responsible for |
| --- | --- |
| • Catering<br>• House management (operations such as arranging access for trucks)<br>• Traffic management<br>• Cleaning | • Selling space at the exhibition<br>• Putting the exhibition together (usually through a conference organizer)<br>• Dismantling the exhibition |

Among the questions the client organizing the exhibition has to consider are:

• What is the target number of visitors to the exhibition?
• How much floor space will be needed?
• How will the floor space in the exhibition be sold?
• How much car-parking space will be required?
• What range and level of catering will the event require?

Among the questions NEC Limited has to consider are:

• Will the exhibition clash with another similar event?
• How will the client's needs be met in the drawing up of a floor plan?
• What security arrangements will be required?
• How do the client's needs fit in with regulations about heights of stands?
• Will the plans meet all the necessary health and safety requirements?

## Meeting the needs of clients

Some of the events held at the NEC, such as the launch of a new model of car, are intended to have a dramatic effect. Sometimes this means special arrangements have to made to set up exhibition halls as the clients want them.

For example an Auto Sport exhibition created a track that ran inside and outside one of the halls. A moto-cross exhibition shipped in tonnes of soil to construct an indoor moto-cross circuit. A Ford car launch moved in tonnes of sand in order to create an indoor desert setting as a background.

A range of services will also be required by clients. The NEC provides many services on site, including:

• A British Telecom Office with ISDN lines installed
• Two Business Centres offering secretarial and translation services
• An American Express Bureau de Change
• A NatWest Bank and cash machines
• A newsagent
• A DHL office providing delivery and collection services
• A Post Office
• Information services through the Birmingham Convention and Visitor Bureau

## Activities

The British International Motor Show is held every two years at the NEC. In 1996 it attracted 623,000 visitors.

Divide your group into teams of between three and five people. Each team represents a small company intending to produce a new sports car to be sold in kit form and assembled by the purchaser. The company has decided to pay for a stand at the Motor Show with the main purpose of winning orders for its new product.

1 Discuss the markets you think your car will appeal to. You might find that doing a SWOT (their strengths, weaknesses, opportunities and threats) analysis for kit cars compared with ready assembled vehicles might help you to assess this.

2 Brainstorm ideas for the main message that you want to put across at the Motor Show.

3 Outline plans for the design and layout of your stand.

4 Suggest (a) marketing materials and (b) on-stand activities that you think would help you to achieve your objective of winning orders for your product.

5 Suggest a method of measuring whether it is worthwhile for a small company to take a stand at a national exhibition.

# Module 2
# LEISURE FACILITIES

## Introduction

## Case study 5
### The Derngate Centre, Northampton – an arts centre

## Case study 6
### Hull Arena – an expanding leisure facility

## Case study 7
### Oxford United Football Club

## Case study 8
### Knebworth House and Gardens

This module covers the following components of the syllabus:

2.1  Factors determining the level and range of local leisure provision
2.2  Operation of leisure facilities
2.3  Staging events

# What is leisure?

Everyone has a certain amount of time available to them. The activities they undertake during this time can be divided into things they *have* to do and things they *choose* to do. The things people have to do may include sleeping, eating, working, studying and looking after children. If there is any time left over after they have done all these things, they are usually described as being at *leisure.*

How they choose to spend this leisure time may depend on a number of things, such as:

- How old they are
- How much free time they have
- What special interests they have
- What they can afford to do
- What facilities are available locally to cater for their leisure interests

# The demand for leisure facilities

The demand for leisure facilities has grown in recent years, mainly because there are more people among the population as a whole with the time and money to pursue sports, hobbies and other leisure pastimes. The huge increase in car ownership means that leisure facilities can be developed on out-of-town sites which are still accessible to main population centres.

The demand for leisure facilities may not be the same in all groups. For example, it is not difficult to find reasons why women, racial minorities, the elderly, the unemployed and the disabled may make less use of leisure facilities than other groups.

While the demand for some kinds of leisure facilities, such as public parks, may remain fairly constant for long periods, other leisure interests fluctuate considerably. For example, a look at Football League or cinema attendances over the last 30 years would show dramatic rises and falls in public interest.

# Types of leisure facility

Leisure facilities are the sites and venues that are designed to be used for leisure activities by individuals, groups and organizations. They will include places where people can actively participate, such as dance studios or snooker halls, as well as places where they can watch sports or arts performances. They can probably be divided into a number of categories, which include:

- Outdoor sports facilities
- Indoor sports facilities
- Venues for spectator sports
- Theatres, cinemas and concert halls
- Pubs and clubs
- Gardening and DIY centres
- Restaurants
- Municipal parks, gardens and allotments
- Casinos, bingo halls, and betting shops
- Community centres

These facilities cater for sports, the arts, and a range of hobbies and pastimes. Some offer mainly events and activities that are professional and for which visitors and spectators are charged for admission. Others are mainly intended to provide for community use and a proportion of their costs may be met by local or national government.

Some people would argue that shopping malls should now be included in any list of leisure facilities because many shoppers treat the experience as a chosen form of entertainment rather than the necessary duty of buying goods essential for daily living.

# Seasonal variation in use of leisure facilities

Many leisure facilities are only in use for part of the year. For example, professional sports grounds are most heavily used during the summer or winter, depending on the main sports that take place in them. For obvious reasons, open-air facilities such as swimming pools and bowling greens are likely to get heavier use in summer than in winter. Indoor facilities may be more popular during the colder months. Facilities such as restaurants and clubs often attract more people over holiday periods, especially at Christmas and the New Year.

Facilities such as garden centres stress different features of what they have for sale in order to extend the more popular times for buying plants. Table 1 shows how a garden centre sets out to retain its year round appeal:

*Table 1*

| Time of year | Main attractions |
| --- | --- |
| January | Seeds, propagation units |
| February | Young plants |
| April – mid June | Bedding plants |
| June – August | Planted containers, hanging baskets |
| mid August – end of October | Bulbs |
| November – December | Flowering houseplants, Christmas decorations |

# Who provides leisure facilities?

Leisure facilities are usually provided from one of three sources – local or national government (the public sector), commercial companies (the private sector) or voluntary organizations (the voluntary sector). In recent times there has been a move towards developing joint ventures between two or more of these sectors.

Traditionally local authorities provided facilities such as swimming pools, parks and sports centres. They did so as part of their responsibility to provide services for the local community. Commercial companies have operated facilities such as cinemas, night clubs and bowling alleys. The purpose of these operations was to make a profit. Voluntary organizations often used public sector facilities in order to provide activities for special interest groups such as cricket clubs or youth groups.

The provision of leisure facilities now is commonly a joint activity. The local authority may own a sports centre but it is quite likely to be managed by a private management team which has to meet certain targets set out in a contract. Cleaning and catering within the centre may in turn be contracted out to other private specialist companies.

The same is often true of the development of new leisure facilities. They are often funded by a mixture of grants from local or national government or even from European funds, and investment by private companies. Even voluntary organizations, such as amateur sports clubs, may seek the status of a commercial charity. This means that they can carry out various business activities in order to raise funds.

## Activities

1 Draw up and conduct a survey among your fellow students, designed to establish the following:

   - What proportion of their time is spent on leisure activities

   - Which leisure facilities they make use of

   - Which facilities not currently available they would like to see developed locally

2 Make a photocopy of a map of the area surrounding your school or college.

3 Divide leisure facilities into a number of categories, e.g. spectator/participant; arts/sports; free/making a charge.

4 Mark the location of all leisure facilities on the map.

5 Look again at the results of the survey you conducted earlier about your fellow students' use of local leisure facilities.

   Prepare a short presentation, possibly including some transparencies for overhead projection, to be made to representatives of your local authority leisure or recreation department, identifying the demand for leisure facilities in your age group and the extent to which existing facilities meet this demand.

6 Discuss who might consider providing the types of leisure facility you have identified and what benefits or drawbacks they would need to take into account before they invested in such developments.

**The Derngate Centre, Northampton – an arts centre**

## Location

The Derngate Centre stands right in the centre of Northampton (Figure 5.1). It opened in 1983, next to the Royal Theatre. Opposite is the Museum. There are also plans to develop a studio theatre on the same site which are waiting for approval and adequate funding. The closeness of these facilities suggests that there is a policy to create an 'arts district' in this part of Northampton.

Research suggests that the audiences for the majority of performances at the Derngate Centre generally live within 40 minutes' driving time. Approximately half of those who attend the Centre come from within the town of Northampton itself. Despite the fact that some people think car-parking spaces are limited in the town centre, about 90% of visitors to Derngate use their own cars.

There are actually two theatres on the same site, the Derngate Centre and the Royal, but each is run independently. While the Royal concentrates mainly on drama, the Derngate Centre offers a broader programme including classical music, ballet, dance, comedy shows and musicals. It also acts as a venue for conferences, presentations and other business events.

There are no other major arts centres close to Northampton, although there is a plan to open one in Milton Keynes in 1998.

## Types of theatre

Theatres can be divided into two main types – **receiving houses** and **repertory theatres**.

A receiving house is one that acts as a host for finished products. In other words, theatre companies, dance companies or rock bands bring completely developed per-

*Fig. 5.1 The Derngate Centre*

formances and the theatre supplies stage staff and, where they are required, sound and lighting equipment. Receiving houses are generally expected to operate as commercial concerns. In other words they may, like the Derngate Centre, receive some funding from a local authority, but they are expected to generate most of their income through attendance charges and retail activities such as catering and selling products related to different performances.

A repertory theatre is one that takes responsibility for developing its own productions. This provides a higher level of artistic control. The theatre management can choose which productions to put on and can decide which actors should take which parts and what the design of the stage sets should look like. A receiving house will have to select its programme of events and performance by considering overall profitability or risk of loss. Repertory theatres usually receive a higher level of subsidy, sometimes from organizations such as the Arts Council, and this enables them to put on performances that they think have artistic merit but that may not attract large audiences.

The nearest receiving houses to the Derngate Centre are in Birmingham and Oxford so its location is good for companies planning national tours and seeking to use a number of different venues, each likely to attract a different audience. Audience research suggests that people come to the Derngate from a variety of towns in the region, including Milton Keynes, Bedford, Rugby, Leicester and Cambridge.

# Community relations

The Derngate Centre was, until 1993, under the direct control of Northampton Borough Council. That meant most of its funding came from local taxation. In other words all members of the local community who paid council tax were contributing directly to meeting the Centre's running costs. The Centre then became a charitable trust. Funding from the Council was reduced and an increasing proportion of the Centre's income was derived from admission charges, bars and catering, and retail services associated with the various productions put on.

This means that most of the Centre's income now comes from people who are actually *attending* the Centre. Establishing and maintaining a good relationship with the local community is clearly very important. Ways have to be found of getting all sections of the local community to sample what the Centre has to offer and then of encouraging their initial interest to become a habit. It is less expensive in advertising terms to attract regular attenders than it is to bring in first time visitors.

There are a number of ways in which the Derngate Centre develops good community relations. Some of the most common examples are shown below.

# Performances

The facilities are offered to local drama groups, orchestras and choirs at a lower cost than that charged to commercial companies. A quarter of all performances in the Centre are put on by local groups. These include offerings from the local operatic society, Northampton Symphony Orchestra and several local choral societies.

During the winter 1,000 tickets for the pantomime were given to under-privileged children from the town and discounted tickets were provided for similar groups from Milton Keynes.

# Charity performances

Up to four charity performances are put on each year (Figure 5.2) with only a minimum charge for use of the Centre facilities. For example, the Royal Institute for the Blind recently put on a fund-raising charity performance.

# Education programme

The Derngate Centre employs an education worker, sponsored by a local company, R. Griggs and Co., manufacturers of Doc Marten's footwear. Educational activities include a Children's Theatre Group held each Saturday and a programme of dance and music activities devised by local groups which are performed in local schools. The education programme also funds a certain number of courses, for example, a demonstration of how to make pantomime costumes.

**Fig. 5.2 A flyer for a charity performance by the Central Band of the Royal Air Force**

## Work placements

During 1994–95 over 30 students took advantage of offers of work placements at the Centre. All of these were planned to match individual interests. Students worked in stage management, marketing, front-of-house customer service and administration sections.

## Providing for People with Disabilities

An area of the main auditorium is set aside for wheelchair users. Discounted tickets and free parking on request are also available. Help is also provided for people with sensory impairments. This takes the form of signed performances for the deaf and described performances (providing extra details of sets, costumes, etc.) for those with impaired vision.

## Activities

Study the advertisement in Figure 5.3 for the Derngate pantomime 'Jack and the Beanstalk'.

Now read again about the ways the Derngate Centre already supports different local community groups.

1 Choose a community group that you think might welcome some extra support or entertainment at Christmas time.

2 Outline an activity using some aspect of the production – for example rehearsals, performers themselves, the theme or story of the pantomime – that could be developed in order to benefit a particular sector of the local community.

3 Work in small groups to draw up a list of the practical things that would need to be done to put the activity into practice.

These activities could be developed into a longer project by completing any or all of the following tasks:

4 Draw up a schedule for this activity.

5 Identify the main costs of running such an activity and suggest ways in which these costs might be met.

6 Suggest a variety of ways in which the Derngate Centre might seek to make its part in offering an activity similar to the one you have proposed more widely known.

7 Evaluate each of these methods in terms of:

● Practicality

● Effectiveness in presenting the Centre in a good light

● Cost

**Fig. 5.3 Advertisement for 'Jack and the Beanstalk'**

# Programming

One of the most important aspects of running an arts complex such as the Derngate Centre is the effective programming of performances (Figure 5.4). For a number of reasons this is a very complicated process. First of all a balance has to be struck between performances that are mainly put on for *artistic* reasons and those that are mainly put on for *commercial* reasons.

Table 5.1 shows some of the issues that affect the planning of a varied programme which will both attract a range of audiences and bring in an acceptable financial return.

**Fig. 5.4 Programming of performances**

**Table 5.1**

| Issue | Result |
| --- | --- |
| Performance and rehearsal times | Both performances and rehearsals using auditorium space have to be filled in on the programming schedule first. |
| Classical music performances | Major orchestras perform in the Centre some ten times a year and such events often have to be planned a year in advance. |
| One night performances | If an orchestra plays a single concert, as they do in the Derngate 10 or 12 times a year, a weekly show, such as a musical, cannot be booked for any of those weeks. |
| Performances by local orchestras | Have to be scheduled so that they do not immediately precede or follow concerts by major orchestras. |

**Table 5.1 Continued**

| Issue | Result |
|-------|--------|
| Amateur performances by local groups | Amateur performers are often at work during the week and so only have Saturdays and Sundays available for rehearsing in the main auditorium, but weekends are the most commercially profitable days for 'live' performances in the Centre. |
| Professional dance companies | Have to be booked between 12 and 18 months ahead and the Centre aims to feature different companies, such as the Ballet Rambert and the Northern Ballet Theatre, at contrasting times of year, perhaps one in February and another in October. |
| Once major and traditional events have been given dates | The Centre managers consider all other interesting options, such as musicals, small dance companies and opera and slot the most appropriate ones into the spaces remaining. |
| West End musicals | After two or three years are often taken on tours of provincial theatres and arts centres. The Derngate Centre may stage up to six a year because they are nearly always a financial success. They are usually accompanied by high secondary spend on bar, catering and products associated with the shows. |
| The presence of a repertory theatre next door | Means that the Derngate Centre does not put on a lot of classical drama, because it would be competing for the same audiences. It therefore focuses more on things like music, dance, comedy and variety. |
| The costs of overheads in the Centre are high | It is important to maximize its use and ensure that there are very few evenings when there are no performances taking place. |

# Budgets and contracts

Deciding what to include in the programme is not just a matter of ensuring variety. Each performance has to be considered in terms of whether it will break even or make a profit, or whether it carries the risk of running at a loss. One of the main factors in deciding costs of different performances for a receiving house is the price and terms agreed in the contract. Most performers will have an agent who acts on their behalf in agreeing the actual terms of the contract.

There are three main ways in which a contract between the Centre and a performer or group's agent might be drawn up.

# An inclusive fee

The agent and the Centre will agree a guaranteed set fee for a particular performance or series of shows. For example, the Centre might agree to pay a comedian £3,000 for an evening show. Agents tend to be keen on this kind of deal because it guarantees a minimum payment regardless of how many people there are in the audience. The Centre would be less keen because there is a higher risk of loss for it if the turnout is low.

# Splitting the Box Office takings between performer and the Centre

In a receiving house this might mean 20-30% of the takings on the night going to the Centre and the rest going to the performer or performing company. The percentage level would probably depend on the reputation of the performers. This kind of arrangement carries less financial risk for the Centre, because it is guaranteed to receive some income, although it would still lose money if few people attended.

# First and second call arrangements

This kind of contract is a combination of the other two methods. A set guaranteed fee, the first call, is agreed with the performers. Once the box office takings rise above this sum the Centre takes the second call, again a guaranteed fixed sum. Any income above these two amounts is divided, according to an agreed percentage split, between performers and the Centre.

 **Activity**

Suppose that the Lighthouse Family agree a contract to perform at the Derngate Centre for five nights. The auditorium is arranged in a layout which sets the seating capacity at 1,200. Tickets are to be sold at the following price levels:

300 @ £15

450 @ £20

350 @ £25

100 @ £30

A contract is agreed which gives the band a first call payment of £25,000; the Centre has second call on the next £10,000 and the remainder of the box office takings are split, with 70% going to the band and 30% to the Centre.

1  If all five performances were sold out, what would the total box office takings be?

2  If the average attendance over all the performances was 70% and the ticket sales were distributed evenly over the four different price bands, estimate what the expected takings would be.

3  If all five performances are sold out, work out from the contract how much the band would receive and how much the Centre would expect to receive.

4 If the performances were 70% sold out, with ticket sales evenly distributed over the four price level bands, how much would you then expect the band and the Centre to receive?

# Planning process for a specific performance

The first task in assessing whether to put on a particular performance is to assess its financial viability. This is done by means of an **event budget forecast.** This may be quite a complicated process, especially if the terms of the contract involve first and second call division of takings. A slightly simplified example of an event budget forecast for a production of Shakespeare's *Romeo and Juliet* can be found on page 96.

Once the Centre and the agent acting for the performers have agreed a deal, a contract covering such things as the financial agreement, insurance, health and safety, publicity, and legal details is sent out and signed. This is the **main contract.** A receiving house such as the Derngate Centre will then need to know what specific arrangements are required for specific performances. A rock band, for example, will probably bring a lot of technical equipment of its own and sometimes a whole stage set. Performers such as rock bands will have a **rider** attached to their main contract. This will specify all the technical and operational details for the performance. It will cover things like sound, lighting, merchandising and catering.

The Centre staff then have to react to the main contract and its rider. Each department will have to make arrangements to satisfy its particular areas of the contract. All operational departments will meet once a week to go through all the details of the current week's work and the following week's productions. Some departments are mostly concerned with the main contract; others work from the terms of the rider:

- The **main contract** mostly affects programming, finance and marketing departments
- The **contract rider** mainly affects stage, front-of-house, customer services, bar and catering departments

The Stage Manager will coordinate all the technical requirements for each performance. The Front-of-House Manager will look after all merchandising and security arrangements. Figure 5.5 shows the auditorium of the Derngate Centre.

***Fig. 5.5  The auditorium of the Derngate Centre***

**The Derngate Trust**  **Event Budget Forecast**

| Event | Romeo & Juliet | No. of performances | 7 |
|---|---|---|---|
| Promoter | Midlands Shakespeare Company | Format | Lyric, no pit |
| Dates | Mon 2 – Sat 7 June 1997 | Deal | Guarantee, 2nd call, split |
| Per. time | M/T//Th/F/S 7.30 T & Th 2.30 pm | Event code | 31612RJ |

## INCOME

| No. of seats | Price | Income | Price | Income | Price | Income | Concessions |
|---|---|---|---|---|---|---|---|
| 581 @ | £16 | £9,296 | £15 | £8,715 | £12 | £6,972 | 5% |
| 355 @ | £14 | £4,970 | £13 | £4,615 | £11 | £3,905 | 5% |
| 72 @ | £12 | £864 | £11 | £792 | £10 | £720 | 5% |
| 110 @ | £10 | £1,100 | £9 | £990 | £8 | £880 | 0% |
| 52 @ | £9 | £468 | £8 | £416 | £7 | £364 | 0% |
| 1170 | | **£16,698** | | **£15,528** | | **£12,841** | 0% |
| Performances | 2 | **£33,396** | 3 | **£46,584** | 2 | **£25,682** | |

| | Seats | Maximum possible income |
|---|---|---|
| **Total** | 8,190 | £105,662 |

| **Deductions** | Concessions = 4.52% | £4,775 | £100,887 |
|---|---|---|---|
| | VAT @ 17.5% | £17,655 | £85,861* |
| | Net Box Office income | | £85,861 |
| | | | **£51,516** |
| | Net Box Office income assuming 60% full | | |

| Gross Box Office target | @ 57% | £60,227 |
|---|---|---|

## EXPENDITURE

| | Guarantee | £25,000 |
|---|---|---|
| | 1st call – promoter | 0 |
| | 2nd call – Derngate | £7,500 |
| | Split – 60% to promoter | £11,410** |

| **Total artist's fee** | | **£36,410** |
|---|---|---|
| | Gross profit | **£15,106** |
| | Number of days | 5 |
| | Profit per day | £3,021 |

\* To calculate net amount after the VAT deduction divide by 117.5 and then multiply by 100.
\*\* £51,516 – £25,000 – £7,500 × 60%.

# Health and safety

The Derngate Group is required by the Health and Safety at Work Act (1974) to provide and maintain safe and healthy conditions for its employees and all who enter its premises. The Group has a **health and safety policy** which sets out aims and objectives in terms of five main areas:

- Good management
- Active support of staff
- Training and instruction
- Supervision
- Monitoring the effectiveness of the policy

Senior managers are responsible for ensuring that the policy is put into practice in all departments of the Centre. Employees also have a responsibility for their own health and safety and that of others. They have to follow agreed procedures and take reasonable precautions. Figure 5.6 shows how responsibility for different areas of health and safety is allocated.

# Risks and hazards

One of the main purposes of any health and safety policy is to identify hazards and reduce risks:

- A **hazard** is something with the potential to cause harm, e.g. chemicals, electricity, working high above ground, regular use of display screens
- A **risk** is the likelihood that harm will result from any particular hazard

Risk assessments are carried out to identify potential hazards. In the Derngate Centre this is done for all tasks carried out by each department. Those responsible then have decide whether they have taken sufficient precautions already or whether they need to do more.

Risk assessments at the Derngate Centre can be split into three categories as shown in Table 5.2.

**Table 5.2**

| Level of risk | Action required |
| --- | --- |
| High | • Set out written procedures, e.g. number and type of staff required, training needed, protective clothing required |
| | • List methods of operation, e.g. auditorium lift |
| Medium | • Hazard control information distributed on a single sheet |
| Low or none | • Monitored to ensure that operational or task changes do not increase the potential to cause harm |

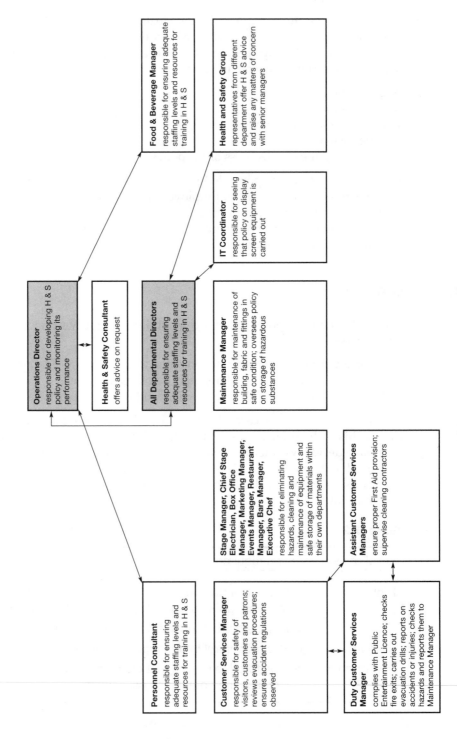

**Operations Director**
responsible for developing H & S policy and monitoring its performance

**Health & Safety Consultant**
offers advice on request

**Personnel Consultant**
responsible for ensuring adequate staffing levels and resources for training in H & S

**Food & Beverage Manager**
responsible for ensuring adequate staffing levels and resources for training in H & S

**Health and Safety Group**
representatives from different department offer H & S advice and raise any matters of concern with senior managers

**IT Coordinator**
responsible for seeing that policy on display screen equipment is carried out

**All Departmental Directors**
responsible for ensuring adequate staffing levels and resources for training in H & S

**Maintenance Manager**
responsible for maintenance of building, fabric and fittings in safe condition; oversees policy on storage of hazardous substances

**Customer Services Manager**
responsible for safety of visitors, customers and patrons; reviews evacuation procedures; ensures accident regulations observed

**Stage Manager, Chief Stage Electrician, Box Office Manager, Marketing Manager, Events Manager, Restaurant Manager, Bars Manager, Executive Chef**
responsible for eliminating hazards, cleaning and maintenance of equipment and safe storage of materials within their own departments

**Assistant Customer Services Managers**
ensure proper First Aid provision; supervise cleaning contractors

**Duty Customer Services Manager**
complies with Public Entertainment Licence; checks fire exits; carries out evacuation drills; reports on accidents or injuries; checks hazards and reports them to Maintenance Manager

*Fig. 5.6 Allocation of responsibility for different areas of health and safety at Derngate*

## Activity

A musical based on the story of Joan of Arc is due to be performed at the Derngate Centre. It will have a cast of 50 and will include both crowd scenes and a simulation of the heroine being burnt at the stake.

Divide into two groups, one to review health and safety issues back stage and the other to look at health and safety issues front-of-house.

1 Draw up a list of potential hazards that might exist in the area being reviewed by your group.

2 Discuss the level of risk involved in each of the hazards you have identified and place them in one of the following categories: high risk, medium risk, low or no risk.

3 Suggest a range of appropriate actions and precautions that would need to be taken to reduce any risk to performers, staff or audience to a minimum.

4 Use a word processor to prepare a memo to all staff at the Derngate Centre, informing them of the actions and precautions that will be in place for this performance.

# Funding issues

To manage the Derngate Trust successfully it is important to keep a check on which activities generate **income** and what the main **costs** are of running the Centre.

### Table 5.3

| Income | % | Costs | % |
|---|---|---|---|
| Joint events | 51 | Artists' fees | 40 |
| Northampton Borough Council Grant | 19 | Wages and salaries | 26 |
| Trading | 16 | Other overheads | 10 |
| Recharges | 10 | Trading | 10 |
| Auditorium hire | 3 | Marketing | 7 |
| Sponsorship | 1 | Other events | 7 |

Table 5.3 suggests approximately what proportion of the total income and costs are associated with different areas of the Centre's operation for the financial year ending in March, 1995.

There are a number of ways of assessing the financial performance of a centre like the Derngate. The two simplest measures to show how well the Centre is doing are figures for the **gross box office income** and figures for **attendances**.

Clearly the amount of box office income rises or falls according to the type of performance and the time of year. The box office figures need to be looked at alongside the proportion of different types of performance offered during the financial year. For example, box office takings could be very high one year because a high proportion of the performances were popular entertainment. This would be good in terms of income but might cause concerns about whether the Centre was offering a reasonable *variety* of entertainments. In another year the box office takings could be lower

**Table 5.4**

| Type of performance | % |
| --- | --- |
| Popular | 31 |
| Pantomime | 17 |
| Musicals | 14 |
| Local groups | 9 |
| Classical music | 7 |
| Drama | 7 |
| Other types of hire, e.g. exhibitions | 7 |
| Ballet/hire | 5 |
| Opera | 3 |

because more time was given to local performances or less popular shows.

Table 5.4 gives a breakdown of the types of performance offered at the Derngate Centre in 1994/5.

## Activities

Study Figure 5.7 relating to gross box office income and attendances.

1 What is the increase in annual gross box office takings between 1990–91 and 1994–95?

Now calculate what this represents in terms of a percentage increase.

2 What factors might help to explain the changes in attendance figures from year to year?

3 For each year given in the two graphs estimate as accurately as you can an actual figure for the box office income and for the attendances.

In each year divide the income by the number of attendances in order to arrive at a figure for the **amount of income per visit**.

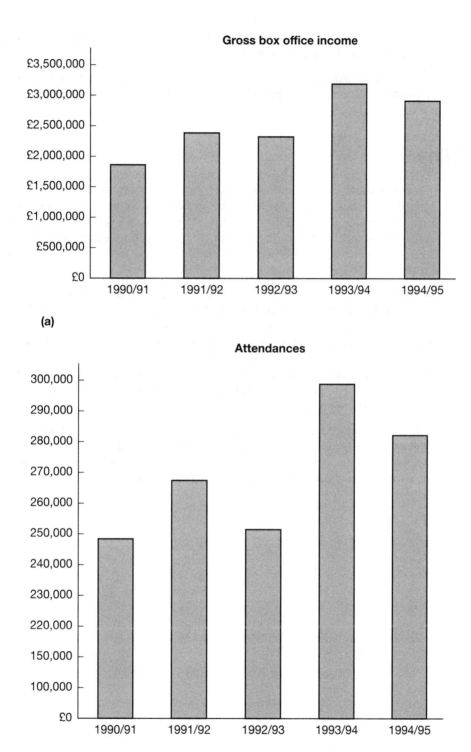

**Fig. 5.7  Gross box office income (a) and attendances(b)**

4 Discuss the results of these calculations, suggesting for both what conclusions you think can be drawn from them.

5 What else would you need to know before you could decide whether the Derngate Centre's financial performance was improving year on year?

# Flexibility

The main auditorium in the Derngate Centre is not just used as a conventional theatre. It was designed so that its shape and layout could be mechanically altered to meet the needs of different types of performance or event. It can also be used for conferences, meetings, seminars, product launches, presentations and conventions.

Figure 5.8 shows some of the different ways the floor space and seating can be arranged:

- The **Lyric** format would be used for events such as major company presentations;
- The **flat floor** format would be used for events such as trade exhibitions which require all the floor space for setting up stands
- The **arena** format would be used for events or performances taking place in the centre of an audience, such as a snooker tournament
- The **concert hall** format would be used for events such as rock concerts or orchestral performances requiring both plenty of stage space and also which could be watched from any angle.

It is not only the stage, seating and floor spacing that can be altered. Reflectors above the heads of the audience can be adjusted to change the acoustics of the building. For example a presentation given by individual speakers may need to amplify the sound more than a concert given by a heavy metal rock band.

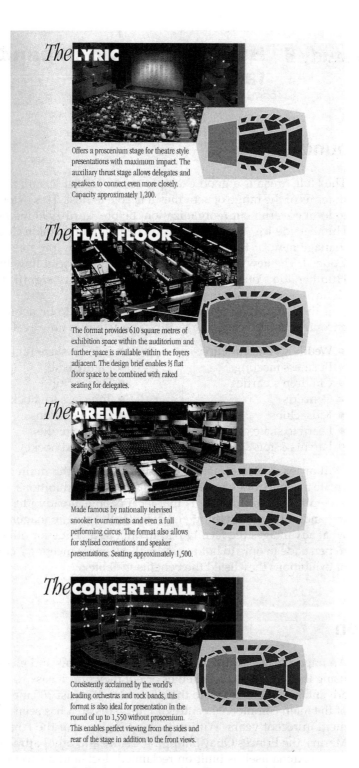

**The LYRIC**

Offers a proscenium stage for theatre style presentations with maximum impact. The auxiliary thrust stage allows delegates and speakers to connect even more closely. Capacity approximately 1,200.

**The FLAT FLOOR**

The format provides 610 square metres of exhibition space within the auditorium and further space is available within the foyers adjacent. The design brief enables ½ flat floor space to be combined with raked seating for delegates.

**The ARENA**

Made famous by nationally televised snooker tournaments and even a full performing circus. The format also allows for stylised conventions and speaker presentations. Seating approximately 1,500.

**The CONCERT HALL**

Consistently acclaimed by the world's leading orchestras and rock bands, this format is also ideal for presentation in the round of up to 1,550 without proscenium. This enables perfect viewing from the sides and rear of the stage in addition to the front views.

**Fig. 5.8 Different ways the floor space and seating of the Derngate Centre can be arranged**

The Derngate Centre, Northampton – an arts centre **103**

**Hull Arena – an expanding leisure facility**

## Background

The Hull Arena is a good example of a specialist leisure facility that has diversified in terms of the range of activities it is able to host. This extension of use is partly due to local government reorganization. Before April 1996 the facility was known as the Humberside Ice Arena and was owned by Humberside Council. After that date the management of the facility was taken over by the newly established Hull City Council. The new council had a different view about how the facility should be run. Humberside Council had subsidised the facility significantly whereas Hull City Council wishes to see the Arena break even.

If the financial target of breaking even was to be achieved it was important to encourage wider use of the facility. The activities now available include:

- Weddings and functions
- Business meetings
- Children's parties
- Concerts
- Kids' clubs
- Learn to skate group courses
- Parents & tots sessions
- Leisure skate nights
- Figure club
- Dance club
- Top class ice hockey matches
- Disco sessions
- Theme nights
- Disabled hockey

In order to attract users other than skaters the main Arena floor is covered to create a venue for events such as concerts and exhibitions. One of the problems with extending use in this way is that local people already identify the facility with skating and not with anything else. The Hull Arena management team had to identify what advantages the facility had to offer as a venue for other activities. For example, to persuade people to hold weddings, business meetings, children's parties, concerts or exhibitions they listed the benefits in Table 6.1.

## Location

An important factor in deciding which individuals and groups might be attracted to using the Hull Arena is whether or not they find it easy to get to. The facility has the advantage of being close to the city centre. It is just 300 metres (350 yards) south-east of the main commercial centre of Hull. This area has seen a great deal of redevelopment in recent years. Within walking distance of the Arena are the Humber Dock Marina, the Princes Quay Shopping Centre and other attractions.

The Arena itself is built on reclaimed dockland adjacent to other leisure facilities and retail outlets (Figure 6.1, on page 106). The interior of the Arena is shown in Figure 6.2 (page 107).

**Table 6.1**

| Weddings | Business meetings |
|---|---|
| • Excellent catering | • Easy to reach (central location) |
| • Warm, friendly atmosphere | • Telephone/fax/photocopier available |
| • Pleasant surroundings | • Fully equipped Function Suite |
| • Seating for up to 250 people | • Accommodation nearby |
| • Late licence (upon application) | • Food and drink available |
| Children's parties | Concerts/exhibitions |
| • Fun on the ice | • Arena capacity 3,750 |
| • Soft play in the Function Room | • Excellent sound and lighting |
| • Several choices of menu | • Easy loading/ off-loading |
| • Warm, friendly welcome | • On-site coach/car parking (400 spaces) |
| • Above all, it's different! | • Bookings office |

The location of the facility, on the edge of the city centre, means that the majority of visitors to the public skating sessions at the Arena arrive on foot. Only about 25% of customers for these sessions arrive by car. Significant numbers of customers visit the Arena as part of a trip to central Hull which may include shopping and other leisure activities.

The large proportion of visitors arriving by foot is also explained by the age structure of the customers. Large numbers are young people who do not own cars and are visiting the Arena as part of a night out in the city centre.

The Arena has good relationships with local public transport providers and is well served by buses to suburban areas. Buses call at The Arena and arrivals and departures are coordinated with the beginning and ending of public skating sessions and other events.

However, not all the visitors to the Arena are young people attending the skating sessions. The facility is used as the home base for the Humber Hawks ice hockey team. The supporters of the Hawks tend to come from a much wider area, some coming from more than 50 miles (80 km) away. In addition, the away side, depending on how far away from Hull they are based and how successful they are, will bring some supporters with them. For ice hockey matches the proportion of supporters arriving by car may be as high as 60–70%. However, many still use the bus services so it is important to coordinate these so that buses are timed to arrive in the period leading up to the start of the game and depart in the period immediately after its completion.

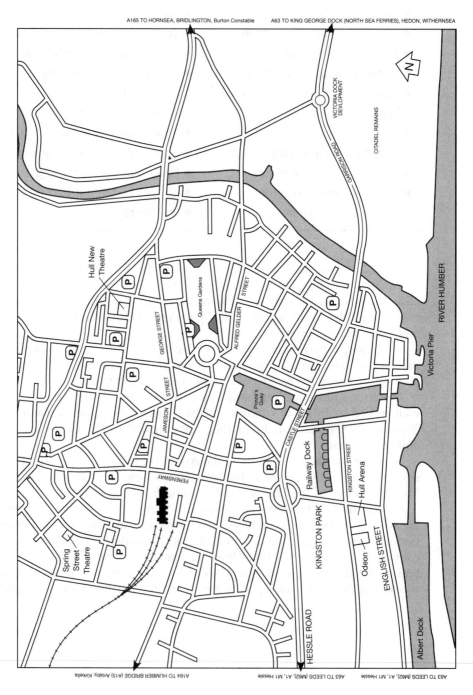

*Fig. 6.1 Location of the Hull Arena*

*Fig. 6.2 Interior of the Arena*

## Activities

Look back at Table 6.1, where the benefits of using the Hull Arena for weddings, business meetings, children's parties and concerts or exhibitions are listed

1 Discuss and list the special transport and access requirements that each of these types of function might require. (For example a wedding party might require a covered dropping off point where, in bad weather, guests arriving by car could alight and be welcomed without getting wet.)

2 Describe any construction work, any training and allocation of Arena staff and any services that might need to be provided to meet the requirements you listed in activity (1).

# Management and staff structures

A number of changes have affected the Hull Arena as a result of Hull City Council, through Hull City Services – Sport and Leisure Management Division, taking over the management of the facility. Hull City Services also has the responsibility for managing other leisure facilities in the city. In particular the objective of enabling the Arena to break even has resulted in a reduction of staff and a different approach towards recruitment.

Flexibility is a key quality looked for in new recruits to the workforce. People who are willing to work in different roles and venues and to gain sufficient training to operate a wide range of equipment make it easier for Hull City Services to allocate staff to the different leisure facilities in the city. People can be moved to where there is greatest need. To make sure that new employees are aware that they may be called on to work in more than one facility job descriptions are written in a very flexible way. For example, the job description for Leisure Assistants includes the following statements:

(a) These principal duties do not include or define all tasks which may be required to be undertaken by the postholder. These may, therefore, vary from time to time without changing the general character of the duties or the level of responsibility.

(b) Although designated Leisure Assistant the job holder may be required in any post of a similar nature and responsibility at such other place of employment within the Hull City Services as required by management.

(c) The Council operates various shift systems throughout the Sport and Leisure Management Division and reserves the right to amend or alter shift patterns together with the hours of working to meet the requirements of the Centre or the needs of the programme.

The desire to boost revenue is also reflected in the staff structure at the Arena. A high proportion of the employees who work there have a customer services role of some sort, whether it be serving food, selling skating equipment, hiring out skates or working as receptionists.

The staff structure diagram in Figure 6.3 shows the main areas of employment at the Arena and also indicates how many hours each employee currently works. Although this shows that those in management positions are contracted to work 37 hours a week, in practice they work much longer than this. This is essential because the Arena stays open from 6 in the morning until midnight on most days of the week.

Most staff now applying for jobs at the Arena will be expected to have obtained an NVQ level 2 in Sport and Leisure. Staff training on activities specifically related to ice skating is provided in-house. This includes sessions on maintenance of the ice and on advice and procedures relating to hiring skates out to the public. However, it is also important that they have the ability to support the non-skating events that take place in the Arena. The person specification in Figure 6.4 (on page 110) shows the range of skills, experience, qualifications and characteristics that are looked for when new leisure assistants are recruited. It also shows how the people doing the recruiting find out whether candidates possess these.

Some job roles within the Arena are particularly important. One is that of the Technical Officer who has the key task of maintaining the unit that freezes the ice. Obviously if anything were to go wrong with this unit it would severely disrupt the programme of activities taking place at the Arena.

## Activities

The programme for the Hull Arena shows that for a week in November the facility was open at the following times:

| | | | |
|---|---|---|---|
| Monday | 6.00 am – 12.00 midnight | Friday | 6.00 am – 10.30 pm |
| Tuesday | 6.00 am – 11.45 pm | Saturday | 6.00 am – 10.30 pm |
| Wednesday | 6.00 am – 12.00 midnight | Sunday | 6.00 am – 10.30 pm |
| Thursday | 6.00 am – 10.45 pm | | |

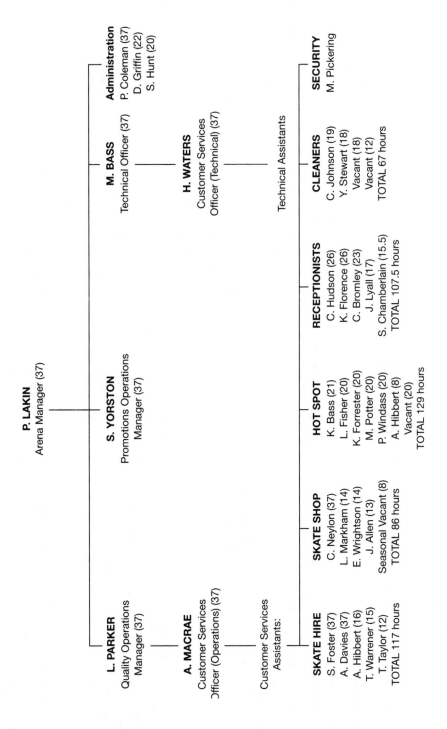

**P. LAKIN**
Arena Manager (37)

**L. PARKER**
Quality Operations
Manager (37)

**S. YORSTON**
Promotions Operations
Manager (37)

**M. BASS**
Technical Officer (37)

**Administration**
P. Coleman (37)
D. Griffin (22)
S. Hunt (20)

**A. MACRAE**
Customer Services
Officer (Operations) (37)

**H. WATERS**
Customer Services
Officer (Technical) (37)

Customer Services
Assistants:

Technical Assistants

**SKATE HIRE**
S. Foster (37)
A. Davies (37)
A. Hibbert (16)
T. Warrener (15)
T. Taylor (12)
TOTAL 117 hours

**SKATE SHOP**
C. Neylon (37)
L. Markham (14)
E. Wrightson (14)
J. Allen (13)
Seasonal Vacant (8)
TOTAL 86 hours

**HOT SPOT**
K. Bass (21)
L. Fisher (20)
K. Forrester (20)
M. Potter (20)
P. Windass (20)
A. Hibbert (8)
Vacant (20)
TOTAL 129 hours

**RECEPTIONISTS**
C. Hudson (26)
K. Florence (26)
C. Bromley (23)
J. Lyall (17)
S. Chamberlain (15.5)
TOTAL 107.5 hours

**CLEANERS**
C. Johnson (19)
Y. Stewart (18)
Vacant (18)
Vacant (12)
TOTAL 67 hours

**SECURITY**
M. Pickering

***Fig. 6.3 Hull Arena staff structure diagram***

HULL CITY SERVICES - SPORT AND LEISURE MANAGEMENT DIVISION

**Person specification**

**Job tiitle:** Leisure Assistant

| Attributes | Essential | How identified | Desirable | How identified |
|---|---|---|---|---|
| RELEVANT EXPERIENCE | | | Previous experience in the Leisure industry | Application and reference |
| QUALIFICATIONS | RLSS Bronze Medallion Qualification | | RLSS Pool Lifeguard Qualification A.S.A.* Teachers Certificate Coaching qualifications Sport & Leisure NVQ level 2 | Application and certification |
| SPECIAL SKILLS AND ABILITIES | Physically fit Competent swimmer | Competence test | | |
| SOCIAL SKILLS | Team worker Caring nature Committed to service industry | Interview Personality test | Mature Confident Interested | Interview |
| MOTIVATION | Committed and enthusiastic | Interview | Self-motivated and possessing initiative | Interview |
| PHYSICAL CHARACTERISTICS (where appropriate) | Polite manner Smart appearance | Interview | | |

**Fig. 6.4 Person specification**

Generally, staffing needs are greater in the evenings and at weekends. Most part time staff are employed at evenings and at weekends.

1  How many hours is the Arena open during this week?

2  What is the minimum total number of hours worked by all employees according to the staff chart of Figure 6.3? (You should not include jobs that are currently vacant.)

3  What is the average number of staff on duty over the week, assuming everyone works only their minimum hours?

4  If it was necessary to have skate hire available all the time the Arena was open, someone from another area might have to help out. How many hours would they have to work?

5  'Hot Spot' is a cafeteria in the Arena. Suppose that the 129 staff hours were allocated as in Table 6.2:

## Table 6.2  Hot Spot – staffing requirements

| Monday | Tuesday | Wednesday | Thursday | Friday | Saturday | Sunday |
|---|---|---|---|---|---|---|
| Open 8.30 am Close 9 pm | Open 8.00 am Close 9 pm | Open 8.00 am Close 9 pm | Open 8.00 am Close 9 pm | Open 8.00 am Close 10.30 pm | Open 7.00 am Close 10.30 pm | Open 7.00 am Close 10.30 pm |
| Staff required: one | Staff required: one | Staff required: one | Staff required: one | Staff required: one up to 6.30 three from 6.30 to 10.30 | Staff required: one up to 11 two from 11 to 3 one from 3 to 6.30 three from 6.30 to 10.30 | Staff required: one up to 11 two from 11 to 3 one from 3 to 6.30 three from 6.30 to 10.30 |
| Total hours = 12 $\frac{1}{2}$ | Total hours = 13 | Total hours = 13 | Total hours = 13 | Total hours = 22 $\frac{1}{2}$ | Total hours = 27 $\frac{1}{2}$ | Total hours = 27 $\frac{1}{2}$ |

(a)  Using the hours allocated on the staff chart, draw up a roster of duties for the week.

(b)  What possible suggestions can you come up with to cover the 20 hours' time allocated to a post that is currently vacant? What are the implications of each of your suggestions?

(c)  List some of the other problems you might come up against in carrying out this task.

# Pricing Policy

The Arena does not operate a discount or season ticket scheme. Research has shown that customers do not require these. Also, because the facility is being used increasingly for activities other than skating, season tickets are not seen as a way forward.

Generally, similar prices are charged for a variety of different types of skating session as shown in Table 6.3.

**Table 6.3**

| Activity | Price |
| --- | --- |
| Patch Ice (for advanced skaters only) | £2.20 an hour |
| Public Skate | £2.50 per session (generally two hours) plus £1 skate hire |
| Parents & Tots | £2 per adult & £1 per child per session |
| Hockey Training | £3 per person |
| Schools Out (early evening session) | £2 per session plus £1 skate hire |
| Dance Club | £1 or £3 with Public Skate session that follows |
| Disco Session | £3 plus £1 skate hire |
| Beginners Hockey | £3 an hour |
| Family Fun | £2.50 plus £1 skate hire or Family ticket @ £2 per person |

If a leisure facility is to have a long-term future it is important for consideration to be given not just to the present generation of users but to think about the people who might be using it in 10 or 20 years' time. The management of the Hull Arena has started a Saturday AM Club. This club for children has exclusive use of the ice between 10 am and 12 noon on Saturday mornings. Members pay £3 to join and in return they get the following benefits:

- Reduced admission on all skating sessions
- An official membership card
- AM Club points each time they visit which can then be exchanged for goods or services within the Arena
- The chance to spend AM Club points at a bi-monthly auction
- Games, prizes, competitions and gifts
- Free invitation tickets on birthdays
- Theme parties throughout the year
- Free skate hire

The system of collecting points for every visit made encourages regular attendance. A notice on the door of the Arena suggests some of the goods and services that points can be exchanged for and explains the terms and conditions that apply to the scheme.

## AM Club     Points List

| | |
|---|---|
| Burger, chips and coke | 155 |
| Free admission voucher | 200 |
| Skate grind | 250 |
| Hockey/figure laces | 275 |
| Skate guards | 325 |
| T shirt | 650 |
| Sweatshirt | 1450 |
| Ice hockey shirt | 3250 |
| £40 skate voucher | 4150 |
| (redeemable in the Skate Shop off any pair of skates) | |

- For each visit using a club membership card 10 points will be electronically added to your account
- Lost or damaged cards must be replaced at a cost of £4
- Any club member banned from the Arena will lose all Club benefits
- Membership cards must be produced on all visits to obtain benefits

## Activities

The first session on the ice each day at the Hull Arena is called Patch Ice. It lasts from 6 am until 9.45 am on Mondays to Fridays and finishes an hour earlier on Saturdays and Sundays.

These sessions are for advanced skaters only and generally attract people in the age group between 15 and 30 years of age. Some of these skaters employ skating coaches. The coaches are self-employed and collect fees on an individual basis from the skaters they train.

1  What do you think are the possible advantages to the Arena of having sessions for advanced skaters?

2  Suggest reasons why these sessions are held early in the morning.

3  Discuss the possible reasons why the Arena does not employ its own skating coaches but permits self-employed coaches to charge skaters using the facility.

# Health and Safety

Probably the only way to avoid accidents in a popular skating rink is to prevent people from using it at all! People to tend to collide and fall over from time to time when they are on the ice. At the Arena there may be as many as 1,500 people on the ice during busy sessions. Some 95% of accidents at the Hull Arena take place on the ice. The remainder mainly happen while people are walking to and from the ice.

However, serious accidents can generally be avoided by ensuring that all users of the facility and all the staff supplying them with skating equipment are aware of and keep to a sensible safety policy. The Arena operates a good practice policy in relation to skates, laces and other equipment hired to the public.

There is no legal requirement to supervise people using the ice during public sessions. Ice marshalls are volunteers only and have no statutory responsibility.

The Arena makes use of a computer-controlled system for preventative maintenance. This system details the routine maintenance to be undertaken on a daily or weekly basis (Figure 6.5). It lists the checks to be made to things such as air conditioning, interior and exterior lighting, and servicing ice-making machines.

For pop concerts and other similar events the centre operates under the *Guide to Health and Safety at Pop Concerts Regulations*. Concerts attract between 2,000 and 3,000 people, with a maximum allowed of 3,750. Stewards are required at a rate of one for every 100 people.

## Activity

1 List the main hazards you can think of that are present during a busy public skating session.

2 Suggest some basic rules of good practice that would encourage safety on the ice.

# Promotion

Since the 1996 reorganization the marketing focus at the Arena has been on the all year round viability of the facility. The name of the facility was changed from the

**Fig. 6.5 Cleaning and smoothing the surface of the ice**

Humberside Ice Arena to the Hull Arena in order to emphasize the fact that it was no longer just an ice rink but could now be used to host a variety of events and meetings.

Although the facility was designed as an ice rink, the ice can be boarded over in 90 minutes to provide a flexible facility.

Various events have been held at the Arena, such as:

- **Trade shows,** including a three day careers convention
- **Boxing**, shown live on Sky television
- **Pop concerts,** including performances by Manic Street Preachers, M People, Pulp, Blur

Several methods of promoting this range of activities are used. A close relationship has been established with the local commercial radio station, Viking Radio. This has two main advantages. Firstly, the radio station's studios are very close to the Arena. Secondly, market research has shown that the profile of the listeners, mainly a young audience, is very similar to many of the customer groups who use the Arena. This means that promoting events at the Arena through Viking Radio automatically targets many of the people who would be most likely to attend them.

A database has been established that includes details of people who have attended large events and concerts. It is then used to generate addresses so that flyers can be sent to keep them informed of future programmes.

The local press is also an important medium for promoting the Arena. A weekly advertisement is placed in the *Hull Daily Mail* to keep the public informed of forthcoming events. These advertisements will sometimes carry a promotional offer, such as a voucher admitting two people to a skating session for the price of one. The use of such offers can be a help in assessing how valuable a particular advertising medium is. The number of vouchers presented for admission provides a way of measuring the response to the advertisement.

## Activities

An important aspect of promotion for the Arena is the opportunities it brings for improving secondary spend in the facility.

As a result of diversification the Hull Arena now hosts pop concerts, conferences, exhibitions, children's parties, business meetings and weddings, in addition to the ice-related activities like skating and ice hockey training and matches.

1 Discuss the various opportunities for increasing secondary spend that this kind of diversification might bring.

2 List any problems which you think the Arena might encounter in trying to get visitors to spend more money while they are in the facility.

3 Draw up a list of criteria which you think the management of the Arena might apply before deciding whether or not to make the sale of a product available on the premises.

## Case study 7 Oxford United Football Club

## Aims and objectives

People often think of a professional football club as an organization that exists to provide entertainment for the public. This is of course one of its aims, but football clubs are also businesses. They spend money on wages and salaries, ground maintenance, administration and marketing. They receive income from gate receipts, sponsorship, catering, merchandising, television fees and grants. They can only continue to provide entertainment as long as they have enough money to do so. If they run up debts and directors, banks and sponsors decide that they can no longer cover the interest payments on these debts, the club will go out of business.

In order to survive financially a football club will generally aim to achieve a number of other things:

- Success on the playing field
- A comfortable and safe environment for spectators
- A good relationship with all sectors of the local community, including other businesses
- An attractive leisure product at a price regarded as good value for money
- A good level of customer service

## The aims of Oxford United Football Club

The aims of Oxford United are closely linked to the development of a 15,000 all-seater stadium, due to open in August 1997. The new complex will be available for use by both local residents and local businesses. It will host a range of activities, including League football, conferences, exhibitions and banquets. The site will include a health and fitness club, a hotel and an adjacent leisure park. There will be parking space for 2,000 cars.

The new stadium is located three miles (5km) from Oxford city centre. It lies in the heart of commercial Oxford, sandwiched between the traditional motor-related industries of Rover and Unipart in Cowley and the new generation science and technology-based businesses of The Science Park. This area of the city also contains a large residential population. So the site is ideal for the Club to attract interest from both the residents and the business community.

In terms of success on the playing field Oxford United have achieved much in their short history. Admitted to the League as recently as 1962, they reached the old First Division for a period of three seasons in the 1980s and won the League Cup at Wembley in 1986.

The Club hopes that moving to a new ground will both encourage further playing success and attract wider media coverage. Sky Sports television will be covering Nationwide League matches in 1997–98.

# The new stadium

A plan of the new stadium, indicating its main features, is shown in Figure 7.1.

## South Stand

This will be the stadium's main stand. It will offer 30 executive boxes providing dining for 10 people and a private balcony from which to view the action. It will also be the base for the region's largest Conference and Exhibition Centre, The Quadrangle. There is also 3,000 square feet (280 sq. m) of exhibition space ideal for product launches. There will also be a cafe, lounge bars and a business centre. Concerts, recitals, summer balls and jazz festivals are planned.

*Fig. 7.1 Ground plan of new stadium*

## East Stand

This stand is behind the 'home goal'. It will include 400 'business seats'. These are behind glass and enable guests to have a pre-match meal overlooking the pitch and a drink from the private bar, and then to take their places in the comfort of theatre-style seating.

On the first floor there are extensive bars and function rooms. The Club plans to hold over 100 non-football events every year, ensuring that it is the social heart of the community.

## West Stand

The West Stand is next to the leisure park and is intended to attract new family supporters. It will also be home to a 20,000 square feet (1,860 sq. m) Health and Fitness Club. There are plans for an extensive spa area, a large gym and aerobic studio, beauty centre and sports injury clinic.

## North Stand

The North Stand will be mainly for visiting supporters. The design is flexible so that it can also be put to other uses.

## Activities

Oxford United Football Club describes its aims for the new stadium like this:

**For our fans**, we aim to provide a total leisure experience rather than build a soulless soccer shed.

**For our corporate clients**, we aim to provide 'fit-for-purpose' business facilities.

**For our sponsors**, we aim to tailor-make promotional packages designed to promote their products and services in the best light.

**For our community**, we aim to create a landmark of which they can be proud.1 Discuss the possible benefits each of the four groups identified above might gain from the Club's move to a new stadium.

2 Use a word processor to prepare a draft text for a letter to be sent to selected representatives of each of the identified groups *who already have contact* with Oxford United, informing them of these benefits

3 Use a word processor to prepare a draft text for a letter to be sent to selected representatives of each of the identified groups *who do not currently have any contact* with Oxford United, informing them of these benefits

# Owners

Football clubs, especially those outside the Premier League, are often owned by individuals or groups whose main source of wealth is through some other activity. Often they have built up their own businesses and the football club is something they have got involved with out of personal interest. The turnover of a club like Oxford is generally somewhere in the region of £2–£3 million which, when set against all the costs the club has to meet such as salaries and ground maintenance, means that they are often run at an operating loss.

# Role of the General Manager

The work responsibilities of Oxford United's General Manager, Ian Davies, give an idea of how much there is to do in the running of a modern football club. He divides his time between three main areas of activity:

## General administration of the club

This involves accounts, marketing, personnel appointments and training, the Club lottery, Oxford United Social Club and liaison with supporters.

## Editing the Oxford United matchday programme

This involves research, writing, editing and liaison with advertisers, photographers and printers.

## Supporting where it is needed on matchdays

This may involve working in the Club shop, helping out with cleaning or socializing with invited guests.

# Ticket and pricing policy

Season ticket holders are vitally important to a football club. They bring a number of advantages:

- They provide a valuable supply of cash before the Club has to pay out expenses on putting on matches and maintaining daily operation of the club and ground.
- They provide information about a market segment known to be interested in the Club's activities.
- Their use of swipe cards saves time on match days, both in admitting them to the ground and in handling cash received in payment.

Each new season decisions have to be taken about how much to charge for tickets. A number of factors have to be taken into account (Table 7.1).

**Table 7.1**

| | |
|---|---|
| **Historical factors** | • How much was charged last season? |
| | • Did spectators find these charges acceptable? |
| **Social & economic factors** | • Have the local earnings and employment situation changed? |
| | • What can local people afford to pay? |
| **Factors relating to the Club** | • What division is the Club playing in? |
| | • Have the facilities been improved and do they now offer greater value for money? |

A number of other factors affect Oxford's pricing policy. Football League regulations mean that the Club cannot discriminate against away supporters. This means that they cannot charge them more for the same facilities they are offering to home supporters. Home games are very important in League matches, since, apart from a percentage levy paid to the Football League, the takings go to the home club. Cup matches, on the other hand, split the takings between home and away sides, with a percentage also being paid to the organizing body. In the case of the FA Cup this would be the Football Association.

Oxford United's home games are divided into Category A games and Category B games. Category A matches include those that take place on popular football-watching days such as Boxing Day or Easter Monday. They also include games where a higher than average crowd might be expected. Lower prices are charged for Category B games in the hope of attracting more people to attend.

Pricing for the 1997–98 season will have to take account of the fact that the Club will be playing at a purpose-built new ground with much improved facilities. It could be argued that people will expect to pay more for the better surroundings. Given that over 60% of supporters travel more than 15 miles (24 km) to watch Oxford United and only a third live in the city, improved car-parking should be welcomed.

However, the real pricing difference will be that the move will enable the Club to charge a wider range of prices. It will be able to hold down some prices for those who cannot afford much of an increase. Other areas of the ground will be used for medium or higher-priced tickets. Many of those willing to pay higher prices, for example those using boxes in the new ground, are expected to be new customers. Table 7.2 shows how the pricing policy for the new ground might work:

**Table 7.2**

| Most expensive ← | | | | → Least expensive |
|---|---|---|---|---|
| Boxes (South Stand) | South Stand | North Stand | East Stand | Family Stand |
| • Business and company groups | • Highest capacity | • Mainly away fans | • Popular support | • Less expensive |
| • Private parties | • Superior quality | • Can be split for complimentary tickets | • Mainly season ticket holders | • For adults accompanied by children |
| • Mostly new market | | | | |

## Activities

1  Why do Football League clubs offer season tickets at a discounted price?

2  What are the advantages and disadvantages to the football supporter of buying a season ticket?

3  Discuss the likely effects of promotion or relegation on the pricing policy of a Football League club.

4  Why do football clubs sometimes admit schoolchildren free of charge for selected games?

5  How do you think the club would select which game or games they intended to offer free tickets for?

# Safety and security

Before a football club is allowed to put on matches, its ground must receive a safety certificate. This is usually issued by the local council. In the case of Oxford United a local Safety Advisory Group, chaired by a senior planning officer from Oxfordshire County Council, sets out the minimum safety requirements for each area of the ground.

The Home Office publishes a document titled 'Guide to Safety at Sports Grounds'. This document provides detailed guidance for local authorities, ground managers and technical advisers to help them to assess spectator safety at sports grounds. It deals with issues such as:

- Inspection of grounds
- Safe entrance to and exit from grounds
- Ramps, steps, seating and barriers inside sports grounds
- Fire safety
- Communications
- Stewarding
- Crowd behaviour
- Safe ground capacity

Ensuring the safety of everyone who visits or works in a football ground is easier in a new ground than an old one. The older a ground is, the more it is likely to be in need of repairs and additional maintenance. New grounds can be *designed* to be safer. The lessons learned from football ground disasters such as Hillsborough and Bradford have made football administrators and ground designers more aware of such issues as the need to be able to evacuate the ground rapidly and safely.

# Stewards and their training

In the 1970s and 1980s football grounds largely depended on the police to keep order during matches. In more recent times the government has decided that it is unfair for public taxes, paid by the whole population and not just football fans, to be used to pay for the policing of matches. The police authorities were made more accountable, which meant they had to charge football clubs the real cost of providing policing on match days. Most clubs, especially those in lower divisions, found these costs increasingly beyond their means. The solution was to replace the police with club stewards, who were trained by the clubs themselves (Figure 7.2).

Oxford United employs 120 stewards for their home League matches, double the minimum number required by the Safety Advisory Group. The stewards receive extensive training, some of it delivered through a computer-aided package developed by the Football Safety Officers' Association.

Stewards are trained in all the following areas:

● Where all important exits, entrances and facilities are in the ground
● How to provide emergency first aid
● How to use fire-fighting equipment
● What to do in the event of an emergency
● How to provide good customer service
● What dress code is required for stewards at the Club
● How to interpret laws and regulations relating to football grounds

Training exercises include the setting up of different scenarios to test how a team of stewards should react. One scenario used in a recent training session is shown below:

Oxford have been drawn against Swindon Town in a Third Round Cup Tie. A large crowd is expected, both because it is a Cup game and because there is some local rivalry between the clubs.

How should your team of stewards respond to each of the following possible events:

(1) a major road accident delays the arrival of the majority of away fans;
(2) the turnstile counter system fails 45 minutes before the kick off;

**Fig. 7.2 Stewards working on match days – looking after a young supporter**

(3) the Chief Safety Officer is taken ill during the game;

(4) the referee takes the players off the field with 20 minutes to go as a result of thickening fog.

Stewards are empowered to eject people who do not obey the ground regulations. They are entitled to search fans for fireworks or banners. They are required by the Football Offences Act (1975) to report occurrences such as racial chanting, going on to the pitch or drinking alcohol to the police. However, their main responsibility is to ensure that people sit in the right places and that crowd density and movement in any area of the ground do not represent a threat to safety.

# Communications systems

Oxford United, like most football clubs of similar size, uses closed circuit televison to monitor crowd movement and behaviour both inside and outside the ground. Linked video recorders and zoom lenses mean individual incidents can be replayed and offenders identified. Some stewards in each part of the ground are in constant radio contact with the control room.

The new stadium will contain a number of improvements to aid communications within and around the ground. A zonal public address system will enable messages to be relayed to supporters in individual sections of the ground. For example, away fans can be given instructions about leaving the ground at the end of the game without this message being broadcast around the whole ground. A new emergency telephone system enables stewards to use phones at key points around the ground to contact the control room.

## Activities

The following extract comes from the *Oxford United Safety Handbook* which all stewards are required to have with them whenever they are on duty. This section covers what stewards need to know about Acts of Parliament which relate to football matches.

### THE SPORTING EVENTS CONTROL OF ALCOHOL ACT (1985)

SECTION 2 AND 2A

It is an offence ...

(a) to possess alcohol or an article* entering or attempting to enter a designated ground during the designated time, or to possess the above in an area from which a person can directly view the pitch.

(b) to possess fireworks, smoke bombs or similar devices.

(c) to enter or attempt to enter or to be in any designated ground during the designated time while drunk.

* 'article' refers to anything which may be thrown or used to cause injury and includes bottles, cans, glasses etc. It does not include a thermos flask or containers with medicine.

Note...legal advice is that stewards make no arrest until after an offender has passed through the turnstiles in possession of alcohol. Officers or stewards may warn persons on the outside of the ground of the consequences of taking alcohol into the ground.

## FOOTBALL OFFENCES ACT (1991)

### SECTION 2

It is an offence for a person at a designated football match to throw anything at or towards...

(a) the playing area, or any area adjacent to the playing area to which spectators are not generally admitted.
(b) any area in which spectators or other persons are or may be present.

### SECTION 3

It is an offence to take part at a designated football match in chanting of an indecent or racialist nature...

(a) 'chanting' means the repeated uttering of any words or sound in concert with one or more others.
(b) 'of a racialist nature' means consisting of or including matter which is threatening, abusive or insulting to a person by reason of his colour, race, nationality (including citizenship) or ethnic or national origins.

### SECTION 4

It is an offence for a person at a designated football match to go onto the playing area, or any area adjacent to the playing area to which spectators are not generally admitted, without lawful authority or lawful excuse...

ALL OF THE OFFENCES GIVEN IN THESE ACTS ARE ARRESTABLE OFFENCES.

However it is the view of the Thames Valley Police that stewards should not become too involved in arresting people for these offences. They prefer that actual arrests should be made by police officers. Stewards have an important role in identifying and reporting offences and may be called as witnesses if offenders are taken to court.

1 Discuss the problems stewards might have in identifying each of the offences covered in these sections of Acts of Parliament.

2 Imagine you are about to act as a steward for the very first time. List a number of questions you might want to ask before your first game. You could include things such as:

- Do we allow people to bring umbrellas into the ground?

- Don't so many people make what could be classified as indecent remarks about players and referees that everybody expects it and trying to eject an individual for this would just create trouble?

- Does going on to the playing area include before and after the game?

3 Compose answers that you think offer sensible advice in response to each of the questions you listed in (2).

# Community relations

Oxford United Football Club is directly involved in a number of schemes designed to support particular sections of the local community. All the players' contracts include a clause requiring them to take part in community activities. For example, they might be asked to:

- visit a local primary school
- be a guest at a local event
- take part in a charity event, such as a sponsored walk
- run a football training or coaching session

Among the community schemes the club is involved in are the following:

## Trax

The Blackbird Leys estate is not far from the site of the new ground development. For a while it achieved some notoriety as a result of some highly publicized car theft and joy-riding incidents. The Trax scheme was designed to use the interest in cars of some of the offenders and channel it into some more constructive activity. Participants in the scheme were assisted in the restoration of old cars so that they could take part in banger racing events. OUFC's part in the scheme included fund-raising through events such as charity games and serving on the Trax publicity committee.

## Leisure credits

Oxford City Council pioneered this scheme, intended to encourage a number of different community projects. These included activities such as developing picnic areas in local parks, clearing out local streams and constructing pathways for wheelchair users. No cash payment was made to participants in the scheme. Instead they were given leisure credits that they could exchange for free access to facilities in the city's leisure centres and swimming pools. The football club helped to publicize this scheme and to recruit people to take part in it.

## Oxford Common Purpose

This is a new scheme, but there are many similar ones in other towns and cities. It is a forum for local industry and community leaders to review some of the problems faced by the local community and to look at possible solutions. The football club has close connections with local industry. Unipart is the club's main sponsor and other business partners are closely involved in the development of the new ground and The Quadrangle Conference and Exhibition Centre.

# The impact of the football club on the local community

There is always some impact on the local community when several thousand people arrive in their locality at the same time. One of the most obvious effects is that parking in the side streets near the ground becomes very difficult for three or four hours. However, this occurs only on the 25 days a year when there are home games, so another way of looking at the issue is to say that there is no impact on about 340 days of the year!

The influx of so many people does benefit local traders. The shops, food outlets and three pubs close to the Manor Ground all have many extra potential customers before and after Oxford's home matches. One of the advantages for the football club of relocating to a site on the edge of the city is that it has no shops and food outlets nearby. This means more people attending the match will spend additional money on food, drinks and retail products within the new ground development. This extra spending, in additional to paying for admission to the facility, is often referred to as **secondary spend**.

# Football and the local business community

Unipart, one of the largest employers in the Oxford region, is the main sponsor of Oxford United. It sees support for the local football team as part of its own wider community relations programme. Companies increasingly make use of football ground facilities, especially hospitality boxes, in order to entertain important clients and reward their own successful employees.

Oxford United runs an organization called the Manor Club and membership is open to a limited number of local business people. Membership provides access to an Executive Suite and the organization acts as a kind of local chamber of commerce. Members can enjoy the football and perhaps set up one or two possible business ventures at the same time!

# Youth development

An important aspect of running any professional football club is to ensure that there is a supply of good quality young players coming through (Figures 7.3 and 7.4). This is necessary to ensure that the team's fortunes do not decline as more experienced players retire or move on. It is also regarded as a potential financial investment. Every club outside the Premier League hopes to discover a talented player every now and then whose value on the transfer market may cover the club's potential financial losses for several seasons.

*Fig. 7.3  Pre-match soccer activities for children*

*Fig. 7.4  Peter Rhoades-Brown (Football Community Officer) providing a 'virtual tour' of Oxford United's new stadium*

Oxford United works with young people in three main areas:

- Centre of Excellence
- Soccer courses
- Football in the Community

The club employs a Youth Development Officer, two Soccer Course Directors and a Football Community Officer to manage and run these youth programmes.

## Centre of Excellence

The Centre of Excellence provides coaching and training for 9–16-year-olds. The Football Association insists that up to the age of 13 young players must live within an hour's travelling time of the Centre. Players who have been recommended to the Centre receive coaching one evening a week from ex-professional players.

The players attending the Centre also play for age group teams representing the Oxford United Club. Those who are thought good enough may be offered two-year schoolboy contracts when they are 14. This gives the Club the option to sign them on a two-year apprenticeship scheme once they are 16. Such schemes usually involve some day-release study and students on post-16 courses, such as 'A' level, are encouraged to complete their studies.

## Soccer courses

In 1995 Oxford United introduced a programme of soccer courses. These included:

- Evening courses – these are offered to primary school children (aged 4–11) at 12 different venues. They run in term time for one hour after school has finished.
- School holiday courses – these are offered at venues throughout Oxfordshire during the school holidays and are for 6–13-year-olds.
- Saturday specials – these courses coincide with Oxford's home games. They include coaching, lunch and a complimentary ticket to the game.

The main aim of these courses is to provide enjoyment, but outstanding players may also be offered a place at Oxford's Centre of Excellence.

## Football in the Community

The Club is involved in a wide range of community activities. The job of the Club's Football Community Officer means that he is involved in:

- Coaching in schools
- Providing tours of the Club's ground
- Organizing complimentary tickets for different community groups
- Organizing pre-match activities for groups such as children
- Arranging competitions such as Christmas Card designs or local school five-a-side competitions
- Developing school project work based on the Club and ground
- Providing talks and coaching to special schools
- Providing information for the Community Programme Page

## Activities

Oxford United encourages school groups to visit its new ground. An experienced teacher has been recruited and will work full time for the club, supervising and running educational activities from a classroom in the Community Stand.

1  Write a list of the responsibilities which you think this new appointment should cover.

2  Find *three* examples of themes or topics occurring in National Curriculum subjects that you think could be appropriately studied by linking them to aspects of a professional football club.

3  Choose one of these themes or topics and design an activity or project that could be based on a professional club, suggesting the resources, personnel and time that would be needed to complete it.

# Publicity

Keeping in the public eye is important for any leisure facility dependent on attracting paying customers. With no other Football League side in the town and no other major winter sports team to compete against, Oxford United is in a strong position in terms of keeping itself in the local news. The club gets the message about what it is trying to achieve across to the public in a number of ways:

- Regular coverage on the back page of the *Oxford Mail*
- Frequent items about the club on Fox FM and Thames Valley FM
- An Oxford United Internet page
- A telephone service, Oxford United Clubline
- Information in the match day programmes

# Ticket systems

At one time tickets for football matches were printed in advance. They were separately numbered and purchasers bought individual tickets. Many clubs now use a computerized ticket system where areas of the ground are called up on a computer screen. This shows which seats remain unsold. The details of each purchaser's requirements are printed on a blank roll of tickets as they are ordered. This not only saves unnecessary ticket printing, it also enables more information about the purchaser to be stored. It also gives more rapid information about which areas of the ground are being sold most quickly and indicates what effect price changes are having. This may then help the club in marketing its future matches.

# Relocation

There are two main reasons why Oxford United wished to move from the Manor Ground to a new ground. The first was to improve the potential of the Club to generate income. The second related to the health and safety issues related to having an ageing ground in a busy residential area. The Taylor Report required all First Division clubs to develop all-seater stadiums. The space available at the Manor Ground would not allow much over 5,000 seats if this were carried out. It is also increasingly difficult to provide easy access for emergency vehicles such as ambulances and fire engines at the Manor Ground.

# Commercial effects of moving to a new ground

In order to break even at the Manor Ground Oxford United would need to attract about 16,000 fans to each home game. Current attendances fall well short of that figure and there are few opportunities at the current ground to increase the amount of revenue earned by other methods.

The new purpose-built ground will provide far more opportunities for the Club. The improved facilities are expected to attract larger crowds. There is evidence to show that this has happened at other clubs such as Huddersfield, Middlesbrough or Northampton, where completely new grounds have been developed. Two thousand car-parking spaces will make access into and out of the new ground much easier.

Secondary spend at the new ground will increase if the crowds grow. For example it is estimated that 40% of all attenders buy a programme, so that profit from programme sales if crowds averaged 10,000 for home games could reach somewhere in the region of £100,000 over a season. More importantly, the income from catering and bar facilities at the new ground will benefit the Club. The plan to develop other leisure facilities on the site, such as a swimming pool, means that the complex will be in use for much longer and the catering and bar facilities should attract customers other than those attending football matches.

Because the current ground is surrounded by houses there is no room for any kind of expansion. This means the Club cannot develop leisure or catering facilities unless they are within the structure of the existing Club buildings.

A company is being set up to run the new stadium. Oxford United Football Club will be both a tenant of the new company and will also be a shareholder in it. The stadium company will have a number of important business partners; for example, a separate company will run the catering operation.

An important element of the new company will be The Quadrangle Conference and Exhibition Centre. It will have a similar relationship with the stadium company as the football club, being both a tenant and a shareholder. These arrangements mean that profits made by the catering and conference organizations will boost the profits of the stadium company. This will in turn make money for all the shareholders in the stadium company, including the Football Club.

## The Quadrangle

The main advantage of having a conference centre at the new site is that it can attract business on most days of the year. On match days it will be used for corporate hospitality. Oxford does not have a lot of hotel accommodation and yet, as a famous historic city, it is popular with visitors. It is believed that The Quadrangle will attract conference and hospitality business from people who like the idea of combining work with an opportunity to visit the city centre.

The choice of The Quadrangle as a name shows that the conference centre is independent of the football club. This is important because businesses and other likely clients probably do not associate high quality conference facilities with football clubs. Calling the facility Oxford United Conference Centre might attract fewer users.

The facilities at The Quadrangle are very flexible. The conference suite can be divided into four separate rooms and can accommodate group sizes from 18 to 780. There is sufficient space for banquets for up to 450 people and a large exhibition hall can be used for major events like new car or product launches

Selling the conference facility began at least a year before its completion. The plans were publicly launched at a major national exhibition, CONFEX. A database of local and national companies and other potential users has been set up. A database including details of companies who organize conferences has been purchased. Once the construction company provides a final date for completion of The Quadrangle, it will be possible to begin taking provisional bookings.

The Quadrangle is a non-residential centre, but there will be an 120-room hotel on the site and it will be possible to negotiate special rates with it for block conference bookings. The hotel would reserve some rooms for its own clients and so larger conference events would still require other accommodation.

Oxford United Football Club will be a key client of The Quadrangle. Their activities will take precedence on Saturdays and Tuesday nights, whenever there are home matches. The Centre would be needed on these occasions for corporate and group hospitality before and after the match. Other important clients will be local businesses such as Rover and Unipart.

## Activities

Companies were encouraged to get involved with Oxford United at the Manor Ground on match days. There were various kinds of sponsorship and hospitality arrangements. Companies could sponsor the whole game, or perhaps the match ball. They could advertise on boards around the ground or in the match programme. Some of these arrangements included catering, bar facilities and seats in the best part of the ground.

Imagine the Club wishes to launch a new sponsorship or hospitality opportunity in order to attract companies with no previous links to the Club to try out the facilities on offer at the new ground.

1 Outline the main aspects of a sponsorship or hospitality scheme that are different from those already available.

2 Explain how you would sell the benefits of this scheme to companies you think might be interested in it.

3 Write the text of a letter intended to encourage companies to find out more about your scheme.

4 Draw up either a match day schedule if the scheme involves hospitality or a planning schedule if the scheme involves a new type of sponsorship arrangement.

**Case study 8  Knebworth House and gardens**

## Location

Knebworth House is situated near Stevenage in the north of Hertfordshire. It is 30 miles (50 km) by road from London and the nearest place to join the M25 motorway is 10 miles (16 km) away. Unlike many country houses, Knebworth is very close to a major main road, the public entrance to the Park can be reached by a short link road from Junction 7 of the A1(M).

The closest rail links to Knebworth are through Stevenage British Rail Station, 2 miles (3 km) away. There is also a coach service from London Victoria in the summer.

Figure 8.1 shows the main access routes to Knebworth.

## History of Knebworth House and gardens

Knebworth has been the home of the Lytton family for 500 years. The land was purchased by Sir Robert Lytton in 1490 and he built the present house. Sir Robert had fought at the Battle of Bosworth in 1485 and served the new king, Henry VII, as friend, courtier and Privy Councillor.

The original Tudor red brick house was later covered over by a new stucco exterior in the nineteenth century. However, there is evidence that there was an eleventh century Saxon settlement on the site. The estate that made up the manor of Knebworth passed through the hands of several different noble families before it was acquired by the Lyttons.

Sir Robert Lytton's purchase of Knebworth Manor cost £800 – a huge sum in those days! The building of a four-sided house enclosing a courtyard was begun in about the year 1500. Regular improvements and alterations were made by later generations of the Lytton family.

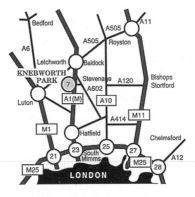

**Fig. 8.1  Main access routes to Knebworth**

Sir Henry Chauncy described Knebworth House in 1700 as 'a large pile of brick with a fair quadrangle in the middle of it, seated upon a dry hill, in a fair large park, stocked with the best deer in the country, excellent timber and well wooded and from thence you may behold a most lovely prospect to the East.'

Much of the original building would still have been recognizable until the beginning of the nineteenth century. In 1810 Mrs Elizabeth Bulwer-Lytton decided that the building was 'old fashioned and too large.' She gave instructions that three sides of the original quadrangle should be demolished. She had the red brickwork of the remaining wing covered with stucco and added some decorative features, such as gothic windows, towers, battlements and a porch (Figure 8.2).

Further additions in the gothic style were added by her son, the novelist Sir Edward Bulwer-Lytton, including domes, turrets, gargoyles and stained glass. Other additions towards the end of the nineteenth century included a third storey to part of the building and a servants' wing. Sir Edwin Lutyens, who became one of the best known architects of the period and who designed buildings as varied in style as Lindisfarne Castle and Liverpool Roman Catholic Cathedral, was related to the Lytton family by marriage and advised on the many alterations to the interior of the house and its decor which were carried out from 1908 onwards.

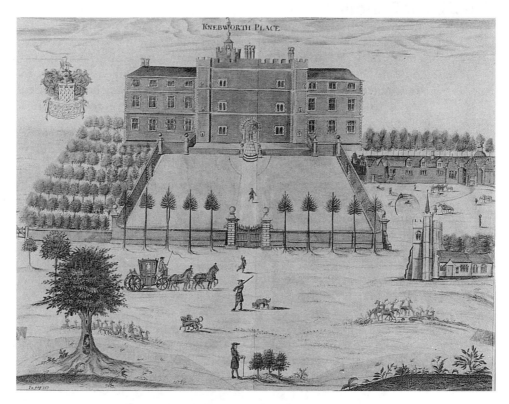

***Fig. 8.2 Earliest known print of Knebworth House***

# The House

There are a number of rooms open to the public at Knebworth. A tour of the House would include the following.

## The Entrance Hall

The Entrance Hall is a drawing room linking the public and private parts of the House. It contains some highly decorated eighteenth century chairs, some eighteenth century German wooden statues and embroidered hangings which were formerly entrance curtains to the Banqueting Hall.

## The Banqueting Hall

This room is famous for its oak screen and the oak decoration of the ceiling. In 1850 Charles Dickens and a troup of actors put on a play in the Banqueting Hall. Sir Winston Churchill's painting of the Banqueting Hall now hangs on the wall there.

## The Dining Parlour

This room has been known as the White Drawing-Room since 1908. It contains embroidery on the furniture said to have come from the state bedroom of King James I. There are tortoiseshell and ivory cabinets made in Italy in the early part of the eighteenth century. The portraits around the walls show members of the Lytton family who owned the House in the sixteenth and seventeenth centuries.

## The Library

Most of the books in the Library were collected by the novelist, Edward Bulwer-Lytton, in the mid-nineteenth century. Some of the House's main treasures are to be found here, including a crucifix given to Mary Queen of Scots by one of her ladies-in-waiting before her execution. A showcase contains the original deed of purchase of Knebworth, dated 17 February 1490.

## Armoury and Staircase

A double flight of oak stairs is surmounted by lions bearing armorial shields and a pair of Nubian slaves. The family coat of arms can be seen in two stained glass windows. A collection of arms and suits of armour stands at the foot of the stairs. Most of these date from the seventeenth century.

# Staircase landing

A picture of Bulwer-Lyttons's wife, Rosina, hangs on the staircase landing. She was heavily committed to the fight for women's rights and wrote many novels and pamphlets challenging the subjugation of women.

# Bulwer-Lytton's Study

There are many examples of Bulwer-Lytton's literary career in this room, including a letter from Charles Dickens containing a new happy ending for *Great Expectations*. Bulwer-Lytton had suggested that he found the original ending too sad.

# The State Drawing-Room

This room is one of the finest examples of early Victorian interior decoration. A stained glass window shows the figure of Henry VIII and indicates the family connections with the Tudors. The ceiling shows coats of arms indicating the family lineage.

# Minstrels' Gallery

The Minstrels' Gallery provides an excellent view of the Banqueting Hall. It contains a skiing exhibition. The Lytton family were much involved in the early years of winter sports development in the 1920s.

# The Falkland Room

This room is hung with hand-painted Chinese wallpaper of the eighteenth century. There is a life-size Dresden model of Empress Catherine of Russia's favourite dog and a small cabinet in the shape of a Chinese pagoda. A wall cabinet contains some fine examples of English and German glass and Austrian porcelain.

# The Hampden Room

This room was the childhood room of Edward Bulwer-Lytton. In it are displayed the family's collection of children's furniture, toys and books. It includes some rare eighteenth century Japanese clockwork toys.

# Mrs Bulwer-Lytton's Room

This room is decorated in Regency style and looks much as it would have done in the early nineteenth century. The room was occupied by Mrs Bulwer-Lytton between 1811 and 1843. When she died her son placed an inscription over the fireplace that reads: '...this room long occupied by Elizabeth Bulwer-Lytton and containing the relicts most associated with her memory. Her son trusts that her descendants will preserve it unaltered.'

## The Queen Elizabeth Room

Recent evidence suggests that Queen Elizabeth I visited the House in 1571. It contains a Tudor-style carved bed, an early map of Ireland on silk, and a 1562 portrait of one of Elizabeth's favourites, Lady Frances Cope.

## The Picture Gallery

This long narrow room contains portraits from the seventeenth and eighteenth centuries. It has also been used for playing and listening to piano music.

## The Indian Exhibition

The Lytton family has many connections with India. This exhibition, put together to mark the proclamation in 1877 of Queen Victoria as Empress of India by her Viceroy, the first Earl of Lytton. The exhibition includes a 15 minute audio-visual presentation showing the involvement of the Lytton family in different periods of Indian history.

## Activities

Study Figure 8.3 of the interiors of some of the rooms at Knebworth House. Note down some of the details and artefacts that visitors might be interested in looking at.

1 Try to match the five photographs with five of the brief descriptions of the different rooms in Knebworth House. The answers are given on page 148.

2 Suggest one way in which each of the five rooms could be made interesting for young children. Discuss whether your ideas would interfere with the ability of adults to enjoy their visit to these rooms.

3 People often want to touch interesting objects in historic houses but this increases the risk of damage or wear and tear. Putting out 'do not touch' notices might spoil the overall appearance of the room. What other suggestions can you make to protect these objects without spoiling the look of the rooms?

4 People come to Knebworth to see what fine houses looked like many years ago. This means the owners will try to preserve the original appearance of rooms that illustrate best the styles of decoration of the past. However, over time furnishings and decorations fade and get dirty and ceilings, walls and floors may suffer structural damage.

Which of the two following points of view do you agree with more and why:

'The most important thing is to preserve an accurate record of the past, keeping objects and buildings exactly as they were, so that future generations can see for themselves what our ancestors achieved...'

'Nothing lasts for ever and the only way of seeing accurately what the best of the past was like is by using modern materials and techniques to mend and restore the best things that were made then...'

**Fig. 8.3  Interiors of some of the rooms at Knebworth House**

# The gardens

The formal gardens and parkland are both features that attract visitors to Knebworth. The formal garden originally contained ornate flower beds, fountains, statues and shrubbery walks. However, this proved very expensive to maintain and in 1908 the design of the garden was simplified by Lutyens. He added avenues of intertwined lime trees, a broad yew hedge and a pergola (Figure 8.4).

A recent addition is a new Herb Garden. This was designed many years ago by a famous garden designer, Gertrude Jekyll, but was never built at the time.

## Activity

1 Suggest some of the groups of people who would be most interested in seeing the formal gardens at Knebworth.

2 In a carefully planted formal garden what problems might arise when it is opened to the public? What measures could be taken to safeguard the appearance of the garden?

# Special events

Knebworth Park is accessible, is not surrounded by housing, and has plenty of space. It makes an ideal setting for outdoor events such as car rallies and rock concerts. These are capable of attracting large numbers of visitors at weekends, but there are risks involved in running them. The English weather is unpredictable, even in summer, and heavy rain is likely to reduce the numbers attending outdoor events.

**Fig. 8.4 The sunken lawn and pleached lime avenue**

There are two main ways of putting on an event at a venue such as Knebworth. Either Lytton Enterprises, the company that manages the business side of running Knebworth, can set up the whole process or it can act as host for an organization or company wishing to use the site as a venue. In the first case Lytton Enterprises would have to meet the costs of hiring all the equipment and groups involved in the event. In the second case they would not have to invest so much in advance of knowing how much revenue the event would bring in.

The second method is far more frequent. It involves a lower level of financial risk for Lytton Enterprises, but still enables it to choose events that enhance the image of Knebworth House. Some events, such as the MG Owners Rally, use the venue for several consecutive years. The location of Knebworth, at Junction 7 of the A1(M), makes it ideal for car rallies because it is central and can be easily reached by road from most directions.

Any event put on at Knebworth by an external business or organization requires clear guidelines about who is responsible for which aspects of the event. The major division of responsibilities is summarized below in Table 8.1.

**Table 8.1**

| Lytton Enterprises are responsible for | The company organizing the event is responsible for |
|---|---|
| • Staffing the main gate<br>• Issuing tickets<br>• Collecting admission fees<br>• Controlling public car park<br>• Staffing the playground | • Setting up required equipment<br>• Supplying and erecting appropriate signs<br>• Roping off show and event areas<br>• Providing stewards |

Other popular events held at Knebworth include craft fairs and gardening shows. Many of these are run by commercial businesses which provide their own equipment, staff and marquees. Their purpose is to generate income from the event and they will share the profits with Lytton Enterprises.

The financial arrangements between Lytton Enterprises and companies hiring the venue for events are determined before any further planning takes place. Lytton Enterprises will always retain control of the main gate, and hence the admission fees paid to enter the grounds. Once the takings have been checked, Lytton Enterprises will distribute the money due to the companies or organizations involved in the event. The gate takings are generally split in the following way:

- A first guaranteed sum is received by Lytton Enterprises as rental for the use of the venue
- A second agreed amount of the total income is split, with approximately 30% going to Lytton Enterprises and 70% going to the company concerned
- Any sum received above this amount is split evenly between Lytton Enterprises and the company

> Example of how revenue for an event might be divided
>
> A special event that generates £50,000 might be split as follows:
>
> | | | |
> |---|---|---|
> | 1 first £15,000 | Knebworth: £15,000 | Company: 0 |
> | 2 £15,000 – £40,000 | Knebworth: £7,500 | Company: £17,500 |
> | 3 £40,000 – £50,000 | Knebworth: £5,000 | Company: £5,000 |
> | **TOTAL** | **Knebworth: £27,500** | **Company: £22,500** |

## Event planning

Good communication between Lytton Enterprises and the company responsible for the event is essential during the planning process. If Knebworth is acting as host to the event there are a number of main issues which will need to be agreed. All of these will involve the development of detailed plans.

Among the most important things to be settled are:

- The ground layout to be used for the event and any practical or safety issues that the proposal raises
- A security system, usually involving passes, which allows access to the Park only to bona fide employees of the company or organization involved
- The catering requirements for the event, including the siting of any mobile food outlets to be admitted
- The setting up and clearing up arrangements, covering requirements such as the need for site workers to camp overnight in the grounds

Major events such as rock concerts cannot be held without a local authority licence. In order to put on such an event, Lytton Enterprises has to satisfy 95 conditions. These relate to many different areas, including traffic management, health and safety, and liaison with relevant local bodies such as hospitals, police and the fire service.

## The programme of special events

The programme of events at Knebworth for 1997 includes car rallies, garden shows, antique and craft fairs and music concerts.

| Special Events | Knebworth Park | 1997 Season |
| --- | --- | --- |
| 4 & 5 May | Knebworth Country Show | |
| 17 & 18 May | Hertfordshire Garden Show | |
| 7 & 8 June | Antiques Fair | |
| 8 June | Classic American Auto Club Rally | |
| 15 June | Vivaldi Four Seasons Concert, with Fireworks | |
| 20 July | Corvette Nationals | |
| 27 July | Fireworks & Laser Symphony Concert | |
| 2 & 3 August | National Street Rod Association Rally | |
| 10 August | Pre-50 American Auto Club Rally | |
| 16 & 17 August | Hertfordshire Craft Fair | |
| 24 & 25 August | Classic Car Show | |
| 31 August | Mustang Owners Club of GB Annual Show | |
| 6 & 7 September | Festival of Flowers | |

## Activities

Study Figure 8.5 showing the layout of Knebworth Park.

1 Taking into account the space and facilities available, choose an event of your own for which you think Knebworth would make an ideal venue.

2 Write a brief description of the objectives of your event.

3 Outline a programme for any performances, demonstrations or other scheduled activities that form part of your event.

4 Make a list of questions that you think would need to be raised at the first planning meeting for your event. These questions should cover the following areas: the siting of the event; access and parking; catering requirements; security provision; set up arrangements; financial management.

# Catering services

Knebworth House makes an interesting setting for conference and banqueting events. Apart from the attractions of the House itself, it is surrounded by 250 acres (100 hectares) of deer park.

The facilities of the House can be made exclusively available for functions and private dinner parties. They can also be combined with functions held in the Barns Conference and Banqueting Centre, using the House to provide a pre-dinner reception, guided tours or a more detailed conference programme using both venues. Banquets, receptions, conferences, themed events, product launches and promotions have all been held within the rooms of Knebworth House.

# KNEBWORTH PARK

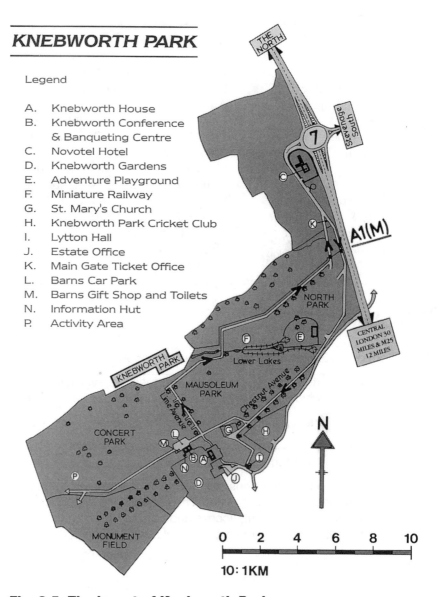

Legend

A. Knebworth House
B. Knebworth Conference
   & Banqueting Centre
C. Novotel Hotel
D. Knebworth Gardens
E. Adventure Playground
F. Miniature Railway
G. St. Mary's Church
H. Knebworth Park Cricket Club
I. Lytton Hall
J. Estate Office
K. Main Gate Ticket Office
L. Barns Car Park
M. Barns Gift Shop and Toilets
N. Information Hut
P. Activity Area

**Fig. 8.5 The layout of Knebworth Park**

The three main rooms used for functions are the Jacobean Banqueting Hall (Figure 8.6), the Edwardian White Dining Parlour and the Victorian Library. These adjoining rooms work well together, are fronted by the grand entrance to the House, and have dedicated access to the formal sunken gardens behind the House.

A family-run business, Lytton Catering, manages the catering and hospitality at Knebworth. They work with private and corporate clients to make sure each event meets their exact requirements. A wide range of menus is available. Clients can choose set menus or they can select items from a much longer list of dishes.

*Fig. 8.6 Jacobean Banqueting Hall: table laid for banquet*

# Conferences

Knebworth has a number of advantages as a conference venue. It is easy to get to by road and has generous parking facilities. The parkland setting is ideal for relaxing after the concentration required by meetings and courses. The historic house has a style and atmosphere that can help delegates to enjoy their stay and that may encourage them to feel more positive about what they are being told.

Knebworth and Lytton Catering combine to offer special packages for conferences. These contain a number of different elements, including:

- Coffee, tea and pastries on arrival
- Mid-morning refreshments
- A buffet lunch or a choice of set luncheon menus
- Afternoon tea
- Drinks as requested
- Conference equipment: overhead projector, screen, TV monitor, video, flip charts, pads and pens, laser pointer, microphones, audio CD and cassette system, staging and lectern
- Activities and entertainments as requested, e.g. archery, team-building games, obstacle course

## Activities

Study the two sample menus on page 144 both available as part of the conference packages offered by Lytton Catering:

```
Menu 1                                         Menu 2
Fresh Cream of Asparagus Soup           Roundels of Chilled Honeydew Melon
Freshly Baked Wholemeal and               offered with Fine Ruby Port
White Rolls and Butter                   Freshly Baked Wholemeal and
                                           White Rolls and Butter
         *****
                                                  *****
Roast Sirloin of English Beef
served with Yorkshire Pudding and Gravy    Roast Crown Lamb Chops
Horseradish Cream                       presented on a bed of Mixed Peppers
                                        and finished with a Tomato and Basilic Sauce
Fresh Seasonal Vegetables
Roast Potatoes                            Fresh Seasonal Vegetables
                                          Buttered Baby Jacket Potatoes
         *****
                                                  *****
Deep Dish Apple Pie
served with Double Cream                      Gateau St Honore

         *****                                    *****

Freshly Brewed Dark Colombian Coffee    Freshly Brewed Dark Colombian Coffee
with Cream                                        with Cream
Lytton Catering Chocolate Mint            Lytton Catering Chocolate Mint
```

1  Suggest two groups who, for different reasons, would probably find neither of these menus acceptable.

2  Draw up one alternative menu to suit each of the groups you identified in activity (1).

# Marketing

Knebworth House uses a variety of methods of promoting both the attractions of the house and gardens and also the special events which are held there. These include:

- Flyer leaflets distributed through Tourist Information Centres
- Advertisements in newspapers
- Representation at trade shows and exhibitions
- Signs alongside the A1(M) that can be updated for different special events
- Advertising events in specialist magazines, e.g. classic car shows are advertised in classic car magazines
- Exit boards by the Park gates advertising forthcoming events
- Issuing special family day tickets

Some features of Knebworth attract families with young children. Leaflets, such as the one shown in Figure 8.7, encouraging people to visit Knebworth often include images of children enjoying themselves.

The exciting children's world of

**FORT KNEBWORTH**

**Children can enjoy hours of fun at 'Fort Knebworth'. This giant Adventure Playground includes:**

● The Fort – with sturdy apparatus where children can let off steam!

● Monorail Suspension Slide. ● Bouncy Castle.

● Sensational sliding experience on the Astroglide – and the new Corkscrew* and Freefall Slides*.

● Skate Board Bowl.

*Extra charge.*

● Tarzan Trail.

● Miniature Railway*.

● Acres of open space for ball games, picnics and play.

**DON'T FORGET... Under 3s are FREE!**

*Fig. 8.7  Leaflet advertising Fort Knebworth*

## Activities

1  Discuss the possible advantages of using a watercolour painting rather than a photograph in this leaflet.

2  List the words used in the leaflet that emphasize having a good time.

3  What reasons do you think there might be for placing the line about free admission at the bottom of the page?

4  Sketch the outline of a page in the same leaflet intended to interest visitors in the House at Knebworth.

# Health, safety and welfare at pop concerts

Knebworth has hosted a number of major rock concerts, attracting up to 250,000 people. Ensuring the health, safety and welfare of so many visitors requires extensive planning. The Health and Safety Commission and the Home Office produce a guide for those intending to put on pop concerts and similar events. It covers such things as:

- Planning and organization
- Crowd management
- Stewarding
- Facilities for people with disabilities
- Communication
- Barriers
- Temporary structures
- Marquees and large tents
- Electrical systems
- Fireworks, lasers and other special effects
- Sound and noise
- Fire safety and emergency procedures
- Traffic and transport arrangements
- First aid
- Food, refreshments and drinking water
- Sanitary arrangements and waste disposal

In planning any event of this size there are some things that the organizers *must* do because they are legal requirements. There are other things that they *should* do because they are thought to be sensible. For example, public music entertainments cannot by law be held unless a licence has been obtained from the local authority. Although providing free drinking water at a pop concert is not a legal requirement, it is regarded as a sensible thing to do. In cramped, hot conditions people easily become dehydrated and this can lead to fainting, collapse and the risk of people being trampled on.

# Crowd management

The most important aspect of crowd safety at a popular concert is setting a sensible **capacity** for the event. This should ensure that crowd density is not dangerous and that evacuation procedures can be managed quickly and safely. Entrances and exits have to be well controlled. Because entrances are the places where the greatest crowd pressures tend to build up, it is important to take steps to reduce the risks. Some of the things that can be done are:

- Open entrances early and advertise this fact
- Keep other queuing points, such as those for food, away from entrances
- Arrange for queuing areas away from entrances
- Use suitable barriers, fences, gates and turnstiles
- Place ticket sales points away from entrances
- Provide enough trained stewards
- Provide information about delays through a public address system
- Arrange suitable space for the removal of prohibited items such as glass bottles, alcohol, etc

# Equipment

Apart from structures such as temporary stages and hospitality marquees major concerts also tend to make use of a lot of potentially dangerous equipment. Complicated electrical systems are required to provide light and sound effects. There are many tasks and checks required to ensure that these systems can be operated safely. Cables have to be protected from contact or damage. The location of the main controls has to be made known to emergency services. The electrical switches have to be protected so that they can only be used by authorized people. Emergency power supplies have to be available in case the main supply fails.

Pop concerts also use special effects, such as lasers, strobe lighting, ultraviolet light, fireworks, smoke and vapour effects and smoke or fog machines. Most of these effects can present some danger either to operators or an audience if strict safety standards are not observed. The venue will not be granted a licence for the event if, in the opinion of the licensing authority, proper precautions have not been taken.

# First aid

First aid should always be available at a big open air concert. People may suffer cuts, bruises, dehydration or sunstroke. Perhaps conditions they are already suffering from may be made worse by their surroundings. Those planning the event have to decide how many first aid staff the event needs. This will depend on the number of people expected to attend, the length of the event, the weather, the age range of the audience and, to some extent, on the degree to which the performance excites those present.

Table 8.2 suggests recommended levels of first aid provision for events such as pop concerts.

**Table 8.2**

| Audience size | First aiders | First Aid Posts | Ambulances |
|---|---|---|---|
| 500 | 2 | 1 | – |
| 3,000 | 6 | 1 | 1 |
| 5,000 | 8 | 1 | 1 |
| 10,000 | 13 | 2 | 2 |
| 20,000 | 23 | 3 | 2-3 |
| 40,000 | 43 | 4 | 3-4 |
| 60,000 | 63 | 4 | 3-4 |

# Food and drink

The majority of the food sold during a concert at Knebworth is bought from mobile units owned by outside catering companies. The details of what kind of food will be available, and how it will be delivered, stored and prepared have to be agreed with the Environmental Health Department of the local authority. The use of mobile units means a number of controls are applied to events where there are large crowds:

- Cans, glass bottles or other dangerous containers may not be used
- Vehicles cannot be moved while crowds are present
- Diets must be available for those with special medical needs, e.g. diabetes

Some events permit the sale of alcohol, but there are always controls involved. Firstly a separate licence has to be obtained. This may grant permission but only if certain conditions are met. These may limit the opening hours and control the types of container in which the drinks are served.

Outdoor events generally require the provision of a supply of drinking water and also of paper or plastic cups. It is recommended that there should be one drinking water outlet for every 3,000 people attending the event.

## Activities

Some pop concerts generate a very high level of noise. This has a number of possible effects. It may disturb people living in the area. It may expose site workers to sound levels that, over time, will have a harmful effect on their hearing. It may also increase the risk for those members of the audience who are exposed to regular high levels of noise at work or in other leisure activities.

The Noise at Work Regulations 1989 require employers to assess noise levels, to provide workers with information and training, and to provide ear protectors.

1  Suggest what you think would be the best way of accurately assessing the noise levels during several days' of rehearsal for a pop concert.

   What problems might you come across in carrying out this task?

2 List the kind of information and training that you think should be supplied to all workers involved in the preparation of the stage area during the period of rehearsal.

3 Can you suggest other forms of protection against the possible effects of exposure to loud noise, apart from providing workers with ear protectors?

Answers to question (1) on page 136: 1 The Entrance Hall  2 The Picture Gallery 3 The Dining Parlour  4 The Falkland Room  5 Bulwer-Lytton's Study

# Module 3

# SOCIAL, CULTURAL AND ENVIRONMENTAL IMPACT OF TOURISM

**Introduction**

**Case study 9**
Uluṟu–Kata Tjuṯa National Park

**Case study 10**
The Gambia

**Case study 11**
Tourism Impact on the Gaeltacht

**Case study 12**
Bali, Lombok and Komodo

This module covers the following components of the syllabus:

3.1 Impact of tourism on society
3.2 Impact of tourism on culture
3.3 Impact of tourism on the environment

# What impacts does tourism have?

When an activity such as tourism grows as fast as it has done in the twentieth century, it is important to be aware of what effects this is having on people, on the quality of their lives and on the places in which they live. Most attempts to assess the results of this growth of tourism have divided its impacts into three main types:

- Economic impact
- Social and cultural impact
- Environmental impact

In each of these three areas tourism has had both beneficial and harmful impacts. The extent to which tourism benefits or harms a particular destination will depend on many inter-related factors, including:

- The rate at which the volume of visitors increases
- The existing infrastructure
- The levels of investment in tourism
- The speed of tourism development
- The strength of the local economy
- The strength of the local culture
- The fragility or robustness of the local environment

# The economic impact of tourism

One direct result of an increased number of visitors to a destination is a growth in the number of jobs available. For example, new hotels may be built to cater for more visitors and will need reception staff, porters, chambermaids, chefs and managers. More tourists generally means more carpark attendants, more ice cream sellers, more tour guides and more shop assistants.

As the population of a tourist destination rises, there will also be a need for better transport services, both to and around the area. This is likely to create temporary jobs for people involved in activities such as road improvement. It should lead to a seasonal increase in the number of jobs required to operate an expanded transport service during the destination's peak season. It may also lead to some permanent jobs when the local population grows as a result of the improved employment opportunities in the region.

In addition to the jobs created directly by tourism there are also ways in which tourism growth affects employment in other industry sectors. As more tourists visit a destination and spend more money on things such as accommodation, so the owners of that accommodation become more wealthy. They, in turn, spend their extra earnings in local shops and showrooms or perhaps employ local people to carry out such tasks as home improvements. In other words the extra earnings from tourism can stimulate employment in a variety of working environments not directly associated with tourism. This process is called the **multiplier effect**.

While tourism is often seen as a potential solution to unemployment problems, especially in areas where manufacturing or agriculture has declined, its apparent ability to employ high numbers of people should be set against a number of limiting factors, such as:

- Some of the employment opportunities are only part time
- In many destinations tourism employment may be seasonal
- Many of the jobs associated with tourism are relatively low paid
- Many of the employment opportunities are in labour-intensive operations, where conditions may result in high staff turnover

# Tourism and national economies

Countries may earn money from tourism in a number of ways. These include:

- Spending by incoming tourists
- Taxation on purchases (e.g. VAT, excise duties) and on additional employees (e.g. income tax)
- Generating added-value foreign currency exchange

International tourism brings money into countries from outside and is highly valued in places where inbound tourists exceed the number of outbound tourists. However, in a country such as Britain, where the native population spends more on holidays overseas than it does on holidays within Britain, tourism may represent a net deficit in terms of revenue.

# The social and cultural impacts of tourism

Culture plays an important part in attracting tourists to many destinations. They may be interested in visiting historic sites such as cathedrals, castles, ancient settlements or monuments. It may be the artistic achievement of the region that draws them to art galleries, museums and performances of dance and music. While this interest is sometimes based on past achievements, people are also drawn to places because their modern culture seems different and exciting by comparison with their own familiar traditions.

Tourism becomes linked to the cultures in tourist destinations in a number of ways. Visitors buy souvenirs of local art and crafts. They attend specially arranged performances of music, dance and drama. They visit churches, temples and sacred places. Perhaps most important of all, they introduce members of the host community to values, standards and ideas that are common in their own cultures but that may not be typical in the tourist destination.

The impact of tourists on a local culture takes a variety of forms. These may include:

- 'The **demonstration effect**' where members of a host community, especially the younger generation, adopt values and beliefs of tourists, often bringing them into conflict with members of their own community.
- The production of '**airport art**', cheap imitations of local crafts made quickly and sold as souvenirs.
- The rediscovery of arts and crafts skills in order to create a new industry selling quality products to tourists.
- The reduction of dances and ceremonies with religious significance to simple performances designed to entertain and be understood by tourists.
- The admission of large numbers of visitors to churches, temples and sacred places, making them more like visitor attractions than places of worship.
- The exposure of language and cuisine to international influences, causing them to risk losing some of their distinctiveness.

Clearly these impacts are both positive and negative. Tourism can encourage changes in cultural traditions and activities that cause a lot of their original significance to be lost. However, it can also revive interest in local cultures, as well as providing funds to encourage the rediscovery and development of arts, crafts and skills.

# The environmental impact of tourism

Tourism development has had a negative effect on the environment in many parts of the world. Many of the main concerns relate to:

- Pollution of the sea through extra sewage, chemicals and water sports
- Excessive demands on resources for light, heat and water
- Destruction of wildlife habitats
- Litter on beaches and in rural areas
- Erosion of coastlines, river banks and footpaths
- Traffic congestion and overcrowding
- Transport noise
- Inappropriate development
- Wear and tear in and around historic sites

Since tourism and, to a lesser extent, leisure demand a pleasant environment in order to provide a fully satisfying experience, it is not surprising that both can have adverse effects on the locations to which people are attracted. From the Caribbean reefs to the deforestation along the trekking trails of the Himalayas, there are many examples of direct physical damage caused by leisure and tourism activities. This impact is made worse by the extra rubbish and sewage generated by visitors and the fact that they make demands on resources such as power and water, often in places where local people already find these in short supply.

The demand for facilities such as hotels and swimming pools has led to many concentrated coastline developments which show little consideration for issues of space, matching shape and materials to land contours, obscuring views or traditional local building styles. Little regulation of the subsequent development of bars, restaurants, souvenir shops, and advertising and directional signs is also responsible for the destruction of the visual attractiveness of many settlements which have become popular with tourists.

The heavy use of air, water and land transport by both leisure and tourism interests often has a harmful effect on the environment. The growth of air traffic raises a number of environmental issues, such as:

- The amount of land required for airport construction
- The energy and water demands of major airports
- Aircraft noise at take-off and landing
- Levels of air pollution caused by aircraft

However, levels of road traffic probably cause greater concerns. While this is a general environmental problem, there are particular locations where tourism during the peak season is the main cause of traffic congestion, noise and air pollution. Specific issues, such as the popularity of mountain bikes and off-road vehicles and the potential erosion they can cause, are a problem in some destinations.

Other leisure activities favoured by tourists can have a harmful effect on the environment. For example, many tourist destinations are affected by the spread of water sports. The small, high-powered boats used for water skiing and power boat racing tend to leave a residue of oil on the water. They are noisy and do not generally improve coastal or lakeside scenery. The wash they create can sweep away plants from the shoreline and destabilize lake and river banks, hastening the process of erosion, as has happened in the Norfolk Broads. The habitats of fish and other marine life are disturbed and areas with extensive coral reefs suffer damage as a result of the popularity of boat excursions.

Sports associated with tourism, such as skiing and golf, have also been the cause of damage to the environment. The ski runs themselves and the construction of resorts represent a threat to the landscape, both by destroying trees and plants and by building unattractive avalanche shelters, pylons, overhead cables, lifts and tows. Golf courses lead to the cutting down of trees. They require a great deal of water to maintain their condition, especially in hot climates. Herbicides and fungicides may be required to keep the grass on the courses healthy and this can lead to a build up of phosphates wherever water drains off the course.

As tourists seek out more remote places, the threat they pose to the ecology of such places increases. Islands are particularly vulnerable. Their animal populations are often small and prone to disturbance. The rapid clearing of land can easily cause rare plants to become extinct. Land clearance can also reduce the available living space and feeding grounds for animals.The introduction of non-indigenous plants and animals can have the same result, in that the newcomers may compete more successfully for the available food, water and light.

Marine pollution represents a threat to to both animal and plant life. Yet the fact that tourists will often pay to see rare or unusual plants and animals is itself an incentive to developers and local people to invest in their conservation.

As with other kinds of tourism impact, not all the effects of tourism on the environment are harmful. Tourism can renew interest in flora, fauna and natural habitats which have become neglected. For example the presence of tourists may lead to the establishment of nature reserves where wildlife habitats and breeding programmes can be properly managed to ensure the survival of creatures under threat. Their presence may encourage the reconstruction of footpaths, so that damage and erosion is reduced. It is becoming more widely recognized, by national governments, regional organizations and authorities and tour operators themselves, that the tourism industry should contribute to paying for the preservation of environments tourists wish to visit.

## Activities

1 Choose an overseas tourist destination which you have visited and think about the ways you think it has probably been changed by tourism.

2 Complete the chart below:

| Name of destination: _____ | | |
|---|---|---|
| Possible impacts of tourism | Positive impacts | Negative impacts |
| Economic impacts of tourism | | |
| Social and cultural impacts of tourism | | |
| Environmental impacts of tourism | | |

3 For each of the possible negative impacts you have listed in your chart, suggest ways of reducing or eliminating the harmful effects.

# Location

Most people have heard of Ayers Rock. It is the largest monolith in the world, rising 348 metres (1,140 feet) above the plain and requiring a 9 kilometre (5.6 mile) walk to circle its base completely. Nearby are the Olgas, another distinctively shaped mountain group. Both of these landmarks are now found inside the boundaries of the National Park bearing their Aboriginal names, Uluṟu–Kata Tjuṯa National Park.

As Figure 9.1 suggests Uluṟu–Kata Tjuṯa National Park is not easy to get to. Ayers Rock itself is some way from any major city, as Table 9.1 shows:

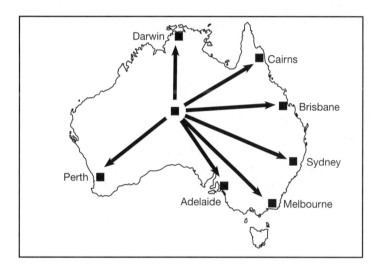

*Fig. 9.1  Location of Uluṟu–Kata Tjuṯa National Park*

*Table 9.1*

| City | Distance to Ayers Rock |
| --- | --- |
| Sydney | 2,139 kilometres (1,329 miles) |
| Melbourne | 1,953 kilometres (1,213 miles) |
| Brisbane | 2,185 kilometres (1,358 miles) |
| Darwin | 1,395 kilometres (867 miles) |
| Perth | 1,674 kilometres (1,040 miles) |
| Cairns | 1,788 kilometres (1,111 miles) |
| Adelaide | 1,265 kilometres (786miles) |
| Alice Springs | 445 kilometres (276 miles) |

Its position in the centre of Australia means it takes more than a day to drive there from most of the coastal Australian cities. The Ghan train takes 14 hours just to get from Adelaide to Alice Springs. The building of an airstrip clearly made the area much more accessible. It is now possible to fly from Adelaide to Yulara, the resort on the edge of the Uluṟu–Kata Tjuṯa National Park in 2 hours 40 minutes.

# History

Central Australia has been inhabited by Aboriginal people for at least 60,000 years. Archaeologists working to the north of Uluṟu in 1987 suggested that people had lived in the region for 22,000 years.

Non-Aboriginal presence in this part of Central Australia is relatively recent. It was not until 1862 that John McDouall Stuart completed the first return north–south crossing of Australia. An overland telegraph line between Darwin and Adelaide was constructed between 1870 and 1872. Alice Springs became an important base on this line and further exploration of the surrounding area began. The purpose of most of the exploration was to find new land to farm.

In 1872 William Giles first saw Kata Tjuṯa. He named the highest mountain in the range Mount Olga (Figure 9.2). In the following year William Gosse reached Uluṟu and named it Ayers Rock after the then Chief Secretary of South Australia, Sir Henry Ayer. Between 1872 and 1885 much of the land around Alice Springs was taken over by the farming industry. However, the area around Kata Tjuṯa was too harsh to be farmed successfully. Uluṟu and Kata Tjuṯa were included in the South West Reserve, one of system of reserves set aside for Aboriginal people. This meant that until the 1940s very few non-Aboriginals visited the area.

The expansion of farming around Alice Springs led to a number of conflicts between Aboriginal and non-Aboriginal people. Most of these were either about

*Fig. 9.2 Mount Olga/Kata Tjuṯa*

water or about hunting grounds. However, it was the expansion of mining that was to have a more significant impact. In 1940 the size of the Aboriginal reserves was reduced to allow mineral exploration. A number of tracks made by miners extended to Uluru and Kata Tjuta and tour companies were quick to see the opportunities these offered for organized tours.

The size of the Aboriginal reserve was further reduced in 1958. In the following year an airstrip was built north-east of Uluru and the first motel leases were granted. Over the next three decades the number of visitors to the area rose from 5,462 in 1962 to 312,000 in 1995. Several unsuccessful attempts were made in the 1960s to move the Anangu people from the Park to a government settlement on the Docker River.

By 1973 concern over the environmental impact of tourists on the environment around Uluru resulted in a government inquiry which proposed that all accommodation facilities should be moved to a site 27 kilometres (17 miles) away. The resort of Yulara, complete with its own airstrip, was opened in 1983.

The growing number of tourists led the Anangu people to make formal protests about the desecration of sacred sites around Uluru. During the 1970s progress towards the restoration of land rights to the traditional Aboriginal owners of land around Uluru and Kata Tjuta was made. However, Uluru and Kata Tjuta themselves were crown land, part of a national park, and as such could not legally be given away. Finally in 1983 land inside the Uluru National Park was returned to the Aboriginal people. The deeds to the land were handed over in 1985 and the lands were then leased back to the Australian National Parks and Wildlife Service for 99 years. Since that time the Park has been managed jointly by the Anangu people and the Australian Nature Conservation Agency staff.

# Park management

The lease arrangement between the Anangu people and the Australian Nature Conservation Agency (ANCA) contains a number of objectives intended to make sure that the Anangu people benefit from the arrangement. The lease ensures that ANCA:

- Encourages the maintenance of Anangu tradition through protection of sacred sites and other areas of significance.
- Maximizes Anangu involvement in Park administration and management, and provides necessary training.
- Maximizes Anangu employment in the Park by accommodating Anangu needs and cultural obligations with flexible working conditions.
- Uses Anangu traditional skills in Park management.
- Actively supports the delivery of cross-cultural training by Anangu to Park staff, local residents and Park visitors.
- Consults regularly with Anangu.
- Encourages Anangu commercial activities in the Park.

An Anangu design by Jennifer Taylor, in Figure 9.3 shows the way the Anangu see the joint management of the Park.

***Fig. 9.3 The Anangu design by Jennifer Taylor, 'Working Together'***

The central circle of the design represents Uluru–Kata Tjuta National Park. The ten seated figures surrounding the circle are the members of the Board of Management: six Anangu and four non-Anangu. They have surrounded the Park with two windbreaks representing the way decisions and policies protect the Park.

Waiting and listening to the Board's decisions are the Anangu and non-Anangu rangers. The white rangers wear shoes, representing their land management training and western scientific knowledge. The Anangu rangers are barefoot, representing their close connection with the land and their training and knowledge from thousands of years of looking after the land.

Surrounding all are two more windbreaks representing the protection and support of Tjurkurpa and the National Parks and Wildlife Conservation Act. Both laws are working together to guide and protect Uluru–Kata Tjuta National Park.

## Activities

Two of the first things the Anangu set out to achieve through joint management of the Park were:

- Taking away references to non-Aboriginal names such as Ayers Rock and the Olgas, so that everyone would use the Anangu names, Uluru and Kata Tjuta

- Encouraging visitors to respect their culture by not climbing Uluru

1 Discuss what obstacles the Anangu might have faced in trying to achieve each of these objectives.

2 Suggest some practical ways in which the Anangu might have tried to persuade non-Aboriginals of the importance of these two issues.

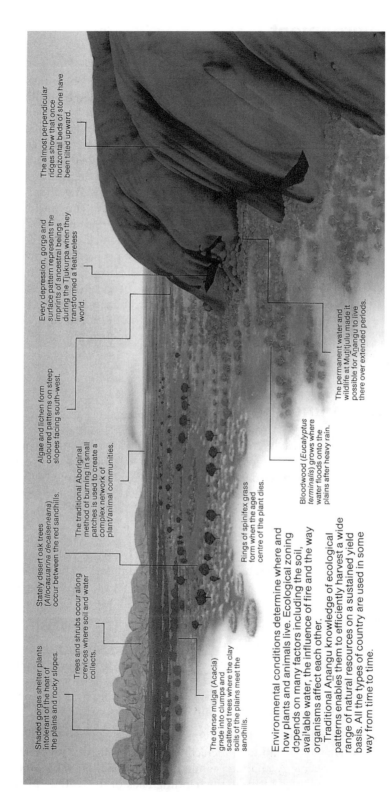

The almost perpendicular ridges show that once horizontal beds of stone have been tilted upward.

Every depression, gorge and surface pattern represents the imprints of ancestral beings during the Tjukurpa when they transformed a featureless world.

Algae and lichen form coloured patterns on steep slopes facing south-west.

The traditional Aboriginal method of burning in small patches is used to create a complex network of plant/animal communities.

Stately desert oak trees (*Allocasuarina decaisneana*) occur between the red sandhills.

Trees and shrubs occur along crevices where soil and water collects.

Shaded gorges shelter plants intolerant of the heat of the plains and rocky slopes.

The dense mulga (Acacia) grade into clumps and scattered trees where the clay soils of the plains meet the sandhills.

Rings of spinifex grass form when the aged centre of the plant dies.

Bloodwood (*Eucalyptus terminalis*) grows where water floods onto the plains after heavy rain.

The permanent water and wildlife at Mutitjulu made it possible for Anangu to live there over extended periods.

Environmental conditions determine where and how plants and animals live. Ecological zoning depends on many factors including the soil, available water, the influence of fire and the way organisms affect each other.

Traditional Anangu knowledge of ecological patterns enables them to efficiently harvest a wide range of natural resources on a sustained yield basis. All the types of country are used in some way from time to time.

***Fig. 9.4  The Uluru environment***

# The environment

Uluru and Kata Tjuta are the remains of a huge bed of sedimentary rock (Figure 9.4). Most of this is now covered by debris and wind-blown sand. The features of the 36 individual domes of Kata Tjuta have been formed by millions of years of weathering and erosion. The Anangu believe that Uluru and Kata Tjuta were created during the Tjukurpa or creation period and that their individual features are the imprints and physical proof of the activities of ancestral beings of the Tjukurpa.

This part of Central Australia is often described as a harsh environment. It is hot, with temperature ranges varying from 4 to 20 degrees Celsius in the coldest month, July, to 21 to 38 degrees in the hottest, January. The area is also very dry, sometimes having no rain for much of the year. Much of the land is made up of sand dunes which means it is easily eroded. A tarmac road has now been built around Uluru and to Kata Tjuta and it is illegal to drive vehicles off the road.

Despite these harsh conditions the area is host to a variety of plants and animals. At the latest count 150 different kinds of birds, 22 mammals, many reptiles and frogs, and nearly 400 plant species have been recorded in the Park area.

For the Anangu people to survive in this area they had to develop a deep knowledge of the properties and habits of the flora and fauna of the region. Nowadays many of these skills are passed on to rangers and visitors and the knowledge helps in the fight to preserve rare species.

# Understanding the countryside

Much knowledge of the environment of Kata Tjuta has come from the Anangu. The rarity of rain at most times of year makes the Anangu very sensitive to the importance of weather changes and the effects these have on habitats and wildlife. This knowledge is vital in finding enough food and water to survive.

## Habitats

There are six main habitats in the National Park as described in Table 9.2.

## Wildlife

Many of the plants in the Kata Tjuta region are rare. They have to rely on irregular rainfall and some depend on fire in order to reproduce. Animals and reptiles have often adopted secretive and nocturnal habits in order to survive.

A number of medium sized mammals have disappeared from the Park. Three possible reasons are generally put forward to explain this:

- They have been killed by predators such as foxes or cats.
- They have had too much competition for food from other species such as rabbits.
- The ecology changed while the traditional Anangu land burning practices were not allowed, prior to the handing back of the National Park.

**Table 9.2**

| | |
|---|---|
| ● *Puli* (rocky areas, gorges, stony slopes) | These areas have shallow, barren soils and so are not good feeding areas for animals. They do, however, provide water holes and shelter and so attract birds and animals after rain. |
| ● *Pila* (spinifex plains, low areas between dunes) | This is the most common habitat, dotted with trees and shrubs. These provide seeds and sweet resins for food. Many small animals and reptiles live in these areas. |
| ● *Karu* (creeklines and run-off plains) | The creeks are normally dry but water can be obtained here by digging. These areas are important sources of grass seeds, firewood and timber. |
| ● *Tali* (sand dunes) | This habitat is very fragile. Spinifex and green shrubs grow here. Many animals survive here by burrowing into the sand. It is also the home of a number of reptiles. Some creatures only come to the surface after rain. |
| ● *Puti* (open woodlands) | These areas often covered by thick patches of mulga trees with grasses at ground level. This is where *tjala* (honey ants) and *maku* (witchety grubs) are found. After rain the areas with hard ground hold water for a time and animals come to drink. |
| ● *Nyaru* (burnt or regenerating areas) | *Pila* and *tali* become *nyaru* after they are burned. The planned burning of patches of land encourages new growth of many types of food plants, including edible seed grasses and succulents. |

The last reason was associated with the rapid growth of tourism in the 1960s and 1970s. Better management of the environmental resources of the region can help to preserve both flora and fauna.

# Managing environmental resources

## Patch burning

The traditional Anangu practice of starting controlled fires in a series of small areas had two main purposes. It stimulated new growth in burnt plants. It also helped to create fire breaks so that larger fires could not spread over much wider areas.

## Wildlife management

Rare species and their habitats are offered special protection. Guided walks, information boards and covered walkways are used to emphasize the threat to some species and the best ways of ensuring their survival. This includes trying to educate people not to introduce weeds and feral animals into the area, since these can have a very destructive effect on the native plants and animals.

## Water-holes and rock-holes

Water is a scarce resource in Uluru/Kata Tjuta. Knowledge of where rock-holes and waterholes are enables the Anangu to carry out the important work of ensuring that they are in good condition. This may involve tasks like cleaning out dirt, rocks, grass and rubbish from water-holes.

## Land regeneration

Areas of land around Uluru/Kata Tjuta that have been damaged by visitors are undergoing a process of repair. There are three main activities involved:

- Restoring the original water flow and run-off patterns of the land
- Replanting areas with native species
- Restricting and controlling access to some land areas

## Activities

Read the article below about World Heritage sites.

In 1994 Uluru – Kata Tjuta National Park became only the second national park in the world to be listed as a cultural landscape. This status was meant to draw attention to the close links between humankind and the environment in this region. It emphasized the religious, artistic and cultural importance of the land-scape itself to the local people.

Since its beginning in 1975 over 100 countries have now signed the World Heritage Convention. There are 440 sites around the world listed as World Heritage Areas. The main aims of the World Heritage Convention are:

- To protect and conserve important world heritage sites
- To identify important heritage properties and protect their future
- To ensure that cultural heritage has a place in national planning programmes
- To use appropriate methods to protect cultural and natural heritage from damage.

The listing of Uluru – Kata Tjuta made special mention of the way traditional Anangu land management practices have begun to reverse the environmental damage caused in the region in the last 50 years.

The effects on tourism of listing the Park as a cultural landscape should be to emphasize the importance of the cultural experience of the visitors. An increas-ing number of visitors will leave with an experience of Anangu culture – their art, their beliefs, and their intimate knowledge of and relationship with their surroundings. Fewer people will drive out, climb to the top of Uluru, and take a few photographs. There will be more emphasis on getting visitors to appreciate how the Anangu interpret their surroundings.

The listing may also bring some financial benefits in terms of regional, national and international funding for conservation projects in the region.

1 Suggest *three* other sites in the world that you think might qualify as World Heritage sites. (You may include sites which you know have already been granted this status.)

For each one give a brief description of why you think it should have this status.

2 Choose *one* of these sites and discuss how each of the two following visitors might think differently about its importance:

(a)  a local person for whom the site has some religious or cultural significance;

(b)  an overseas tourist visiting the site for the first time.

# Yulara Resort

The building of the tourist resort at Yulara was completed in 1984 (Figure 9.5). It was sited outside the boundaries of the National Park, some 20 kilometres (12 miles) from Uluru and 30 kilometres (19 miles) from Kata Tjuta. The choice of site was a deliberate attempt to take some of the pressure off the damaged areas in the immediate vicinity of Uluru. However, given that up to 5,000 people a day can be accommodated in the resort, there was always the risk that it would simply create environmental problems elsewhere. Several features of the design of the resort were intended to reduce its environmental impact.

## Building development and environmental protection

Prior to the development of Yulara, a collection of old and sub-standard motels had grown haphazardly in the shadow of Ayers Rock.

Vehicles and visitors had gradually caused damage to the flora that prevented the sand-dunes from drifting, and the animal life retreated to safer and more peaceful grounds.

When Yulara was sited outside the National Park boundaries the old motels were closed down and the landscape returned to its natural state.

There were a number of reasons for choosing the site where Yulara was built:

● It was acceptable to the Aboriginal people
● It was close to underground water sources
● It provided visitors with views of Uluru and Kata Tjuta

Yulara Resort,
Ayers Rock

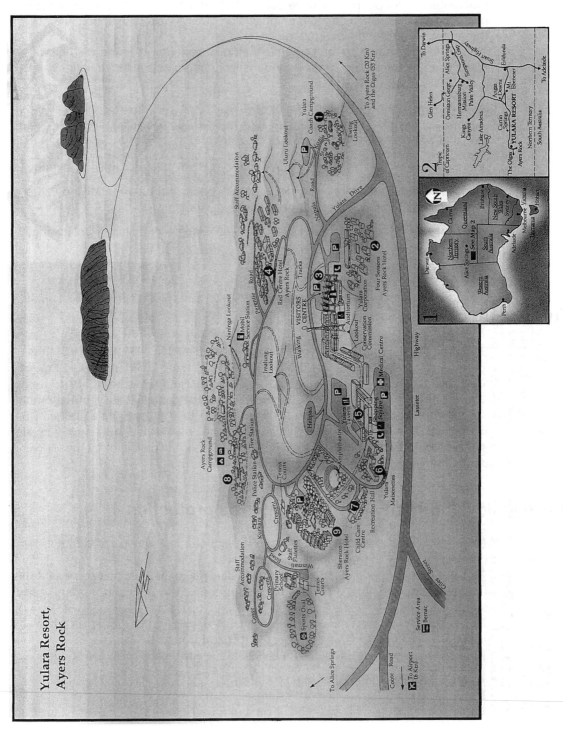

**Fig. 9.5 Yulara Resort**

# Design of Yulara

The design of Yulara, by Australian architect Philip Cox, was intended to be as compatible as possible with the surrounding landscape. The main plan consisted of a central core of sand-pink buildings winding around the base of a long sand-dune formation. Its colour was intended to blend in with the background and its position to make it invisible from behind the next ridge of the sand dunes.

The resort development consists entirely of low-rise buildings which follow the contours of the dunes. Much of the main complex is topped by immense white sails, anchored horizontally over roof lines and walkways to provide shade and maximize the movement of breezes.

# Energy conservation

Very high temperatures with occasional cold nights mean that energy consumption in hotels of conventional design could be high, having to provide both cooling and heating systems. In Yulara buildings were placed in positions where they could provide shade for each other. Large windows were placed in walls with protection from the sun. Balconies were used to provide shade for both guests and external walls. All of these design features contributed to reducing energy requirements.

With almost a guarantee of regular sunshine, solar power provides about 70 per cent of hot water and air-conditioning requirements in the central complex, reducing demands on the resort's power station.

Swimming pools, green lawns and landscaping comprising more than 120,000 Australian native plants have been made possible in this arid environment by a complex water-treatment usage and re-usage system in which nothing is wasted.

All hotel rooms have coded swipe cards that serve as keys. These deactivate the electricity supply to individual rooms as visitors leave them.

## Activities

Visitors travel from Yulara to Uluṟu and Kata Tjuṯa either by coach or car. There is a tarmac road which links the three (see Figure 9.6). Which of the following points of view would you support and which would you oppose? Give your reasons.

(1) 'The main attraction of this area is that it represents the ancient part of this continent...how it was millions of years ago. The presence of buses and coaches in this landscape is completely out of place...'

(2) 'Endless coaches are bound to cause some damage, but you can't stop the tourists coming. Besides it's too hot most of the time to expect them to walk everywhere. A monorail system would be the perfect answer...'

(3) 'If you improve the transport systems more people will come into this area and the damage will increase. The only real way of protecting Uluṟu and Kata Tjuṯa is by controlling the transport and accommodation available. If you can close the caves at Lascaux to protect the ancient wall paintings and open a replica somewhere else, why not consider the same strategy for Uluṟu and Kata Tjuṯa...'

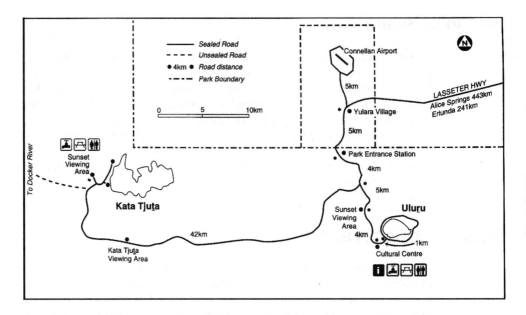

**Fig. 9.6 Access by road to Yulara, Uluṟu and Kata Tjuṯa**

# Tourism and Aṉangu culture

Until the handing back of Aboriginal lands and the beginning of joint management of Uluṟu – Kata Tjuṯa National Park the majority of visitors would probably have had little contact with Aṉangu culture. By the 1960s the only Aṉangu contacts with the tourism industry were either through the sale of artefacts or through working as labourers.

However, things are very different now. In October 1995, to mark the 10th anniversary of the handing back of lands to the Aboriginals, the Uluṟu– Kata Tjuṯa Cultural Centre was opened. Visitors are recommended to make this their first port of call. It provides them with some insight into Aṉangu culture and the significance of Uluṟu to its traditional owners before they begin their tours of the area.

## Tjukurpa

The culture of the Aṉangu people and the cultures of the majority of visitors to Uluṟu and Kata Tjuṯa are very different. The contrast means that visitors see things differently and are often not aware of the full meaning of features of the landscape or ways of behaving to local Aboriginal people.

The basis of Anangu culture is *Tjukurpa*. It is a difficult word to translate because it refers to many complex things. It provides rules for behaviour and for living together. It refers both to the time of creation and to the present. The landscape provides visual evidence of ancestral beings who travelled widely, creating all living species. The Aṉangu are the direct descendants of these beings and are responsible for the protection and appropriate management of these ancestral lands. Teaching about the ancestral beings is passed on through story, dance, song and ceremony.

> **What the land means to Anangu people**
>
> This is how the Anangu describe the way their land was created:
>
>> The world was once a place with no features. None of the places we know now existed. Our ancestors travelled widely across the land and created the forms of the world which we see today.
>>
>> Our land is still inhabited by these ancestral beings. Their journeys and activities are recorded at sites linked by iwara (tracks). Different groups of our people are associated with animals, snakes and birds. They travel around on the traditional routes. As they do this, they are aware of the exploits of ancestral beings in the places they pass through.
>>
>> All the knowledge of the land, and the behaviour and distribution of plants and animals is preserved and passed on through ceremony, song, dance and art.
>>
>> We identify with land and our kinship system tells us how we should behave towards other people. We regard everyone who speaks the same language as part of our family group.

Uluru and Kata Tjuta are part of a wide network of important places linked by *iwara* (tracks) made by ancestral beings during their various travels. The Anangu believe that Uluru and Kata Tjuta are part of a timeless representation of the past, the present and the future and the relationship of all beings to one another.

*Tjukurpa* is also the Law explaining how to behave. Four of its beliefs conflict with common tourist practices at Uluru see Table 9.3.

### Table 9.3

| *Tjukurpa* says... | Tourists... |
|---|---|
| ...the route by which people climb to the top of Uluru is the traditional one taken by Mala men on their arrival there. It has great spiritual significance and so Anangu rarely climb Uluru. Anangu prefer visitors not to climb the Rock, both because of its cultural significance and also because, as traditional owners of the land, they have a duty to protect the safety of all visitors... | ...many tourists come on organized tours, in which climbing the Rock is featured as one of the highlights. Most are unaware before they come that there are any objections to this activity, apart from any concern about their physical health... |
| ...much of the area of Kata Tjuta is associated with ritual information and activities that should be known only to initiated men. Therefore no details of ceremonies associated with Kata Tjuta can be made public and sacred sites should only be visited by particular Anangu men or women... | ...tourists are asked not to deviate from the marked path around Kata Tjuta and not to climb the domes or attempt to visit the men's and women's sacred sites. Despite these requests visitors sometimes attempt to explore freely and are not always quiet and respectful in their behaviour... |

**Table 9.3 Continued**

| Tjukurpa says... | Tourists... |
| --- | --- |
| ...Anangu do not like to be photographed and ask visitors to respect this wish. It is also against Anangu law to photograph areas of spiritual significance... | ...many visitors photograph everything they see! There are now guidelines published by the Board of Management suggesting what is appropriate photography practice in the Park... |
| ...Anangu people are the guardians of traditional lands. They regard all rocks and plants as essential parts of the landscape and believe that these should not be damaged or removed... | ...visitors are sometimes guilty of defacing rocks, uprooting rare plants and removing stones as souvenirs of their visit... |

## Language

The Anangu people speak two dialects of what is called the Western Desert language. These are called Pitjantjara and Yankunytjatjara. *Anangu* means 'people' in Pitjantjara. There are about 4,000 speakers of these two dialects. The language remained purely a spoken language until the late 1930s when linguists made the first attempts to write it down.

There is no word in either dialect for 'tourists' so the Anangu named them *'minga'* which means 'ants'. They chose this word because the lines of visitors climbing the single route up the side of Uluru looked like ants.

## Activities

This is how Anangu sum up the way they would like visitors to think of the climb up Uluru:

> When we leased the Park to ANCA we agreed to continue to allow people to climb Uluru because we know that some visitors come to the Park especially for that purpose. Rather than close 'the climb' we ask visitors to respect the *Tjukurpa* and learn about our land and culture through alternative activities. We are happy that an increasing number of visitors do not climb Uluru. It shows us that they understand and respect our view and see our land as more than just a place of amazing geological and ecological features, with a climb and a sunset view.

1  Write a dialogue between two English tourists visiting Uluru for the first time.

   One wants them both to climb the Rock the following morning to experience the dramatic views from the top. The other feels that the wishes of the Anangu should be respected and that they should find other ways of enjoying their visit.

2  The Anangu comments mention learning about culture 'through alternative activities.'

   Suggest a range of activities that might prove as attractive as 'the climb' to a range of visitors to Uluru.

3 For many people, churches and cathedrals are sacred places. Yet many receive large numbers of visitors interested in their historical and artistic importance, as much as their religious significance.

If you were a regular member of a church or cathedral congregation, what do you think you would judge to be appropriate behaviour and activities for visitors?

How would you set about seeking to persuade them to act in accordance with your wishes?

# The Uluru – Kata Tjuta Cultural Centre

The Uluru – Kata Tjuta Cultural Centre contains examples of Anangu art, artefacts of wood, tile and glass, and various kinds of display and presentation showing the interaction between Anangu, the landscape and the Park rangers.

The design of the centre imitates the shape of two ancestral beings, *Kuniya* (the woma python) and *Liru* (the poisonous snake). Arts and crafts can be purchased from the Maruku Arts and Craft Centre. Table 9.4 describes some of the items for sale.

**Table 9.4**

| | |
|---|---|
| ● **Hunting spears** | These are about nine feet (3 m) long and made from the flexible branches of the tecoma vine. The spearhead is made of hardwood and fixed to the shaft with spinifex resin and kangaroo or emu sinew. |
| ● **Clubs and chisels** | These are made from mulga wood and have a variety of uses – hunting, fighting and as tools. A sharp piece of quartz is often set into the handle to provide a cutting edge. |
| ● **Spearthrowers** | Made from mulga wood, these implements are also used for cutting meat, mixing ochre and in the process of fire-making. They could also be used to sharpen spears and to deflect other people's weapons in combat. |
| ● **Shields** | Both the face and back of these mulga or bloodwood shields are covered with traditional designs. Their main purpose was to parry spear blows in armed combat. |
| ● **Boomerangs** | Contrary to popular opinion, the desert boomerangs do not come back. They usually have designs relating to the maker's ceremonies or birthplace on them. Apart from their use as hunting weapons, they are also sometimes used to beat out a rhythm to accompany music. |
| ● **Bowls** | Women make bowls from white gum, mulga or river red gum root. Patterns are burnt into the wood using heated wire. The designs are traditional interpretations of landscape and popular stories. |

***Table 9.4  Continued***

| | |
|---|---|
| ● **Carved animals** | These are carved from sections of root of the red river gum. They are made with basic tools and are covered with traditional designs or with the natural markings of the animals. |
| ● **Music sticks** | These are traditional Aboriginal instruments used during ceremonies. Made from eucalyptus or mulga wood, they are played by holding one stick loosely in one hand while striking it rhythmically with the second stick. |

The Maruku Arts and Crafts Centre is a good example of the way a lively industry can be built on the basis of traditional skills. It was established in 1984 and employs people to travel throughout the region, buying artefacts and art from their makers. These works are returned to Uluṟu – Kata Tjuṯa, where they are documented, and then are either sold locally to visitors to the Centre or else are sold wholesale to shops and galleries throughout Australia. One important feature of the centre is that it is an Aboriginal owned cooperative. This means all income from sales is invested in the further purchasing and marketing of Aboriginal crafts.

## Activities

1 Discuss the original uses of the artefacts and implements for sale at the Maruku Arts and Crafts Centre. You might consider how many are likely to be still in current use or how the range of products would differ from arts and crafts shops elsewhere.

2 Discuss ways in which the fact that these artefacts are now being produced mainly to function as *house decorations* might affect the ways they are made and designed.

# Case study 10  The Gambia

## Introduction

Labelled by the travel trade as the *Smiling Coast*, The Gambia is a popular 'winter sun' destination, attracting thousands of package holidaymakers from northern Europe every year to its beautiful beaches (Figure 10.1).

This is Africa's smallest independent country and one of its poorest. Away from the glamorous tourist strip on the shores of the Atlantic Ocean lies a world of rural villages with none of the amenities we take for granted such as running water and electricity. Even in the tourist strip, the run-down back streets of the towns and suburbs are very different from the comfortable hotel facilities that are too expensive for most Gambians to afford.

Thirty years of tourism development along its coastline have not yet produced prosperity for the vast majority of Gambians, despite the best efforts of its people. This is due partly to The Gambia's economic circumstances and partly to the nature of the international tourist industry. But even if tourism has not made the country wealthy, it certainly plays a significant role in Gambian society. Less than 1% of The Gambia's population of just over one million people earns money from tourism in one way or another; but thousands more are affected by tourism's economic impact, or by the changes in lifestyle it has brought.

*Fig. 10.1  Tourist brochure photograph of The Gambia*

# Life in The Gambia

The Gambia has a diverse population of West African peoples such as the Fulani and the Wolof, speaking over ten different languages between them. Although English is only spoken by around 5% of the people, it is the official language of government, education and business. This is the result of 200 years of colonial rule by Britain, which ended when The Gambia became an independent state in 1965.

Gambians are strongly united, through a shared religion – Islam. Over 90% of the people are Muslim, and particularly in rural areas, religious traditions govern the way people dress and behave. It is a very important part of Gambian life.

## Coast and country

Despite the fame of its beaches, The Gambia is not really a coastal state. Most of its 11,000 square kilometres (4,240 sq. miles) of territory (roughly the size of Cornwall) lies inland along either side of the Gambia River, never getting wider than 50 kilometres (30 miles) from north to south (Figure 10.2). Apart from where it borders the ocean, it is completely surrounded by its large neighbour, Senegal.

There are no high hills to be seen, but the flat landscape has plenty of variety, from the sandy coastline to the wooded grasslands of the African savannah, with salt swamps and mangroves lining the Gambia River and its estuaries. There are still some pockets of virgin tropical forest, but trees everywhere are becoming scarce as people cut them down for fuel or to make way for fields of cash crops.

At the mouth of the river is the capital, Banjul, not far from the main tourist and commercial centres of Bakau and Serrekunda. Stretching for 24 kilometres (15 miles) southwards from Bakau are the beaches. Yundum Airport, the main gateway for tourists visiting The Gambia, is located a few kilometres south from Banjul. A ferry connects Banjul to the northern shoreline and a network of roads and river boats links it to townships down river such as Georgetown and Basse, and on into Senegal.

## Climate, tourism and agriculture

The Gambia's two main sources of income, tourism and agriculture, are highly dependent on its two contrasting seasons. The sub-tropical climate ensures dry, sunny weather between mid-November and mid-May, with an average temperature of 25 °C, ideal for beach tourism. In the months of the wet season, heavy tropical rainstorms are common. Tourism winds down, but agriculture gets into top gear, as crops are harvested and food stored for the long dry months ahead. The Gambia's climate is getting noticeably drier and, although this may seem good news for holidaymakers, it is causing general concern. A drop in annual rainfall could in the long run badly affect water supplies to the tourist industry as well as agriculture. Climate statistics are given in Figure 10.3 (page 174).

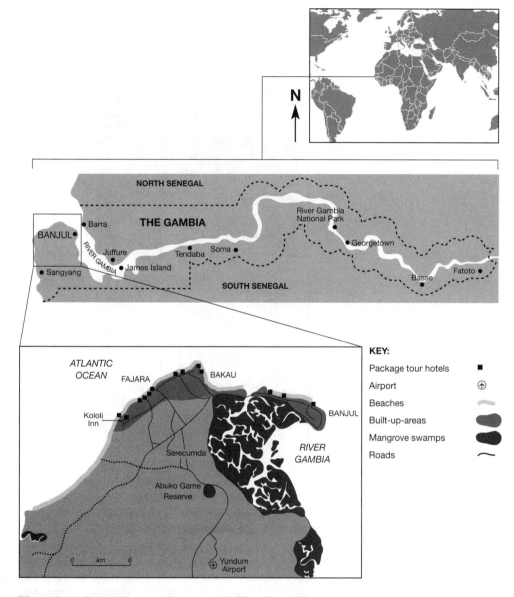

**Fig. 10.2 Location and maps of The Gambia**

# The local economy

Major settlements such as The Gambia's capital, Banjul, and the sprawling township of Serrekunda are growing fast, but most people live in the countryside, in villages that have no access to the basic conveniences of the modern world. Villagers make their living by farming and have little contact with life on the coast.

Beyond the mangrove swamps along the Gambia River and its tributaries, fields support a variety of crops such as rice, but further inland the wooded grassland is not very productive and is prone to drought.

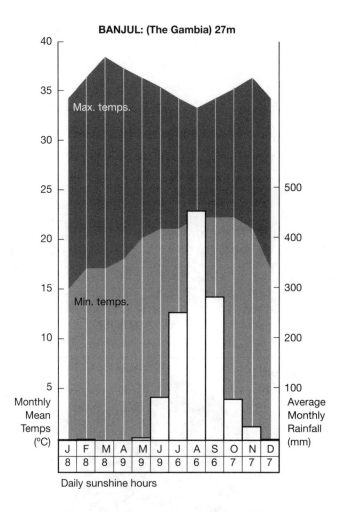

**Fig. 10.3  Climate statistics of Banjul: (a) mean temperatures; (b) sunshine and rainfall**

Families grow staple foods such as millet and sorghum for their own needs, along with fruit and vegetables. There is some livestock farming too, and near the rivers, fishing supplements villagers' diets. When possible, income is earned by selling surplus food or growing The Gambia's main export crop, groundnuts (what we call 'peanuts'). Otherwise little money circulates in rural communities.

Living off the land (Figure 10.4) in the Gambia's interior is not easy, but life on the coast can be just as hard. Fishing provides a livelihood for some communities, but in the towns permanent jobs are difficult to find.

The lack of paid employment is one reason why the majority of people, in both rural and urban areas, are extremely poor. However, families and communities support each other by looking after each other and sharing income or food with their extended families. Those in work have an average of ten people depending on their wages, which are usually very low in the first place – roughly £10 a month in the local currency, dalasi.

*Fig. 10.4 Most Gambians live off the land: rice is the main subsistence crop in The Gambia (Photo: David Young)*

# The Gambia and the global economy

Owing to its location at the mouth of a navigable river, The Gambia has always been a busy trading centre, including a period when the river was an important link in the British slave trade with America. Even so, it is now among the world's poorest nations.

Like many former colonies, The Gambia has traditionally depended on exporting raw materials, in its case groundnuts, as a way of earning foreign exchange. However, international prices for groundnuts have fallen very sharply in recent years. Attempts to grow other cash crops such as cotton and rice have been defeated by the harshness of the dry season, when water shortages are common.

The Gambia's lack of mineral wealth, its location far from modern trading centres and its tiny size have all made it difficult to develop a manufacturing industry. It has very few factories and has to import most goods considered necessary for a modern westernized lifestyle.

## Activities

1 List the ways in which you think life for young Gambians may be different from your own.

2 Suggest reasons why the growth of tourism in The Gambia has had a limited impact on the country's economy.

3 What similarities and differences can you identify between The Gambia and tourist destinations in the Mediterranean, such as Spain, Morocco and Turkey?

# The Gambia as a tourist destination

For some time now, tourism has seemed to offer the best way of earning foreign exchange and creating jobs, and the current government is promoting it eagerly.

Although the country has always welcomed visitors in small numbers, arriving by sea, land or scheduled flights, its tourist industry consists almost entirely of hotel-based package holidays (Figure 10.5). This suits the budget-conscious north European tourist, in search of a beach holiday and guaranteed sunshine.

In many countries, tourism grows slowly and unevenly, but in The Gambia's case it is possible to say precisely when package tourism began.

In 1965, just as The Gambia had become a newly independent nation, a Swedish tour operator set the Gambia's package holiday industry in motion. He realized that its warm temperatures and beautiful beaches would appeal to Scandinavians wanting to escape from their long cold winters. The promise of visiting somewhere more exotic than the Mediterranean, yet at a distance from Europe that was not much further than the Canary Islands, would also be a selling point. Since The Gambia's cost of living was very low, he was able to offer these holidays cheaply, giving The Gambia another advantage over rival winter sun resorts.

That first year, he brought over 300 tourists, and gradually this small number increased as other Scandinavian companies imitated his successful operation. Then British, German, Dutch and French tourists began coming too, attracted by the same factors as the Scandinavians, as well as by the country's growing reputation for friendly hospitality.

> There are no culture shocks in The Gambia. It offers an unpretentious winter sun holiday on a good beach, with enough excursions into the bush on offer to stop the hyperactive from becoming bored, and it has the advantage that it's but 6 hours away from the UK. Which is perhaps why many of our birds winter in the Gambian sun. You should try it!    *Source*: SunMed holiday brochure 1989–90.

***Fig. 10.5  A typical Gambian hotel scene
(Photo: David Young)***

Foreign companies started building accommodation to meet the demand. The government began to involve itself in tourism development to supplement the country's other economic activities. It secured international aid to help build infrastructure such as roads, buildings and power lines and to improve its airport.

In 1972 a Tourism Development Area was established along 15 kilometres (9 miles) of coastline. By the 1993/1994 season, 90,000 package tourists were travelling on holidays to The Gambia, staying mostly in the 17 major hotels scattered along the coast from Banjul. Tourism had come to stay.

# Tourism in The Gambia today

The Tourist Development Area is where today you will find all the main hotels, and this is also the area that is most developed in terms of its local services. There is now a four lane highway from the airport to Banjul, although in The Gambia as a whole, roads are mostly dirt tracks, and there are still few modern facilities.

The hotels along the tourist strip have increased in number and some have changed ownership several times. At one time the government controlled several hotels, but virtually all are now owned either by foreign investors, Europeans who have settled in The Gambia or Gambian businesspeople.

Once at their hotels, package tourists are offered excursions and advice about where to shop and eat out. The shops and restaurants chosen are often linked closely to the tour operators or hotels. Tourists may get a good deal and be assured of good service, but this situation makes it very difficult for small entrepreneurs to make their services known to package tourists.

Besides the big hotels there are smaller hotels and guest-houses, both on the coast and inland. Most of these are not used by the package tour operators, but are patronized by foreign independent travellers or African visitors. The people who stay in these establishments spend their money more widely, but they form a small minority of the total number of visitors to the country.

**Table 10.1 Tourist arrivals in The Gambia by air charter**

| Nationality | 1974/5 | 1984/5 | 1993/4 |
|---|---|---|---|
| Swedish | 11,082 | 5,911 | 6,746 |
| Danish | 5,125 | 2,636 | 2,903 |
| Norwegian | 705 | 701 | 955 |
| German | 534 | 2,106 | 7,435 |
| British | 362 | 23,742 | 61,062 |
| French | - | 4,330 | 1,507 |
| Other | 843 | 5,021 | 9,389 |
| **TOTAL** | **18,651** | **44,447** | **89,997** |

*Source*: Central Statistics Department, Banjul.

## Activities

Study Table 10.1 showing arrivals in The Gambia over the past 20 years.

1 Which countries have contributed an increasing number of visitors and which countries have contributed a decreasing number of visitors?

What factors do you think might account for these trends?

2 Work out the percentage of visitors to the Gambia who come from Britain in each of the three years given in the table.

Are there any advantages or disadvantages to the Gambian tourism industry of having a high percentage of tourists coming from the same country?

# Tourism and employment

The Gambia should be able to make money from tourists in a number of ways.
The government can make money from charging **taxes**:

- Paid by tourists
- Paid by tourism businesses

The money it collects is used to provide basic education, health and social welfare services. Expansion of each of these services creates jobs. However, the government cannot risk setting tourism taxes too high, because tour operators and tourists might respond by going elsewhere.

The local population can make money through **employment**, by working in tourism businesses or by providing goods and services to tourists. Tourism creates a number of different types of work in The Gambia.

- **Direct employment**
  - working in hotels, restaurants, souvenir shops, bars, clubs and tour businesses
  - providing goods and services to tourists, e.g. fruit sellers, taxi drivers, unofficial tour guides, market traders
- **Indirect employment**
  - selling goods and services to tourist enterprises, e.g. farmers selling food to restaurants, small manufacturers supplying furniture for hotels, crafts people supplying souvenir shops, musicians
  - maintaining the transport, power and other services used by tourists
- **Induced employment**
  - supplying everyday goods and services to *employees* in the tourist industry

In The Gambia, package tourism provides **direct** and **induced** employment but only limited opportunities for **indirect** employment. Because agriculture and industry are not highly developed, it has been very difficult for local Gambian enterprises to provide the package tour industry with its requirements. Many of the hotels, for example, serve 'international' menus requiring the import of European ingredients.

The general manager of a top class hotel explains why it has not been possible to create more indirect employment among food suppliers:

We bring in virtually all the food eaten by guests in £20,000 consignments. You might say why not use local produce in a country blessed with mangoes, citrus fruits, seafood and the ability to rear poultry and livestock? I wish we could. Nothing I'd like better. But it just won't work.

The mangoes drop from the trees abundantly – in the off-season, when the tourists aren't here. There are no facilities for mass rearing of beef and chickens, no big ranches of the type that make local food so easily available in Kenya. It's cheaper to buy chicken and meat frozen in Europe and pay freight costs and import duty than to buy local.

The costs of providing hotels with facilities of an international standard are very high. Package tourists expect everything from the airport onwards to be of at least the quality they are used to at home.

## Activities

1 Identify the kind of dishes you would expect to find on an 'international' menu and discuss why they have achieved such widespread use.

2 Suggest two ideas that would encourage visitors to be more adventurous in sampling local Gambian dishes.

3 Suppose more major hotels agreed to purchase local Gambian food products. Write a short report suggesting what kind of investment might be needed in local agriculture and how this might affect small farmers.

# Tourism, arts and crafts

Many people in The Gambia make a living from selling souvenirs to tourists (Figure 10.6). In particular, they sell carvings, paintings and decorated cloths, made up into everything from clothes to table napkins.

Sometimes the items sold as traditional Gambian handicrafts are not Gambian at all, but come from neighbouring countries, e.g. jewellery from Senegal, woodcarvings from Ghana, printed cloth from Manchester, Pakistan or China. Or souvenirs may not be traditional, but invented to suit tourists' tastes. An example of this is the sale of pictorial wall hangings which are very popular with tourists. These were introduced by a European artist who taught Gambian women traders how to make them.

Tourists seem quite happy to buy items that look 'African' to them and do not seem to notice the lack of quality in their production. The market traders are very aware that low prices are more popular than high quality and are expert now at supplying what tourists like.

**Fig. 10.6 Colourful Gambian souvenirs:
haggling for a good price is expected (photo:
David Young)**

Supporters of traditional arts and crafts call these goods 'airport art' and complain that they have a bad influence on local artistic standards. The Gambia does have wonderful craft skills to demonstrate, particularly batik and tie-dye, and it is true that tourists are not always willing to pay adequate rates for the beautiful work of its traditional craftsmen and women. It may also be true that if market traders were not so commercially minded, tourists might buy more good quality goods.

Another concern about the souvenir trade comes from the damage to religious or cultural life that can happen when tourists want to buy something sacred because they find it attractive. Just as a visitor to a religious building may cause distress by improper behaviour or dress, so may someone wearing a religious item as an ornament. However, this is not always the case. It may be possible to make money from tourists while keeping the item sacred.

For example, a valued religious item in The Gambia is the '*juju*' – an amulet containing a verse from the Koran, worn to bring the owner good fortune. Tourists often ask to buy these to wear, and so enterprising Gambians now make and sell replica *jujus*.

Since these replicas simply contain bits of newspaper or nothing at all, their sale does not cause offence. It does cause Gambians to wonder at tourists, however – if the *jujus* are stripped of their religious significance, local people cannot understand why tourists want them at all!

## Activities

1 Discuss the reasons holidaymakers may have for buying souvenirs and list them.

  Decide which of these reasons are likely to be most important when they are deciding exactly what to buy.

2 Choose three different tourist destinations you have visited and select three students from your group. Choose a souvenir you would buy each person if you were visiting these destinations. Explain why you would buy these things for them. Discuss with them how they would react to these gifts and what they would do with them.

3 Suppose there are two shops selling Gambian arts and crafts. The owners of these shops each has a different attitude towards the sale of local goods:

*Owner 1 says:* 'Works of art and high craftsmanship take time and skill to make, and therefore deserve to be sold at a price that reflects this. Tourists should be willing to pay a fair price for them.'

*Owner 2 says:* 'It doesn't matter whether 'airport art' is sold, as long as local people earn money from it.'

How do you think the attitudes of the two shop owners would affect the products they sold, the craftspeople who supplied them and the tourists who came to their shops?

# Tourism and the environment

Tourism in The Gambia has had both positive and negative impacts on its natural environment.

> The fragile state state of the land in The Gambia is partly unrelated to tourism, as villagers chop down new trees for firewood, still the prime source of cooking fuel, and to make room for crops. Erosion in coastal areas results directly from the building boom, both of hotels and of new housing by the few wealthy Gambians and by resident foreigners who want to be in on the tourist action.
>
> Hundreds of truckloads a week of building sand is scooped from the most beautiful beaches, some of which are sinking and disappearing. One hotel lost part of its bar area during high summer tide; others are licked by the ocean more greedily each year.
>
> *Souce*: *Panos* magazine, 1991.

Serious environmental problems have been caused by the construction and operation of the coastal hotels. However, tourism also helps with conservation in The Gambia, providing a valuable argument for preserving what is left of the wonderful tropical forests that once covered the land. The Abuko Nature Reserve not far from the airport attracts many tourists. Some are taking time off from sunbathing. Many others come specifically to The Gambia on birdwatching holidays (Figure 10.7).

Apart from Abuko, tourists can visit other reserves far inland along the Gambia River. If these visitors are seen to be contributing to local incomes, there is a better chance that local people will seek to preserve the habitats of The Gambia's remaining wildlife.

*Fig. 10.7  Gambian birdlife*

# The future for tourism in The Gambia

Gambian politicians and planners have had very little control over the type of tourism that has developed, but for some time now they have been trying to become less dependent on package tour operators and their clients.

This policy is explained in the following extract from a press article:

*Gambia minister in fact-finding mission*

The Gambia's new tourism minister has made a fact-finding mission to the UK in a bid to improve and expand the product.

Tourism is The Gambia's second biggest industry but it accounts for only 10% of the gross national product.

The aim is to turn tourism into a more lucrative source of income for the country itself. The minister is hoping to persuade operators, particularly those specialising in activity holidays, to think of The Gambia as a year-round destination by organizing wildlife packages during the summer. He is also hoping to persuade operators to take part in the 'be my guest' scheme where visitors stay not in hotels but with Gambian families in their own homes or at the growing number of bush camps, thus making a direct contribution to the economy.

Meanwhile the government continues to offer attractive terms to foreign investors wanting to build hotels. Land is leased free of charge for 99 years, when the lease is renewable. Hoteliers can operate tax free for the first five years in business.

Nearly 60% cent of tourists to The Gambia are from the UK. The country suffered a 7% decline in the total market of 112,000 visitors last year as a direct result of interest rate rises in Britain. Next year it aims to increase the overall figure by 10% and is attracting package holidaymakers from Italy and Switzerland for the first time.

*Source: Travel Trade Gazette*, July 1994

A peaceful military coup in 1994 showed the risks involved in depending on package tourism when advice by the British Foreign Office led to tour operators withdrawing their flights, despite the evidence to suggest that the situation was quickly under control and there was very little risk to holidaymakers. With nothing to replace the package holiday visitors, hotels were forced to suspend employees without pay. Gambians who provided goods and services to tourists were also suddenly deprived of their source of income.

One way of reducing the dependence on package tourism was to try to expand the tourism product. In other words, an effort was made to develop aspects of the Gambia that would appeal to groups other than those looking for a sun and sand package holiday.

## Activities

1 Suggest a number of new market groups that the Gambian tourism industry might try to encourage to visit the country, and outline the methods and activities they could use in order to attract them.

2 What advantages for The Gambia do bush camp holidays and the 'be my guest' scheme have over the existing package holidays?

   Are there any advantages for The Gambia in encouraging package holidays?

3 Why is it necessary for the Gambian government to offer incentives such as tax 'holidays' to hotel investors?

   What benefits does the government expect to gain, in spite of the loss of tax?

4 Why did interest rate rises affect the number of British visitors in 1993?

# Diversifying the tourist product

Diversifying the types of holiday people could go on would help to spread tourism activity to other parts of the country, and it would lessen the dependence on standard package tourism.

Apart from its beaches, The Gambia has a number of aspects that tourists find attractive and, since the early days of package tourism, hotel guests have gone on excursions designed around these.

The bulk of package tourism's economic impact is restricted to one small region of the country. Many of the excursions take place further inland. If extended and improved, they could attract more visitors who are not interested first and foremost in beach tourism, thus spreading the economic benefits of tourism.

The following points suggest some possibilities for developing different types of tourism in The Gambia:

- The Gambia does not have large game animals such as lions, but it has plenty of smaller animals to observe, from monkeys to crocodiles. More importantly, it is already internationally famous among ornithologists for its huge number of bird species.
- The Gambia River is a fascinating waterway to explore. Already there are a number of tourist lodges and camps along its banks, and boats that offer cruises.
- Gambian musicians are well known in 'world music' circles, and the country has a reputation, too, for beautiful arts and crafts. Music and art workshops already attract tourists.
- Not all visitors to The Gambia want to stay in Western style accommodation, or eat the same food as they would find at home. There are opportunities here for providing simple accommodation in different parts of the country, such as small hotels like the Kololi Inn:

> WELCOME TO KOLOLI INN
> Kololi Inn comprises 8 traditional round huts with thatched roofs. It is built out of local materials in what was originally a fruit garden, where meals are served. We specialise in genuine African cuisine. If you fancy lime in your tea, just reach up over your head and pick your own! We also have an art gallery that displays genuine African art in its most diverse forms, ranging from sand paintings to pottery. We are an ideal base for adventure travellers, students and ornithologists. (Extract from local accommodation brochure.)

# Conclusion

The experience of 1994 certainly demonstrated how important package tourism is to the Gambian economy, but also revealed how easily it can be disrupted. The government is now trying to achieve three main objectives:

- Attracting package tourists from a wide number of countries and tour operators
- Persuading tour operators to run charters over a longer season
- Developing a more varied tourism product

A new Gambian organization, DEEGO ('deego' means 'co-operation and understanding' in the Wolof language), is trying to get the government to provide more financial help and training for small Gambian businesses which depend on tourism, such as transport providers, restaurants, and fruit and vegetable suppliers. The British charities Voluntary Service Overseas (VSO) and Tourism Concern have been helping DEEGO establish itself.

In an interview for VSO's magazine, hotel manager Adama Bah, who is one of the founders of DEEGO, explained how he would like to see tourism develop in The Gambia. He has a vision of tourism development in which both package tour operators and small-scale independent businesses can contribute to a more prosperous future for The Gambia:

'I believe tourism must be planned in such a way that whatever resources are gained must go to help develop the country's other sectors like agriculture and industry, so that in the long run the country becomes self-reliant.

Some tourists who come to The Gambia are not just interested in the wine bar and the beach; they are also interested in going inland, in learning something, in having an exchange. This helps local people because they can build guest houses and small tourist resorts, provide the food from their own gardens, and manage the whole thing themselves. The advantage is that they are environmentally friendly.'

## Activities

1 Study two or three holiday brochures that feature The Gambia and make notes on what they suggest are the main features which would encourage you to visit the destination.

Describe the types of tourist you think they would be most likely to appeal to.

2 Suppose a group of villages along the River Gambia is planning to set up a small scale tourism business offering simple accommodation and a chance to experience village life and culture.

List the things they would need to plan before they decided whether to go ahead and launch the scheme.

3 Discuss what problems they might have in marketing their idea. Describe the kind of support they might need from the government in order to get their scheme off the ground.

## What is the Gaeltacht?

In the sixteenth century the great majority of the population of Ireland spoke Irish. As the English, who first arrived at the time of the Norman conquest, increased their ownership of land, many Irish speakers began to use English, particularly where they thought it would improve their social or economic position. The establishment of a national school system in 1831 placed further emphasis on the learning of the English language.

The great famine of 1845–46 led to the emigration of many Irish speakers so that the census of 1851 recorded that only a quarter of the population spoke the language. By 1911 the proportion was down to one-eighth. The Gaeltacht is the name given to those parts of Ireland where Irish is still spoken. However, nowadays most of these communities are bilingual, with English being the second language.

The area covered by the Gaeltacht is not large. It consists of less than 7% of the land area of the Republic of Ireland. Its population in 1986 was 83,430. It consists of small areas of the west coast of Ireland – in counties Donegal, Mayo, Galway and Kerry – and some inland areas in counties Cork, Meath and Waterford. These are shown in Figure 11.1.

The Irish language is an important part of Irish culture and it has become a government priority to find ways to preserve and extend it. The best way of doing this is to find ways of improving the economy of the Gaeltacht. It is important to do this so that there is sufficient local employment to encourage people to stay in these areas. Many of the gaeltachts, especially those on the west coast of Ireland, contain dramatic coastline scenery which has always attracted some tourists.

The percentage of Irish speakers in the Gaeltacht dropped from 86% in 1961 to 77% in 1981. The reasons for this are thought to be connected to social and economic development. There is more contact with the English language through television. Central and local government conduct most of their business in English. Neighbouring business communities are English-speaking, as are a high proportion of the visitors to the Gaeltacht. Here is an extract from a bi-lingual leaflet about Gael Linn, an Irish language teaching institute:

| | |
|---|---|
| Tá Gael-Linn go sioraí ag iarraidh scéimeanna nua a fhorbairt chun Éireannaigh óga a ghríosadh le staidear a dhéanamh ar a gcultúr agus a n-oidhreacht, chomh maith le cultúir Eorpacha eile. | Gael-Linn is continually seeking to develop new schemes to encourage young Irish people to study their own culture and heritage, as well as the cultures of other European nations. |

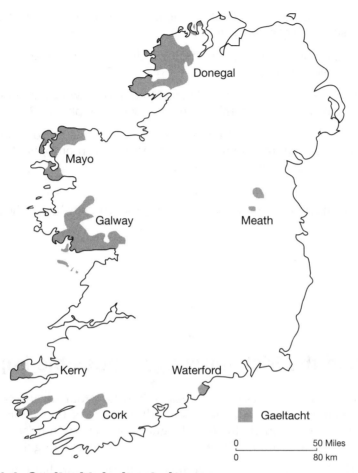

**Fig. 11.1 Gaeltacht designated areas**

## Activities

Read the following comments from non-Irish speakers who have visited some of the Gaeltacht areas:

'The language looks very interesting when you see it written down, but we just couldn't work out how to pronounce any of the words.'

'The guide book provided us with a few simple phrases and we did try these out towards the end of our stay. People sometimes laughed, but usually they seemed to appreciate our efforts.'

'Almost everyone seems to speak English nowadays so there doesn't seem much point in trying to learn another language just for a few days' holiday.'

'Knowing a few phrases of Irish is quite a help. It gets you attention and you can tell if someone's talking about you!'

'It would be a lot easier to pick up a bit of the language if everything – signs, notices, and menus for example – were always in both languages.'

1 Does the Gael-Linn leaflet suggest any differences or similarities between the Irish and English languages?

2 What would you say are the main difficulties involved in learning to speak a new language?

3 If you were due to visit a Gaeltacht area for a two week holiday, what approach would you take to learning some Irish words or phrases?

4 Copy the box below. Write in it as many reasons as you can think of to support the argument that tourism will probably (a) help or (b) hinder the preservation of the Irish language in the Gaeltacht.

| Why tourism may <u>help</u> the preservation of Irish | Why tourism may <u>hinder</u> the preservation of Irish |
|---|---|
| 1<br>2<br>3<br>4 | 1<br>2<br>3<br>4 |

## Tourism and the Irish language – possible impacts

There are very few research studies to show how tourism affects different languages. In Ireland, most opinion seems to fall into one of two camps. Either people say tourism can stimulate the Irish language or they say tourism will contribute to its gradual disappearance. Here are three ways of considering the issue:

● The Irish language is the common cultural factor that links all the areas of the Gaeltacht. This means that it can be used as the basis for developing a tourism product that can be easily understood by potential visitors.

● Tourism can be used to create a fresh interest in the Irish language. This can be done both by encouraging people from outside the Gaeltacht to visit in order to learn Irish and also by persuading local people that speaking Irish can attract more visitors who will help to boost the local economy.

● Tourists in the region very rarely speak Irish. Encouraging more tourism means that more English is spoken and written. It also changes the nature of the spoken Irish language as it encourages the habit of absorbing more foreign words and phrases into the language.

## The cultural attractions of the Gaeltacht areas

The coastal areas of the Gaeltacht, especially Donegal, Galway and Kerry, have a rugged coastline and unspoilt, uncrowded beaches. They have always been popular with visitors who enjoy outdoor activities such as angling, sailing, shooting, golf and mountaineering.

However, it is the culture of these regions that often proves the strongest attraction. They share an ancient folklore, with many songs, stories and poems telling the myths and legends of the region (Figure 11.2). Visitors are also likely to encounter Irish music and dancing. It is not uncommon to find an Irish folk band playing in pubs in the Gaeltacht. Instruments may include accordions, fiddles, tin whistles and wooden flutes. However, the traditional instruments which give Irish music its distinctive sound are described in Table 11.1.

*Fig. 11.2 Siamsa Tíre-Gaeltacht folk theatre*

### Table 11.1 Traditional Irish musical instruments

● The Irish harp or *clairseach*

The harp stands about three feet high. Its frame is made of yew or chestnut, strung with gut or nylon. It usually has 32 strings, covering three octaves. It is smaller than the harps used in concert performances.

● The *uileann* pipes

These pipes take their name from the Gaelic word for elbow '*uile*'. They are made from boxwood. The piper straps a bellows to his right elbow and pumps air into a leather bag under his left elbow. The elbow is used to force air through the pipes.

● The *bodhran*

The bodhran is a native Irish drum made from treated goatskin. The skin is stretched and fastened across a ring of ash wood.

● The bones

Two straight bones are taken from the ribs of a sheep. Each piece is five or six inches long. One piece is held between the thumb and the forefinger and the other between the third and fourth fingers. A sound not unlike that of castenets is made by rhythmic wrist movements

# Other features of Gaeltacht culture

## Irish dancing

There are three main types of Irish dancing: step-dancing, set-dancing and ceili dancing.

### Step-dancing

Step-dances are danced individually. The dancer may include reels, jigs and horn-pipes, all with different rhythms. It is thought that step-dancing originated from country house dancing when the single flagstone in front of the hearth was used by solo dancers to show off their skills. Modern step-dancing has added more complicated foot movements and a lot of high kicking.

### Set-dancing

Set-dances are performed in groups of four or eight. They use polka, reel, jig or hornpipe time. Different types of dance, such as the Clare Set and the Ballycommon Set, were named after the place in which they were developed. Set-dancing may have developed as a result of Irish soldiers returning from the Napoleonic Wars and introducing French dances such as the quadrille.

### Ceili dancing

Ceili dances are carefully planned formal dances for groups of four, eight, twelve and sixteen. Based on the old solo reels, jigs and hornpipes, they were originally danced at crossroads where people from surrounding communities met to socialize, play music and dance.

## Irish art and sculpture

There are many examples of Irish art and sculpture in the Gaeltacht and the surrounding areas. The extreme age of some of these, especially the carvings, is a factor that often persuades visitors to make special journeys to see them.

Carvings dating back to before 2000 BC have been found in County Meath. Gold and other metal ornaments were produced in many parts of Ireland in the Bronze Age (2000–500 BC). The most striking were the lunulae. These were crescent-shaped neck pieces, often with ornamental discs on the ends. Iron Age (500 BC – AD 500) Celtic art created a style and themes which are still imitated in modern jewellery and design. The standing stone at Turoe in County Galway is a good example. Its surface is covered with loops, ellipses and spirals.

## Irish folklore

Irish culture possesses a fund of ancient stories, many of which concern *Daoine Sidhe*, or the Fairy People. There are many different theories about the origins of such stories, but the tradition and characteristics of the 'Good People' have been preserved. They clearly provide the basis for a thriving souvenir industry. The best known fairy characters are:

- The **banshee** – a woman fairy or attendant spirit who follows the old families and wails before a death. An omen which sometimes accompanies the old woman is a black coach, carrying a coffin and drawn by headless riders.
- The **leprechaun** – a fairy shoemaker. He is solitary, old and bad tempered. He is fond of playing jokes on people. His trade makes him rich and he buries pots of gold at the end of rainbows.
- The **leanhaun shee** – longs for the love of mortal men. If they refuse her she becomes their slave but if they consent they cannot escape from her unless they find someone to replace them.
- The **pooka** – an animal spirit that lives in solitary mountain places and old ruins. It often assumes the form of a horse and is easy to tame if kept from the sight of water. If he sees water he will plunge into it and tear his rider to pieces at the bottom.

## Activities

1 Irish music is often played in pubs in the evenings in the West of Ireland. What do you think might be the effects on the musicians of having an audience which contains a high proportion of tourists? Do you think it is ever possible to preserve traditional music in its exact original form?

2 What impact do you think shows like 'Riverdance' have on the way outsiders think of Irish dancing?

3 Which of the following points of view do think is more accurate:

'Tourism encourages people to make fun of Irish folklore.'

'Local people exploit Irish folklore to entertain and attract visitors.'

# Crafts in the Gaeltacht

## Aran sweaters

What are now regarded as handicrafts for sale to visitors usually had an important purpose in the everyday lives of local people. The Aran sweaters (Figure 11.3) that can be purchased in knitwear shops all over the world came originally from the area

**Fig. 11.3 Aran sweater**

around Donegal and the Aran Islands. They were worn by fishermen and their use of heavy, oiled wool was intended to keep out the effects of cold, damp weather.

Patterns on Aran traditional sweaters include a mixture of cable and diamond shapes. The cables represented the fishermen's ropes and the diamonds stood for their nets. The sweaters were hand knitted and different stitches used in each original sweater were believed to have special significance. Some were said to have religious significance while others had a special meaning related to the life of the wearer of the sweater.

Modern factories now mass produce Aran-style sweaters but hand-knitted designs, produced in the West of Ireland, are still much sought after by visitors.

## The Claddagh Ring

The Claddagh Ring, named after an Irish-speaking village in Galway, has been worn for more than four hundred years as a symbol of love. Claddagh, a small community which elected its own king and made its own laws, required all married women to wear a Claddagh Ring. Its design featured a heart joined by two hands with a crown over the top. The motif accompanying this marriage ring was: 'let love and friendship reign'.

The originator of the design is said to be Richard Joyce who was captured by the Moors in the seventeenth century. He was forced to become a goldsmith while in captivity. Eventually he was ransomed and returned to Galway to work as a goldsmith where he is said to have designed the Claddagh Ring.

The way the Ring is worn is said to have particular significance:

- Worn on the right hand with the crown towards the wrist it means the wearer's heart is free
- Worn on the right hand with the crown facing the knuckles it shows the wearer has a marriage partner in mind
- Worn on the left hand the crown always faces the knuckles to show that the wearer is married

Nowadays the design can be seen frequently in Irish jewellers' shops and makes a popular souvenir for tourists.

---

*Louis Mulcahy Pottery – culture and tourism in Baile an Fheirtearaigh*

Louis and Lisbeth Mulcahy left Dublin to set up a pottery studio in Clougher in 1975. Both went to evening classes to learn Irish, and customers in the couple's Dingle craft shop are often surprised when Lisbeth speaks to her assistants in fluent Irish.

The pottery business is in Baile an Fheirtearaigh on the western point of the Dingle Peninsula. It employs 30 people. Potters are trained at the workshop to produce a wide range of pots, lamp bases, tableware and presentation trophies.

The pottery is open every day and attracts many visitors. The annual pre-Christmas sale attracts important off-season visitors to the region from all over Ireland. Local guest-houses and holiday homes are often full over sale week-ends. An added advantage of coming at this time of year is that the narrow roads are free of the very heavy traffic they experience in the summer months.

Lisbeth Mulcahy also runs 'The Weaver's Shop' in An Daingean. Using the seasonal changes and the seascapes surrounding her home as inspiration she designs rugs, shawls, tapestries, table mats and scarves. Three highly trained weavers are also employed in the shop. Its produce is popular with both Irish visitors and those from overseas.

---

## Activities

1 Can you suggest examples of ways in which ancient crafts have assumed value or importance in modern times?

2 What evidence can you find in the examples of Irish crafts provided in this case study to show that cultures change over time? How does this fact affect the arguments of people who say that the best elements of a local culture must be preserved?

# Tourist appeal of the different Gaeltachts

Each Gaeltacht has its own individual characteristics.

# The Donegal Gaeltacht

Donegal is the largest Gaeltacht in terms of the number of Irish speakers. There is an all-Irish theatre in the town of Gweedore. Handwoven tweed is made in the area around Kilcar. Glencolumbkille boasts a folk village and prehistoric remains. There are several Irish colleges in the region and visits to the islands of Tory and Arranmore are popular.

# The Mayo Gaeltacht

The area round Erris has a number of small, unspoilt beaches. The inlets, channels, bays and banks in Blacksod and Broadhaven Bays are popular for all kinds of sea fishing. Tourmakeady, on the banks of Lough Mask, is renowned for its excellent trout fishing.

# The Galway Gaeltacht

This is the largest Gaeltacht in area and the second biggest in terms of numbers of Irish speakers. It is well known for the number of writers and artists associated with the area. The region possesses some striking scenery with areas of bogland alternating with rocky fields enclosed by grey stone walls. It includes the three Aran Islands in Galway Bay – Inis Mor, Inis Meain and Inis Thiar – very popular with tourists seeking to 'get away from it all'.

# The Kerry Gaeltacht

This region includes some very popular tourist areas, such as the Dingle peninsula and part of the Ring of Kerry (Figure 11.4). The Dingle Peninsula was once the retreat of monks and modern-day visitors are drawn to see the surviving beehive stone cells which the monks used for meditation.

Gallarus Oratory (Figure 11.5 on page 197) provides a rare example of sixth century Christian architecture with its gabled roof of overlapping unmortared stones. The dramatic coastline makes the area popular with hikers and the Ring of Kerry is a magnet for car and coach tours of the West of Ireland.

# The Cork Gaeltacht

The inland part of the Cork Gaeltacht stretches over mountainous countryside. It has links with Saint Finbar and the first Irish college was founded here in Ballingeary.

# The Waterford Gaeltacht

This is a small area but one that is strong in local tradition. It has a very distinctive east Munster dialect and its associated with a number of well-known Irish songs. Pony-trekking, hunting and sailing are popular in this region and nearby Dungarvan offers shore and deep sea fishing.

**Fig. 11.4 (a) Walking on the Dingle Way and (b) the Blasket Islands
from Mount Eagle on the Dingle Peninsula**

*Fig. 11.5  Gallarus Oratory*

## The Meath Gaeltacht

Though only 35 miles from Dublin the two small areas of the Meath Gaeltacht are still Irish speaking. The areas were settled by Irish speakers from the west in the 1930s.

## Activity

The West Kerry Gaeltacht covers the part of the Dingle Peninsula known as *Corca Dhuibhne*. The Irish language is spoken daily here and students participate in Irish language schools in the area. However, there is no residential college. Students live in local homes and are taught in local schools. Many visitors are attracted to the Peninsula in order to walk the Dingle Way. Others take advantage of the excellent sea angling facilities around the coast.

A small independent tour operator specializing in activity holidays in the West of Ireland decides to extend the mainly environmental principles of 'Green Tourism' so that tourists pay more attention to cultural issues, such as the preservation of language, traditional dress, music, and dance.

It decides to include a set of guidance notes for visitors in its brochure. Suggest ten principles it could include. An example is given below to help you get started:

1. Learn some key words and phrases of the language of the region you are visiting and remember to take a dictionary or phrase book with you.

# Supply and demand of culture to tourists

All features of Irish culture were part of normal everyday life. They were arranged to suit the people themselves and arose out of regular social gatherings of families, friends and communities. Musicians and dancers were not so much providing a service as enjoying themselves with people who shared their background.

Consider each of the changes in Table 11.2 applying to the performance of traditional Irish music in pubs.

**Table 11.2**

| In the past... | Now... |
| --- | --- |
| • Musicians would often play in pubs for a few drinks, so there was little cost to publicans or hoteliers | • Music sessions are often organized in advance with a fee paid to the musicians, so hoteliers and publicans have to be sure the music will bring in more spending customers |
| • The audience was mostly family and friends and knew the players | • The audience includes holidaymakers, some of whom may expect to be able to talk quietly in a pub |
| • It was easy to clear the floor for traditional dancing | • Tourists are unfamiliar with the dances and may not like having only cramped drinking space |
| • Many of the traditional music skills were passed on within families | • Many young people rely on local musicians providing lessons in traditional music at school |
| • Visitors were mostly independent travellers who were familiar with the sound of traditional Irish music | • Visitors are often on organized tours and may expect to hear a sound they are already familiar with, such as country and western music |
| • Members of traditional communities were used to entertainment starting late and continuing into the night | • Modern visitors often expect their entertainments to begin and end at specified times and not to go on too late into the night |

Similar changes may be seen in the demand for arts and crafts. Artefacts once produced for local daily use, such as pots, knitted sweaters or woven blankets, are now in great demand as tourist souvenirs. One of the results of this huge increase in demand is the mass production of some items. Factory-produced Aran sweaters help to meet the demand but they are not of the same individual quality as the hand-knitted ones. So tourism may encourage craft production in terms of quantity but have a detrimental effect on the quality of the goods produced.

# Tourism strategy in the Gaeltacht

The culture of the Gaeltacht is attractive to visitors. In the music, art and dance of the region they experience something that they cannot in their everyday lives. Also, because this culture has its origins in the past, they are also able to get a sense of what life was like in former times. Yet visitors also tend to expect some of the comforts of home, such as good hotels, restaurants, transport systems and entertainment. Too many visitors might pose threats to the survival of the culture and so it is important to have a tourism strategy. The writers of this strategy must work out a reasonable balance between tourism development and support for sustaining features of Irish culture.

By the 1950s the Irish government came to the view that the only way to preserve the Irish language was by direct encouragement. This eventually led to the setting up of an organization called Údarás na Gaeltachta.

---

*The role of Údarás na Gaeltachta is*

to develop the economy of the Gaeltacht so as to facilitate the preservation and extension of the Irish language as the principal language of the region. To achieve this objective, Údarás promotes productive schemes of employment through the development of local natural resources and entrepreneurial abilities and the attraction of mobile investment and skills to the Gaeltacht.

---

The link between developing the local economy and supporting the language is an important one. It suggests that the local culture is unlikely to survive without help. If the region becomes more prosperous, there will be more money to support projects to sustain and develop Irish language, arts and crafts.

There are four main elements of the Gaeltacht's cultural tourism strategy:

- To develop and market the Gaeltacht as a special and unique tourism product
- To work with local groups to develop tourism in their own areas
- To provide assistance in developing new tourism products, such as accommodation or guided tours
- To provide assistance for initiatives that will 'add value' to any existing tourism activities

These areas of the strategy are intended to encourage and support some practical methods of developing cultural tourism in the Gaeltacht areas. This may take a number of forms:

- Irish language summer schools
- Promotion and funding of Irish art, dance and drama performances and festivals
- Building on existing environmental initiatives, such as those showing the traditional way of life in areas of the Gaeltacht

 **Activity**

Below is a typical advertisement for Irish language courses intended to attract summer visitors to the Gaeltacht.

**Gael-Linn, Gweedore, County Donegal Gaeltacht Language Courses for Adults**

Irish language and culture courses organized in the Gaeltacht area of Gaoth Dobhair in north west Donegal, where Gaelic is the native language, providing an unbroken link with Ireland's past.

Courses are totally conversational and cater for three different levels of ability, aiming to give beginners the capacity to carry on a simple conversation in Irish and aiming to expand the fluency and confidence of people with some previous knowledge of Irish.

It is your responsibility to draw up a programme for a one week course for beginners at the above centre. Discuss the following questions:

1 What proportion of each day should be devoted to language learning and what proportion to 'holiday' activities?

2 What other aspects of Irish culture, apart from the language itself, would you introduce on this course and how would you do this?

3 What range of language-learning methods could you use on this kind of course?

4 Which methods do you think would be most appropriate in this case and why?

5 How would you encourage people taking part to continue their study beyond the beginners' stage?

6 How would you change the advertisement if you wished to place it in a newspaper in an American city such as Boston, where many of the inhabitants have Irish ancestors?

# Indonesia

The islands of Bali, Lombok and Komodo are part of the country called Indonesia. From the point of view of tourism impact they make an interesting contrast. The number of tourists visiting Bali has risen rapidly during the past 20 years. It is a very popular base for surfers. Lombok is much newer to tourism and is much quieter, although hotel development on the island has increased considerably in the last few years. Komodo is more remote and has a smaller population but it attracts people willing to travel overnight in small boats because it is the only place in the world where the giant monitor lizards, known as Komodo Dragons, can be seen.

Indonesia is an unusual country. It has the world's fourth largest population, over 197 million people (Table 12.1). Its 17,000 islands, half of which are uninhabited, are spread across an area the size of the United States. It is the most volcanic country on earth, with almost 4,500 volcanoes. The country contains 60,000 villages. Immigration and colonization have given the country an extremely varied culture. Settlers from India introduced Islamic and Hindu religions. The Dutch colonized the islands in the seventeenth century and the country remained under Dutch rule until independence was gained after the Second World War. There are almost 400 different languages and dialects spoken.

**Table 12.1  Estimated population of Indonesia's main island groups 1994**

|  | Area (sq. km) | Population | Density (per sq km) |
| --- | --- | --- | --- |
| Java & Madura | 132,186 | 113,582,700 | 859.3 |
| Sumatra | 473,481 | 40,100,600 | 84.7 |
| Kalimantan | 539,460 | 10,237,700 | 19.0 |
| Sulawesi | 189,216 | 13,524,900 | 71.5 |
| Bali | 5,561 | 2,879,500 | 517.8 |
| Nusa Tenggara (inc. Lombok) | 68,053 | 7,125,100 | 104.7 |
| Moluccas | 74,505 | 2,047,800 | 27.5 |
| Irian Jaya | 421,981 | 1,892,200 | 4.5 |
| **Indonesia** | **1,904,443** | **191,390,500** | **100.5** |
| East Timor | 14,874 | 826,000 | 55.5 |
| **TOTAL** | **1,919,317** | **192,216,500** | **100.1** |

Tourism is growing very rapidly in Indonesia. In the period from 1990 to 1996 the number of visitors rose by 99%. The amount they spent increased by 148%. In 1995 there were 4.3 million visitors who spent £3.5 billion between them. About 800,000 came from Europe. One sign of the importance of tourism is the fact that there were, by the end of 1996, 41 hotel chains operating in the country. The Economic Intelligence Unit recently predicted that visitor numbers could grow to more than 10 million by 2005 with over 400,000 coming from the UK. This would place enormous pressure on the most popular destination in the country, the island of Bali.

Figure 12.1 shows the position of the islands of Bali and Lombok. Komodo Island is too small to show, but is located to the east of Lombok between the islands of Sumbawa and Flores.

# Bali

The main appeal of Bali as a tourist destination lies in two main areas – its landscape and its culture. It possesses spectacular scenery – live volcanoes, rain forest, white sand beaches and terraced rice fields that follow the contours of the hills. The Hindu culture, which influences all aspects of local life, has resulted in distinctive dances, rituals and ceremonies which can be observed daily. The local crafts are much sought after because of their originality and quality, especially batik, silverware, shadow puppets and woodcarving.

Some 2.8 million people live on Bali in an area of just over 5,180 square kilometres (2,000 sq. miles), the majority of them in traditional houses. As these are single storey and contain a number of separate buildings and shrines within a walled courtyard it is easy to see why there is a growing shortage of land space in Bali.

A volcanic chain of mountains stretches across the island from east to west. The highest peak is Gunung Anung (Holy Mountain) which is 3,170 metres (10,400 feet) high. The availability of water at a high level, such as Lake Batur, part of the water-filled crater of Mount Batur, some 1,740 metres (5,700 feet) above sea level, enables the rice terraces to regulate the amount of water they receive by opening and closing the flow of water from higher levels. Apart from rice, vegetables and copra are the main crops on the island.

**Fig. 12.1  Location of Bali and Lombok**

The main tourist resorts, such as Sanur Beach and Kuta are found in the south, not far from the airport at Denpasar.

Many people are drawn to Bali because of its cultural distinctiveness. Some of the things they come to see are described in Table 12.2.

***Table 12.2***

| | |
|---|---|
| ● **Temple festivals and ceremonies** | There are thousands of temples on Bali, each holding festivals twice a year. These usually involve colourful processions and offerings of food and flowers made to the gods. |
| ● **Dances** | Dancing is considered an art in Bali. Children learn dances based on stories from ancient legend and religious epics such as the *Ramayana*. Hand and eye movements are a vital part of Balinese dancing styles. |
| ● **Woodcarving** | The centre for woodcaving is Mas. Visitors can watch carvers making traditional figures from ebony and other hardwoods. There is a permanent exhibition of the best of Balinese woodcarving in Denpasar. |
| ● **Cremations** | More wealthy families will hold cremation ceremonies for their dead. A tall wooden tower on which rests an animal-shaped sarcophagus containing their remains is burned. |
| ● **Paintings** | The village of Ubud is famous for its painters, some of whom are local and some who came from overseas to settle there. Though styles vary, many of the paintings represent the Balinese landscape. |
| ● **Gold and silverwork** | Many families in the village of Celuk have made gold and silver jewellery for several generations. Many of the pieces are very intricate, using very delicate filigree work. |
| ● **Batik** | This technique of using wax to mask parts of cloth while dying it in order to produce designs originated in Indonesia. Batik can be purchased all over Bali, ranging from cheap machine-made products to expensive original designs made by hand. |
| ● **Stone carving** | Batubalan is the centre of stone carving in Bali. Carvers use traditional designs to create statues, tombstones and ornaments. |
| ● **Puppet figures** | Puppet shows are an important part of Balinese culture. They tell traditional stories but the puppet master, who speaks all the voices, will often include comment on modern times as well. Shadow puppets, made from buffalo hide and richly decorated, are popular as gifts. |

Bali's landscape has always been a major attraction. Inland it is dominated by terraced rice fields, with rivers and artificial irrigation streams criss-crossing a very green landscape. A chain of volcanoes crosses the centre of the island. The summits, often shrouded in mist, are believed to be the home of the gods. The highest peak, Gunung Agung, is 3,170 metres (10,400 feet) high.

Many of the most interesting cultural and landscape sites on Bali are inland. Every year thousands of visitors set off on tours to visit them. Figure 12.2 shows where some of the most popular tourist attractions are located. The key below gives the name and a brief description of each attraction.

| | | | |
|---|---|---|---|
| 1. **Denpasar** | Administrative capital of Bali. Art centre and market | 16. **Padang Bai** | Port for Bali–Lombok ferry |
| 2. **Datubalan** | Centre of stone carving | 17. **Tenganan** | 'Bali Aga' village – origin of Balinese society |
| 3. **Celuk** | Centre of silverwork | 18. **Amlapura** | Former capital of Karangasem Kingdom |
| 4. **Mas** | Centre for woodcarving | 19. **Ujung** | Site of Karangasem Water Palace |
| 5. **Ubud** | Centre of Balinese painting | 20. **Penelokan** | Spectacular viewpoint at rim of Mt Batur crater |
| 6. **Bedulu** | Former capital of Pejeng Dynasty | 21. **Batur** | Mt Batur volcano and Pura Ulun Danu Temple |
| 7. **Tegalalang** | Noted area for colourful painted woodcarvings | 22. **Kintamani** | Famous market town on edge of Mt Batur cratur |
| 8. **Pliatan** | Training centre for Legong dancers | 23. **Tampaksiring** | Gunung Kawi Memorial and Tirta Empul holy springs |
| 9. **Sangeh** | Pura Bukit Sari Temple and monkey forest | 24. **Mengwi** | Pura Taman Ayun Temple from 1634 |
| 10. **Bangli** | Ancient capital and site of Pura Kehen Temple | 25. **Tanah Lot** | Important temple built on rocky islet |
| 11. **Pejeng** | Site of monastery and 'Moon of Pejeng' – 1,000-year-old drum | 26. **Mt Batukau** | Second highest mountain in Bali |
| 12. **Klungkung** | Centre of Gelgel Dynasty, Bali's most important kingdom | 27. **Penebel** | Panoramic view of rice terraces |
| 13. **Besakih** | Bali's 'Mother Temple' – complex of over 30 temples | 28. **Bedugul** | Ulu Danu Temple on Lake Bratan in mountains 2,020 metres (6,600 feet) high |
| 14. **Kusamba** | Colourful fishing village | 29. **Sangsit** | Pura Beji Temple with superb sculptures |
| 15. **Gelgel** | Original capital of Gelgel Dynasty | 30. **Sanur** | Quiet tourist area with sheltered beach |

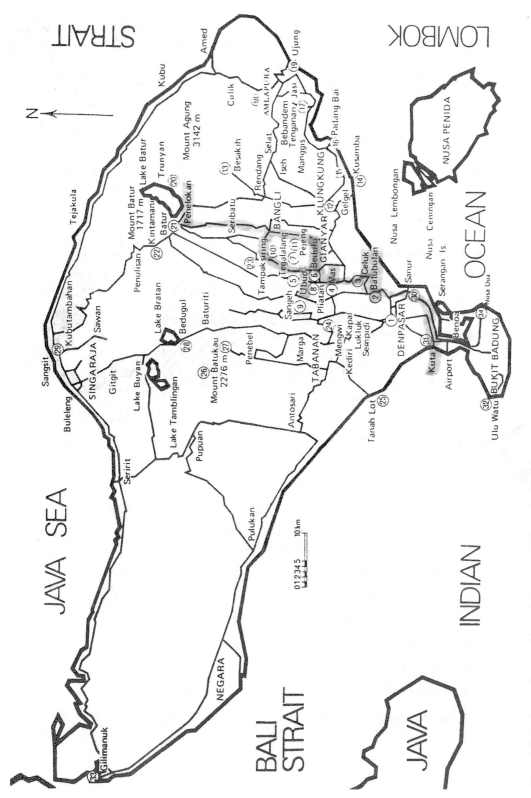

*Fig. 12.2 Location of tourist attractions in Bali*

| 31. **Kuta** | Surfing beach and favourite shopping and nightlife area | 33. **Gilimanuk** | Terminus for Java ferry service |
| 32. **Ulu Watu** | Pura Luhur Temple and route along scenic cliffs | 34. **Nusa Dua** | Newly developed beach resort |

Outside Denpasar and Kuta Beach the most popular tourist sites include Tanah Lot, Penelokan, Tampaksiring and Sangeh.

The roads in the interior are often narrow and there are many bends as the roads follow the contours of the landscape. The main methods of transport available to people who wish to tour the island are:

- **Taxis** – these can be hired by the hour or the day, usually with a minimum charge.
- **Self-drive car hire** – these services were introduced more recently. A daily rate is charged and an international driving licence is required for foreign drivers.
- **Motorbikes/scooters** – these are common and relatively cheap to hire, especially on a weekly basis.
- **Dokars** – these are small horse-drawn carts which carry three or four people. They are mostly found in larger towns.
- **Bemos** – these are six to eight seater buses which run along main town and sub-urban routes. They are inexpensive and stop on request.
- **Local buses** – these are inexpensive and often crowded. The vehicles are generally old but provide a good chance to meet local people.
- **Bicycles** – these can be hired from the main towns by the day or week. They provide access to side roads and tracks.

## Activities

Study the five tours in Figure 12.3.

1 Photocopy the map in Figure 12.2. Plot the routes taken by each of these tours.

Mark on the map sites you think would attract the greatest number of visitors travelling by hired transport or public buses.

2 Discuss which routes and sites would become most congested.

3 Draw up a suitable itinerary for a tour for each of the following groups:

- A Hindu group visiting from India
- A couple wishing to experience the variety of Bali's landscape
- A family with three young children
- An importer of arts and crafts

4 Suggest some possible ways of reducing the crowds at some of the more popular tourist sites on Bali.

Besakih Temple tour
Duration: 7 hours

The Besakih Temple is the biggest temple in Bali and located on the slopes of Mount Agung. The sight of the over one-thousand years old 'mother-temple' against the background of the mountain is awe-inspiring. On festival days coloured banners add a touch of gaiety. In the main courtyard is the Hindu Trinity shrine wrapped in cloth and decorated with flower offerings.

Stops along the way to Besakih will be made at the Klungkung Kerta Gosa, the court of justice of the 18th century, and the Goa Lawah Bat Cave at Kusamba.

Sangeh & Mengwi tour
Duration: 4 hours

Tour to the towering nutmeg tree forest of Sangeh, home to hundreds of spirited monkeys and bats. Following this will be a visit to Mengwi, the Royal Family Temple of Taman Ayun, famous for its stone-carved figures, gateway and moat.

**Fig. 12.3 Tours in Bali**

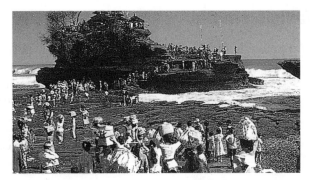

Tanah Lot & Alas Kedaton tour
Duration: 4 hours

A half-day tour to the sacred forest of towering nutmeg trees at Alas Kedaton, home of hundreds of monkeys and large groups of fruit bats hanging from the branches high above. An old temple is found here. The tour continues on to Mengwi for visit to the Royal Family Temple of Taman Ayun, one of the most beautiful temples on the island, then on to the famous and breath-takingly beautiful seaside temple of Tanah Lot.

Tanah Lot & Jatiluwih tour
Duration: 7 hours

Tanah Lot – Alas Kedaton Tour, extended to Jatiluwih, which means 'extraordinary', because it overlooks a shimmering view of terraced ricefields, stretching in endless contours over hills and valleys. This tour also includes a visit to Pura Luhur, halfway up Mount Batukau, the royal temple of the Tabanan Dynasty.

Barong Dance & Kintmani tour
Duration: 8 hours

The Barong Dance depicts the never-ending fight between good and evil, and your stop at Batubulan to watch the performance by some of the best Balinese dancers will be unforgettable.

This journey takes you to the beautiful mountain village of Kintamani, nestled on the slopes of Mount Batur. The view of this volcano and its surrounding lake is breathtaking. Stops *en route* include visits to the Pura Kehen temple of Bangli, the Bedulu Elephant Cave, the Holy Spring at Tampaksiring and Bali's three main artists' villages: Mas, famous for wood carvings; Celuk, the centre of hand-crafted gold and silver jewelry; and Ubud, Bali's major art centre.

# Religion in Bali

Religion plays a much stronger role in daily life on Bali than it does in many places. The majority of the population believe in the Hindu religion. They worship Tintaya, Brahma the creator, Shiva the destroyer and Vishnu the preserver. Tourists to the island will see daily evidence of Balinese beliefs as offerings like baskets of fruit are regularly made to the gods and at the shrines of ancestors. Hinduism in Bali involves a large number of gods and spiritis, including Dewi Sri, goddess of rice, Dewi Ratih, goddess of the moon, and Dewi Melanting, goddess of shopkeeping.

## Cremation ceremonies

Cremation ceremonies are an important part of Balinese village life. Families who can afford the cost will pay to give their dead relatives a lavish send off.

On a date that is regarded as favourable, tall wooden towers are decorated with colourful tinsel, glitter and cloth. They are carried round the streets in a procession and shaken or spun at every crossroads. Gamelan music is played on bamboo or metal instruments, which sound like xylophones.

The purpose of the ceremony is to enable the souls of the dead to begin a new life as they are reborn in a different and possibly better form. Hindus believe in an endless cycle of birth and death.

The Brahman priest, or pedanda, says prayers and offerings of rice and sweets are made to the gods. The dead relatives' bodies are dressed in white cloth and anointed with perfume. They are given money and goods for their long journey to the next world. Each body is then placed in a tower, whirled around so that the spirits will not be able to find their way back home, and torched by flames.

At dusk the ashes are taken to a river nearby and the surviving relatives usually celebrate the occasion with a meal and some rice wine.

## Tourism and ceremonies

Ceremonies are part of daily life and have a holy purpose. They are attractive to visitors because they are colourful and full of energy. They are not serious occasions. They are often intended to welcome and encourage the presence of the gods, so that music, laughter, conversation and prayer are all part of the process.

Dress is very important for all ceremonies held in holy places. Visitors are encouraged to observe these dress formalities. Professor Adnayana Manuaba, writing in *In Focus*, the magazine of Tourism Concern, describes the sort of dress and behaviour that would be appropriate for tourists witnessing ceremonies in Balinese temples:

> The minimum standard of dress for visiting men and women is the same: a sarong, a sleeved shirt preferably not a T-shirt, a waist belt or sash tied on the outside of the shirt and clean, neat hair. It is customary to bathe directly before dressing for temple...
>
> Inside the inner temple is where we bring our offerings and pray. When visiting the inner temple please move about as unobtrusively as possible, for it is distracting and disrespectful to wander around as other people are praying or meditating. Find a place to sit discreetly with others. If you stand, stand back from those who are praying, so as not to block people's path.

Also sensitivity and discretion should be used when photographing people taking part in ceremonies. We recommend not taking flash photos because it disturbs people's concentration. And of course, throughout your stay in Bali, but especially in holy places, please dispose of rubbish responsibly.

### Temples

Some of the Hindu temples on Bali, such as the eleventh century shrine of Pura Agung at Besakih, are closed to non-Hindus. Others, like the sixteenth century Tanah Lot, standing on a rocky outcrop sticking out into the sea, are frequently crowded with tourists.

The more popular temples often make a small entrance charge. Visitors are sometimes required to wrap a sarong around their clothes as a mark of respect. Because these sites attract a constant stream of visitors there are usually very persistent sellers of souvenirs of all kinds at the entrances and around the perimeters.

### Religious values

Concerns are sometimes expressed that the growth of tourism will affect the traditional values of the Balinese. Customs and beliefs are passed from one generation to another through the practice of *Adat*, or custom law. *Adat* shows that there is a clear difference between what is holy and what is impure. Things that are high, such as the summit of Gunung Agung, are thought of as holy. The head is the most holy part of the body and the feet the most impure.

The sense of purity and impurity is very strong. Very sick people, those who have suffered a recent death in the family, open wounds, babies less than 42 days old, and menstruating women are all considered impure. Balinese people in any of these impure conditions are not allowed to enter sacred places such as temples. Some of the more sacred sites on the island display notices requesting tourists to respect these beliefs by not entering sites if they are in what the Balinese would consider an impure condition.

## Activities

1 Find a tour operator's brochure that features Bali as a holiday destination.

2 Briefly summarize the information that the brochure contains about religious ceremonies on Bali.

3 Discuss the extent and level of advice that the brochure gives to visitors about how they should behave when they are present at ceremonies or in holy places.

4 Write a short section to be added to the brochure that would encourage visitors to be more aware of the beliefs of Balinese people.

# Performance in Bali

Two of the best known traditional Balinese dances (Figure 12.4) are regularly performed for tourists in open air theatres. These are the Barong dance and the Kecak

*Fig. 12.4  A Balinese dancer*

dance. They feature performers in elaborate costumes and take place to the accompaniment of gamelan music. In order to help the audience to understand what they are watching leaflets containing summaries of the story are distributed at the beginning.

- The **Barong dance** represents the eternal fight between good and evil. Barong, a mythological animal, represents a good spirit and Rangda, a mythological monster represents an evil one. Animals, witches and gods appear in the story. Characters have the power to change their outward appearance from human to animal. In the end the fight between good and evil remains unfinished.
- The **Kecak dance**, also known as the Monkey Dance, involves a troupe of over 100 men singing and chanting a story from the epic Hindu poem, the *Ramayana*. The story tells how King Rama sets out to rescue his captured wife, Sita. He is helped in this task by an army of monkeys led by Hanuman.

Other commonly performed dances include:

- The **Kidang Kencana Dance** – this dance shows what the life of a herd of deer in the forest is like.
- The **Margapati Dance** – this dance represents the cruelty of the tiger, traditionally believed in Indonesia to be the King of the Jungle.
- The **Gopala Dance** – this dance shows three young men responsible for a herd of buffaloes, suggesting how they amuse themselves while having a rest.
- The **Jauk Dance** – this dance features a giant who wears long, sharp nails and a frightening mask.

- The **Belibis Dance** – this dance is based on the story of King Angling Dharma who is cursed by his beloved wife and transformed into a duck. He joins a group of wild ducks and learns to fly with them. They come to realize he is not like them and they abandon him.

## Activities

The performance of dances illustrating stories from the Ramayana originally followed strict lines laid down by religious leaders or kings. Modern performances have been influenced by other countries' dance forms and by more individual interpretations of the stories.

1 What arguments can you think of in favour of keeping traditional dances exactly the same?

2 List the factors that could be responsible for the introduction of changes into traditional dance forms.

3 Apart from distributing leaflets, what other methods of helping an audience to understand a traditional dance can you suggest?

4 There are several sites on Bali where daily performances of traditional dances are put on for tourist audiences, usually in open air theatres.

Discuss how you think this use of culture as entertainment might affect the thought and attitudes of:

- The performers

- The audience

- The local resident population

# Lombok

The island of Lombok, which means 'chilli pepper', is a 15 minute flight away or a short ferry crossing from Bali across the Lombok Strait. Lombok is smaller and quieter than its neighbouring island, although the pace of hotel development is now increasing.

Its population of 2.3 million come from a number of different cultures – Islamic Sasaks, Hindu Balinese and people of Malay ancestry. The majority are Muslim. The landscape reveals great contrasts. The south coast, called Kuta, is rocky. The west resembles Bali with its rice terraces, banana and coconut groves and fertile plains. The east is dry, barren and desert-like. The north, dominated by Mount Rindjani, a volcano which rises to 3,745 metres (12,000 feet), has thick forests and dramatic views.

There are many beaches on Lombok. Some are white sand; others are black volcanic sand. A good highway crosses the island from east to west passing through Narmada, the site of a huge complex of palace dwellings built for a former Balinese king. Coral reefs are popular with snorkelers and scuba divers.

## Activity

The Sengiggi Beach Hotel on Lombok has 149 rooms. All of these are in thatched single- and two-storey bungalows. The extensive gardens are carefully planted with palms, shrubs, flowers and bushes so that many of the buildings are hidden from view. The whole site is fenced off to prevent access by non-residents, although the beach itself is public. The hotel has facilities for tennis, volleyball, table tennis and basketball, as well as a swimming pool. There are also other facilities on site such as a souvenir shop, a tour service and travel agency, a currency exchange facility, a postal service, and telephone and telex services.

1 Discuss the description and picture of the hotel shown in Figure 12.5 and write a comment on its appearance, the facilities and why you think it was fenced off.

2 What do you think are the likely results of constructing hotels so that everything visitors need can be found inside their boundaries?

# Wildlife habitats

The British naturalist, Alfred Wallace, noted in the last century that the deepest sea in the area was the deep channel running between the islands of Bali and Lombok. He suggested that this channel, now known as the 'Wallace Line' divided Indonesia into two regions with very different flora and fauna. Nowadays the country is more often divided into three distinct sections, each one having different plants and animals from the others (Table 12.3.)

*Fig. 12.5  Senggigi Beach Hotel and gardens*

**Table 12.3**

| The western islands (Sumatra, Java, Kalimantan, Bali) | The central islands (Sulawesi, Lombok, Nusa Tenggara, Komodo) | The eastern islands (East Timor, Irian Jaya) |
|---|---|---|
| Characteristics similar to south-east Asia – lush jungle, rare orchids, the giant *Rafflesia* (with blooms a metre across), tigers, leopards, elephants, rhinos and thousands of varieties of birds and insects. | A mixture of Asian and Australasian flora and fauna. For example, Sulawesi has both monkeys and marsupials. Komodo has the 'dragons', found nowhere else in the world. | More like Australia with bush-like shrubs and hardy plants. Brilliantly coloured lorries and cockatoos replace barbets and thrushes, and the Australian marsupials become much more common. |

# National Parks

Wildlife habitats in parts of Indonesia have been reduced by deforestation. Timber is a major industry on many of the islands. However there are a number of small National Parks, including Bali Barat National Park. This is how a guidebook describes it:

---

*Bali Barat National Park*

Once upon a time visitors would have come across tigers in this sparsely populated region of Bali. These days the animals you are most likely to see in the 200 sq km of coastal forest are long-tailed macaques, barking and smabar deer, or, if you are really lucky, the Rothchild's mynah, which is Bali's only endemic bird.

Several trails start out from Labuhan Lalang, 15 km from the visitors' centre. Alternatively take the delightful boat trip to Menjangan Island, a 30-minute trip from the mainland. Guides and accommodation can be arranged at the visitors' centre.

The Park is located 134 km north west of Denpasar. Buses take 3 to 4 hours to reach the park headquarters from Denpasar.

*Source*: Thomas Cook Travellers' Bali, Java & Lombok

---

# Komodo Island

Komodo Island lies between the island of Sumbawa and Flores, to the east of Bali and Lombok. It is a remote place. Though more tourists travel there each year, it still requires a lengthy journey. For example, visitors to Lombok in 1996 might have followed this itinerary in order to visit Komodo:

| | | |
|---|---|---|
| 6 am | Fly from Mataram Airport to Bima on the island of Sumbawa – arrive 6.45 am | Small turbo prop planes with local airline such as Merpati |
| | Breakfast | |
| 7.30 am | Drive across Sumbawa to the eastern fishing port of Sape – arrive 10 am | Generally by small minibuses |
| 11 am | Board small boat to sail for Komodo, lunching on board – arrive Komodo Island 6 pm (weather and currents permitting) | Weather conditions and currents, because of the tidal exchange between the Indian Ocean and the Flores Sea, can be variable – not recommended for poor sailors! |
| | Sleep overnight on boat | |

Day 2

| | | |
|---|---|---|
| 6.30 am | Breakfast | Simple food prepared on the boat |
| 7 am | Go ashore on Komodo Island and take guided walk to see the Komodo Dragons | Guides accompany tour parties of about 15 to ensure safety |
| 10 am | Return to boat – snorkelling around the reefs of Komodo Island | Some beautiful, unspoilt reefs in the region |
| 11.30 am | Sail back to Sape – arrive 6.30 pm | |
| 6.30 pm | Drive back to Bima – arrive 9 pm | |
| | Hotel in Bima overnight | Unsophisticated accommodation |

Day 3

| | |
|---|---|
| 7am | Fly back to Mataram Airport, Lombok – arrive 7.45 am |

Komodo Island was given the status of a National Park in 1980. The island itself is about 300 square kilometres (115 sq. miles) in area. Much of the landscape is hilly and rocky with fan-shaped lontar palms being common. Inland there is rainforest on hills that reach up to 800 metres (2,600 feet).

There is a hostel on the island where about 50 people can sleep on the floor under shelter overnight. They have to provide their own bedding.

The Komodo Dragons (Figure 12.6) are actually monitor lizards. They grow up to three or four metres in length and generally feed on deer and wild pig. They lie in wait beside animal tracks and grab the legs of creatures that pass. They can move very quickly over short distances and possess an extremely venomous bite.

For a number of years tourists were taken to a shelter overlooking a gully in which a dead goat would be tied to a tree. The Dragons, attracted by the scent, would come to feed. However, concerns that this was disrupting their feeding patterns and also concentrating numbers in a single area, meant that this practice has now been stopped.

Because Komodo Dragons are reptiles, and very large ones at that, they do not tend to move much until they have warmed up in the morning sun. Perhaps for this reason the guided tours take place in the early morning when the creatures are at their least active. Even so, tourists are warned to be very careful and not to get too close. The guides carry very large sticks and keep a watchful eye on all the members of their group.

**Fig. 12.6 Komodo Dragon**

Recent estimates suggest that there are about 5,000 Komodo Dragons on Komodo and the neighbouring Rinca Island. However, only about 350 of these are breeding females. The biggest danger to their survival is that, because there is a small population living in a very restricted area, any sudden change in their environment could prove very harmful. A fire or a disease in the deer population could threaten their future. If the human population of Komodo grows, people might see the Dragons as a threat and take steps to destroy them. The presence of tourists could be seen both as a threat and a support. The risk is that the habitat of the Dragons might be exposed to change. The support is that money from the tourists can be used to support protection of the Dragons' environment to ensure their survival.

## Activities

1 There seems to be an increasing interest in wildlife tourism, including destinations that are not easy to reach, for example the Galapagos Islands and the Antarctic.

   What factors do you think have contributed to this increasing interest?

2 What aspects of the Komodo Dragons' existence do you think the staff of the Komodo National Park would need to monitor carefully to check that they were not at increasing risk from tourism?

3 List the possible methods of discouraging tourists from visiting Komodo Island. If it was found to be necessary to limit the numbers admitted, what do you think would be the best method of achieving this?

4 Suppose that funds are needed to ensure the survival of the Komodo Dragons and to carry out more research about their habitat. Discuss the different possible sources of funds, who you think should contribute, and what arguments might be used to persuade them.

   You could begin this activity by searching for information about the Komodo Dragons on the Internet.

# Module 4

# EMPLOYMENT IN THE TOURIST INDUSTRY

**Introduction**

**Case study 13**
Holiday Inn, Maidenhead/Windsor

**Case study 14**
Lilleshall

**Case study 15**
British Airways – working for an airline

**Case study 16**
Chessington World of Adventures – working at a major tourist attraction

This module covers the following components of the syllabus:

4.1  Nature and range of jobs in travel and tourism
4.2  Skills and qualities valued in the travel and tourism industry
4.3  Working in a specific travel and tourism context

# What does working in tourism involve?

Tourism is a huge industry. It is said by the World Travel and Tourism Council to employ 255 million people world-wide. The 1996 English Tourist Board says that 1.7 million people are employed in tourism in Britain, providing facilities and services for an estimated 145 million customers each year. Table 1 shows the range of jobs in tourism and leisure.

What do these customers need? Their main requirements are:

- **Accommodation and catering** – hotels, guest-houses, caravan parks, campsites, holiday centres, restaurants, pubs, cafés
- **Travel and transport** – airlines, coaches, rail, travel agents, tour operators
- **Leisure and visitor attractions** – theme parks, zoos, leisure centres, cinemas, nightclubs
- **Heritage and the countryside** – museums, art galleries, religious buildings, historic houses, national parks, urban parks

Because these needs are so varied, this means that the range of jobs available in tourism is very wide. The tourism industry employs all kinds of people at all ages, with different experiences, skills and qualifications.

Tourism is a service industry. This means that contact between employees and customers is frequent. Tourism businesses depend for their success on providing a better level of service than their competitors. Many tourism products, such as package holidays, contain several different elements. Customers expect each element – the flight, the hotel, the transfers – to be satisfactory but they also expect to enjoy themselves. The extent to which they manage to do this may depend on the character and personality of key employees involved in the process, such as the travel agent, the airport check in staff, the cabin crew, the hotel staff and the tour group representative in the resort.

The needs of tourists are not limited to office hours. This means that many jobs in tourism require employees to work some evenings and weekends. Jobs such as those in hotel kitchens are likely to involve shift work since there are busy times at midday and in the evening with a slack afternoon period in between.

Some tourism employment is seasonal. For example, outdoor tourist attractions generally shut down during the winter months. Hotels in British seaside resorts will be much busier during the summer months and over public holidays and will need more staff then than at other times.

# Skills, knowledge, qualities and attitudes

In listing the things they expect to find in new employees companies often do not distinguish very clearly between skills, knowledge, qualities and attitudes. They

**Table 1  The range of jobs in tourism and leisure**

Air Cabin Crew
Airline Manager
Airport Staff
Art Gallery Assistant
Bar Staff
Bingo Club Staff
Boat Hire Staff
Box Office Staff
Caravan and Camping Park
  Staff
Car Hire Staff
Cashier
Catering Manager
Chef and Cook
Cinema Staff
Coach Driver
Coach Operator
Computer Operator
Conference Organizer
Countryside Park Staff
Courier
Cruise Operating Staff
Electrician
Entertainer

Exhibition Organizer
Farm Accommodation Staff
Fast Food Service Staff
Ferry and Hovercraft Staff
Finance and Accounts Staff
Gardener
General Manager – Hotels/
  Tourist Attractions
Groundsman/woman
Guest-house Owner
Health Club Staff
Historic Property Manager
Holiday Centre Staff
Hotel Manager
Housekeeper
Incoming Tour Operator
Interpreter
Kitchen Assistant
Leisure Centre Assistant
Lifeguard
Local Authority Tourism
  Officer
Local Tour Guide (Blue Badge)
Maintenance (e.g. Engineer,

Painter, Modelmaker,
  Builder, Welder)
Manager (all sectors)
Marketing Officer
Motorway Services Staff
Museum Assistant
Museum Curator
Nightclub and Disco Staff
Night Porter
Nurse
Nursery Nurse
Park Attendant
Park Warden/Ranger
Personnel and Training Staff
Pool Assistant
Porter
Publican
Publicity and Public
  Relations Officer
Railway Staff
Reception and Counter Staff
Reservations Assistant
Resort Representative
Restaurant Manager

Retail Assistant
Room Attendant
Sales Representative
Secretary
Security Staff
Self Catering Staff
Specialist Coach
Sports Centre Staff
Steward/Stewardess
Taxi Driver
Technician (Maintenance and
  Operation of Equipment)
Telephonist
Theatre Manager
Tour Guide
Tour Operator
Tourist Information Centre
  Staff
Transport Staff
Travel Agency Clerk
Visitor Attractions Manager
Waiter/Waitress
Wine Bar Staff
Zoo and Wildlife Park Staff

might, for example, say that they were looking for someone 'with personality' or that they wanted someone who was enthusiastic or that they wanted someone 'with a good education'. Table 2 suggests some of the differences between skills, qualities and attitudes:

*Table 2*

| | |
|---|---|
| ● **Skills** | Some skills are a matter of knowing how to do something, e.g. use a word processor. They usually involve something that has been learned. They may be largely mental (e.g. reading, writing, counting) or mainly physical (e.g. carrying six full dinner plates). Some general skills (e.g. problem-solving, information-handling, communicating) are much broader and draw on a range of individual skills. |
| ● **Knowledge** | Knowledge is often acquired by doing the job. Employers in some travel and tourism sectors expect some prior knowledge, e.g. a good knowledge of travel geography for applicants for posts in retail travel. |
| ● **Qualities** | These are the characteristics used to describe an employee's personality. Some qualities, such as an outgoing personality, a sense of humour and confidence, are highly valued in some sectors of tourism. Most travel and tourism employers would say that the ability to get on with other people is vital. Training is often used to try to develop these qualities to a higher level. |
| ● **Attitudes** | Attitudes are often connected with qualities. They involve the way employees express their views and feelings about their work, their colleagues and their working conditions. The areas in which attitudes are seen as important include such things as appearance, reliability and tolerance. |

## Personal skills and qualities

Most travel and tourism employers place personal skills and qualities very high in their list of priorities. These include such things as:

- Honesty
- Good manners
- Confidence
- Being organized
- Having a sense of humour
- Paying attention to detail
- Being reliable
- Getting on well with other people

These skills and qualities are particularly important for tourism employees who work directly with the public. Being cheerful, polite and helpful comes more naturally to some people than others, especially when working under pressure. Sometimes it is something that has to be learned as part of a professional approach to providing good customer service. In other words it is not just a question of personality, but also of attitude towards the job being done.

# General work skills

Other skills that are welcomed in the travel and tourism industry are less a matter of personality, and more to do with techniques which can be learned. Among the most important of these are the following:

### Telephone skills

A lot of tourism business is conducted over the telephone. Skill is required in establishing rapport with the customer, giving and receiving accurate information, keeping the conversation focused on its main purpose and following up what has been agreed.

### Money-handling skills

Money transactions form a vital part of most tourism businesses. Some of these, such as collecting admission fees, selling souvenirs or exchanging foreign currency, involve handling cash. Larger sums, such as hotel bills or airline ticket charges, may be settled by cheques, credit cards or debit cards. Skill is required in ensuring accuracy in all these dealings.

### Selling skills

The prime purpose of many tourism businesses is to sell things. Good selling skills involve establishing rapport with customers, being well informed about products, listening accurately to clients' needs and being persuasive once an appropriate product has been identified.

### Communications skills

Good communication is important in most sectors of the travel and tourism industry and plays a part in most of the other skills identified earlier. Being a good conversationalist is vital in roles such as tour guides, resort representatives or tourist information centre staff. Being able to write clearly and accurately is important in most administrative roles, especially those involving correspondence with customers and other businesses.

# Technological skills

The use of personal computers is widespread in the travel and tourism industry. They are used to generate text, client records and data, marketing information, address lists, graphs, charts, financial accounts, overhead projections, designs and illustrations. They are also used for various kinds of communication, including electronic mail and computer reservations systems.

The most common business uses of computers are for word processing, databases, spreadsheets, desktop publishing and computer-assisted design. Developments in telecommunications are also vital to travel and tourism. Fax, telex, e-mail, the Internet and viewdata services are all in common use in some sectors of the industry.

## Job-specific skills, experience and qualifications

There are some skills that are specialized and that are required in order to carry out particular jobs. For example a driver for a coach company would need to have learnt skills in manoeuvring large and heavy vehicles, a safety officer at a theme park would need to understand the engineering of the mechanical rides, a tour guide with responsibility for incoming overseas visitors would need some knowledge of appropriate foreign languages, and a lifeguard at a tourist beach would need both to be a good swimmer and to have enough first aid knowledge to be able to apply resuscitation techniques.

Clearly these job-specific skills are often important because they relate to the health and safety of tourists. Employers therefore need evidence of these skills. This is shown in the qualifications that job applicants have achieved and through the extent of their previous work experience. Clearly for the more highly technical jobs, such as an aircraft engineer, the qualifications and experience required are also set at a very high level.

## Activities

1 Draw up a list of 20 different jobs available in different sectors of the travel and tourism industry.

 Mark off on a grid whether each of these jobs requires personal, general, technological, job-specific or other skills.

2 Choose *four* contrasting examples from your list and say more precisely what skills holders of these jobs would need (a) when they were first appointed and (b) to be developed over the course of time.

3 Draw up a list of the qualities and skills that you believe you currently possess and indicate whether you think they are highly developed, reasonably developed or fairly basic.

4 Compare your own skills and qualities with those you identified in activity 1. Which of the jobs you listed do you think you would be most suited to and which would you be least suited to?

5 Through your school or college work experience programme, contact *one* individual employed in the travel and tourism industry and ask him or her to describe or write a report of a typical working day. Discuss the range of skills he or she had to use during the various activities described.

# Background

Although the majority of small hotels are privately owned, larger hotels are often owned by large companies. A hotel chain, a group of hotels owned by the same company, has a number of advantages. It is more likely to be able to raise the funds needed to finance developments on prime sites close to major attractions and business areas. It can negotiate reduced rates for food supplies and redecoration. A very important benefit is the ability of the parent company to afford to advertise nationally, using the press and television. It is also more likely to have the funds to be able to invest in computer reservations systems and quality training programmes. The Holiday Inn at Maidenhead/Windsor is part of the Holiday Inn chain and this group of hotels is part of the Bass Group.

There has been a hotel on this site on the edge of Maidenhead since 1968. The first hotel belonged to the Esso group and an Esso petrol station is still located next door to the hotel. During the 1970s the hotel was purchased by the Bass Group and traded as a Crest Hotel. Holiday Inns were acquired by Bass in 1989, at which time the company sold off most of the Crest Hotels, but kept this one in Maidenhead. In 1990 the hotel was rebranded as a Holiday Inn.

One unusual feature of the site is the presence of a thirteenth century manor house, Shoppenhangers Manor (Figure 13.1), within the 18 acres (7 hectares) of grounds that surround the hotel. After the site had been acquired the manor house was first used as a meeting room and restaurant. The restaurant eventually closed and the building is now used as a conference venue. The kitchens are still used to prepare food for delegates attending conferences there.

# Location

The location of a hotel is very important. The hotel overheads remain much the same whether the rooms are full or empty and so it is important to ensure that income flows in at a regular rate. A hotel that is close to a flourishing business area or that is near major tourist attractions has some advantages over one that is in a more remote area.

The Maidenhead/Windsor Holiday Inn is mainly used by business clients during the week. There are a number of computer companies in the area and many of these use the hotel for meetings, conferences, training courses and accommodating business partners and clients.

A hotel serving these business purposes needs to be easy to reach from many different directions. The Maidenhead/Windsor Holiday Inn has the advantage of being very close to where a number of motorways meet. As Figure 13.2 shows, it is a relatively short drive away from the M40, M4, M3, M25 and M1. Maidenhead Station is 1.5 kilometres (1 mile) away, while Heathrow Airport is 26 kilometres (16 miles) by road.

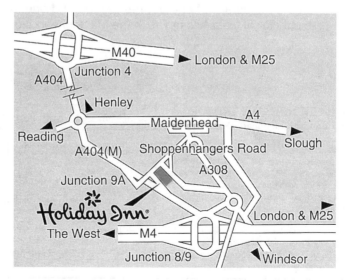

**Fig. 13.1 Shoppenhangers Manor: exterior and the Long Lounge**

**Fig. 13.2 Location of the Maidenhead/Windsor Holiday Inn**

Business use of hotels is very much reduced on Fridays and over weekends. The hotel is able to attract more tourist business at these times because it is near to tourist attractions such as Windsor Castle and Legoland. Ascot Racecourse is 15 kilometres (9 miles) away. There are many pleasant places for walking, for example along the River Thames, at Burnham Beeches or round the National Trust grounds at Cliveden.

# Size

The hotel occupies three floors and contains 189 bedrooms. These are mainly double rooms but an increasing number of weekend family visitors means that requirements may be slightly different then, especially for families with children. A number of rooms now have 'link' beds. These are double beds that can be unzipped to form two separate single beds.

There are 23 meeting rooms, ranging from a small syndicate room for six people to a room capable of accommodating 400.

Although the Holiday Inn Maidenhead/Windsor is mainly a business hotel and is fuller from Monday to Thursday than it is at weekends, its overall occupancy figures compare very favourably with other hotels in the group. Between September 1995 and September 1996 it achieved an occupancy rate of 77% and was one of the three most profitable Holiday Inns in the Europe, Middle East and Africa section of the company.

## Activities

Study Figure 13.3 which appears in the *Holiday Inn Directory of Hotels and Services*.

1 Create the details of one business group and one family group who are planning to stay for at least two nights in the Maidenhead area.

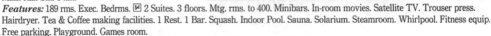

### *U n i t e d   K i n g d o m*

**MAIDENHEAD/WINDSOR**
Manor Lane, Maidenhead, Berks SL6 2RA
Maidenhead (01628) 23444
(01628) 770035                    MDNUK
*Location:* M4, exit junct. 8/9.Take A404(M) M'head West and exit junct. 9A. At mini roundabout turn left, cross bridge and double mini-roundabout. Turn right into hotel by Esso Station. Heathrow Airpt. 26 km. Main Rail Stn. 1 km.
*Features:* 189 rms. Exec. Bedrms. 2 Suites. 3 floors. Mtg. rms. to 400. Minibars. In-room movies. Satellite TV. Trouser press. Hairdryer. Tea & Coffee making facilities. 1 Rest. 1 Bar. Squash. Indoor Pool. Sauna. Solarium. Steamroom. Whirlpool. Fitness equip. Free parking. Playground. Games room.
*Local:* Royal Windsor 8 km. Ascot Racecourse 15 km. Eton College 9 km. Windsor Castle 8 km.
*Rates:* (Pounds Sterling) 1 per. in Std. **122** Tax & Svc. incl.

**Fig. 13.3 Directory entry for the Maidenhead/Windsor Holiday Inn**

2 Discuss the range of questions the organizer of each group might want to ask during the first telephone enquiry to the Holiday Inn Maidenhead/Windsor to find out if it is appropriate for the group's needs.

3 Discuss the range of information that reception staff at the hotel would need to have within reach to enable them to answer these questions quickly and efficiently.

4 Taking turns in the roles of group organizer and receptionist, act out role plays in which the first telephone enquiry is made.

# Category

Hotel chains often put their hotels into different categories and give each group of hotels a different brand name. Holiday Inns, for example, divide their hotels into four different brands: Holiday Inn, Holiday Inn Garden Court, Holiday Inn Crowne Plaza and Holiday Inn Express. Branding helps the company to advertise its hotels without having to describe each location separately. Customers can also expect all the hotels carrying the same brand name to offer a similar range of facilities and services.

The Maidenhead/Windsor Holiday Inn, like all hotels carrying the Holiday Inn brand, offers:

- En suite bedrooms
- A full-service restaurant, bar and lounge
- A swimming pool
- Facilities for meetings of various sizes
- Interactive television, hair-driers, and trouser press in all rooms
- Porterage and 24-hour room service
- Standard rooms and executive rooms with superior furnishings and mini bars

# Facilities and services

The days when hotels consisted just of a place to sleep and a place to eat are long gone. The fact that the Maidenhead/Windsor Holiday Inn is mainly used by business travellers means there is a great demand for services that help them with their work.

Most of the tasks which are carried out in an office can be carried out in the hotel. Typing services can be provided, faxes can be sent and received, and access to computers is available. Individual rooms have modems in them so that customers can use their own portable computers to send electronic mail and faxes. The only practice that is not allowed is for hotel guests to use their own floppy disks in the hotel's computers. This is to prevent viruses from corrupting the company's own computer software.

However, not all business requirements are to do with administration. Meetings, events and conferences often require the setting up of a stage with back projections. These may take up to two days to set up and the event itself may last for less than an hour. Some events, such as book fairs or toy fairs, may need space and furniture to accommodate displays and exhibitions. Sometimes requests are very unusual. For example a Farmers' Association annual dinner dance wanted to exhibit that year's champion cow in the foyer. This was duly arranged and no comment was made on the fact that beef appeared on the menu for the event!

Banqueting is an important part of the services offered by the hotel. Food can be provided for every kind of event from a one to one meeting to large events like weddings or product launches. For conferences, using either the hotel or Shoppenhanger's Manor, inclusive daily rates are offered which include meals and refreshments.

Leisure facilities are an essential part of any hotel catering for business travel and conferences. People who have to spend much of the day sitting in meetings want either relaxation or exercise at the end of their working day. The Maidenhead/Windsor Holiday Inn has a swimming pool (Figure 13.4) with a children's pool, a sauna, a steam room, sun beds, a squash court, a gym area with weights, treadmills and exercise bikes and a snooker and pool room. At weekends, when the clientele includes more tourists, a playroom is opened where parents can take young children to use a variety of toys and games.

Holiday Inns as a group are also developing a video-conferencing facility. This would connect up delegates in a number of different hotels and enable them to conduct meetings and business by means of a video link. The hotels with this facility will include venues as far apart as Edinburgh, Manchester, Birmingham, Leicester, Heathrow and Maidenhead/Windsor. There is clearly a benefit for companies with offices all over the UK because they are able to hold national conferences without everyone having to travel to and stay at one central location.

Another technical facility that has been introduced in the hotel rooms is interactive television. This provides a range of services that can be activated by using the TV in individual rooms. Guests can book wake up calls, view their bills, read messages left for them or their group on-screen, and order room service.

## Activities

Suppose that the Maidenhead/Windsor Holiday Inn has been approached by three clients wishing to use the hotel as a venue for the following events:

*Fig. 13.4  Health and Leisure Club and the Berkshire Suite*

- a three day conference for leaders of European farmers' trade unions to discuss aspects of European Union agricultural policy

- an exhibition and auction of antique furniture

- a banquet to celebrate the centenary of a well-known rugby club

1 List some of the different facilities and services that you think the organizers of these three events might request.

2 What special preparations might the hotel have to make if it agreed to host each of these three events?

3 Select an event or function that you think the hotel might decide it was unable to host. Write a letter to the event organizer explaining why the hotel is unable to help him or her.

# Employees

Running a big hotel is very labour intensive. In other words, compared with other industrial operations, it requires a larger number of employees to make it work successfully. The Holiday Inn Maidenhead/Windsor employs about 125 people, of whom over a hundred are full-time. In addition, further part-time staff are recruited whenever there are large functions or dinners held at the hotel.

The staff in hotels are generally divided up into different departments. The main departments in Holiday Inns are as follows.

## Food and beverage

Hotels often have several food and beverage service areas. These may include a restaurant, bar, room service, banqueting and lounge area serving morning coffee and afternoon tea. As well as being open to hotel residents, the majority of these facilities are also used by non-residents. The reputation of the hotel often depends on the quality of food served and the style and level of service provided.

## Food preparation and cooking

The kitchen will usually be responsible for the preparation of food for a number of service areas, including restaurants, bars, room service and banqueting areas. Hotel kitchens are often split into a number of sections, such as larder, vegetables, pastry and sauce. The type of food to be prepared may vary from specialist cuisine cooked for small numbers to large-scale production for a banquet.

## Accommodation services (housekeeping)

The housekeeping department is very important because it is responsible for the service and preparation of guest bedrooms. The front office department will update housekeeping on a daily basis about the number and type of rooms required. The housekeeping department has to ensure that the right rooms are prepared to agreed Holiday Inn standards and in time for guests to check in to them promptly.

## Conference and banqueting

The conference and banqueting department is responsible for the organization and smooth running of events such as weddings, dinner dances, conferences and exhibitions. They liaise with the client planning the event to see that room set-up, menus, equipment hire and special requirements are provided as requested.

## Human resources

The human resources department has to work out the staffing requirements of all the departments in the hotel. It is responsible for recruiting new staff and then overseeing their training and development so that the hotel is able to meet the company's objectives.

## Sales and marketing

Only larger hotels tend to have a separate sales and marketing department. Its responsibility is to generate new business. The main method of achieving this is by visiting potential clients. It will also attempt to increase the amount of business the hotel receives from existing clients.

## Leisure

Leisure facilities are now standard in most large hotels. Some offer membership to non-residents as well as hotel guests. The leisure department will be responsible for the safe use of leisure facilities and for providing a programme of fitness assessment, activities and classes that meets the needs of people using the facilities.

## Finance

The finance department keeps track of all the revenue taken in different departments of the hotel, checking that every item is charged accurately and that payments are received from clients. It must also ensure that costs such as electricity, stationery and wages are met. The finance department will monitor costs against budgets and revenue reports through the preparation of a profit and loss account.

## Front office

The front office is a key department in a hotel because it is usually the first and last point of contact for all hotel guests. It is therefore a major influence in terms of what impressions of the hotel the guests are given. As well as dealing with the registration of guests on arrival, the front office staff are also responsible for the allocation of bedrooms, the answering of any guest queries, dealing with telephone enquiries, processing payments and the promotion of other hotel facilities.

# The qualities required for hotel work

There are many career routes available within the hotel industry requiring differing levels of experience and qualifications. People generally enter the hotel industry by one of three routes:

- direct from school, joining a Youth Training Programme;
- joining a Youth Training Programme after completing a Further Education course;
- through a graduate management development programme.

The Youth Training Programme may lead to the achievement of a National Vocational Qualification (NVQ).

The qualities needed for any job in a hotel will depend on the particular responsibilities involved. Below are four examples of hotel jobs, showing the work involved, the qualities required and the kind of career progression that is possible.

## Housekeeping department

### The Job: Room Attendant

The primary role of a room attendant is to service guest rooms to a high standard. This involves cleaning and preparing the bedroom and bathroom, replenishing bed linen, towels and complimentary toiletries. In addition the room attendant frequently comes into contact with hotel guests and has to deal with questions about the hotel or the local area.

### The qualities needed

In order to achieve a high standard, a room attendant needs to have a keen eye for detail and be self-motivated as he/she often has to work alone. He/she needs to be well groomed, take pride in his or her work and be physically fit.

### Possible career progression

Room attendants may progress to the position of floor housekeeper in a large hotel, which includes the checking of the rooms, leading on to head housekeeper, which involves taking responsibility for the whole department.

## Front office

### The Job: Receptionist

The receptionist is the focal point for the guest, not only when arriving and departing from the hotel but also when dealing with day-to-day enquiries. The receptionist has to be able to take reservations, allocate bedrooms, deal with telephone enquiries and process payments whether it be cash, credit card or foreign currency, while also promoting other facilities within the hotel.

### The qualities needed

Receptionists need to be friendly, courteous and efficient throughout the shift no matter what is happening around them. They are in the public eye so they need to be able to maintain a high level of grooming, portraying a professional image at all times. Much of the job entails handling cash and recording guest information. It is therefore essential that they possess numeracy and administrative skills.

### Possible career progression

Opportunities include the chance to specialize within a number of front office areas. This may include reservations, switchboard or night audit with the possibility of moving into a supervisory position and ultimately to a front office management role.

## Food and beverage

### The Job: Food & Drink Service

- **Food service** – working in a food outlet may involve a range of different service styles such as plated, silver service or buffet, each requiring specific skills (Figure 13.5).
- **Drink service** – there are many different environments where drinks may be served, such as a cocktail bar, public bar, wine service or banqueting bar and, as with food service, these require different skills.

Whether working in the restaurant, bar or banqueting areas this role involves taking orders, serving food and drink, and clearing tables and service areas. It requires

*Fig. 13.5  Working in a Holiday Inn*

familiarity with all the dishes and drinks available on the menu and an ability to advise the guest using accurate information, as well as a willingness to promote different items. The role often means working under pressure and carrying out several different tasks at the same time, while maintaining a friendly rapport with guests.

### The qualities needed

Food and drink service requires people who are physically active and who have the stamina to work consistently well, often covering split shifts. They must have good grooming standards and excellent interpersonal skills, being polite and efficient at all times.

### Possible career progression

Whichever area of food and drink service is chosen there are opportunities to progress up the ladder from commis waiter/waitress to restaurant supervisor or manager of a food and beverage service area.

## Food preparation and cooking

### The Job: Commis Chef

A chef is a highly skilled and creative person and has often spent many years training. This will probably have meant working around the different sections in the kitchen learning the basic skills before specializing in one area. The range of skills will vary considerably according to the hotel or restaurant. Chefs may be required to prepare anything from French cuisine to the processing of convenience foods.

### The qualities needed

Chefs need to be physically fit as they often have to work long hours. They often have to work to tight deadlines and must be prepared to follow instructions. Working in a kitchen also requires a high degree of teamwork as all the sections are dependent on each other. Imagination and flair are called upon, as well as a genuine interest in food preparation. The training is long and hard and will only suit the dedicated. The rewards can be exceptional as a successful chef can earn very high salary.

### Possible career progression

The prospects for chefs are excellent. Once they have completed their training, depending on their ability, they may be promoted rapidly through the kitchen brigade from Chef de Partie to Sous Chef to Head Chef de Cuisine.

## Activities

Suppose that Holiday Inn had decided to use these four examples as part of a national campaign to try to encourage more people to consider a career in hospitality and catering.

The focus of the campaign is to be a series of posters to be distributed to schools and colleges.

Choose *one* of the four job examples provided on pages 229–231.

1 Sketch the outline of a poster, using this job example, that you think might be effective in achieving the campaign's aim.

2 Write the text that you think should appear on the poster.

3 Discuss the effectiveness of using posters for this purpose, in comparison with other means of trying to get the message across.

# Holiday Inn training programmes

There are two main types of training and career development programmes available to new employees of Holiday Inns: the Youth Training Programme and the Graduate Management Development Programme.

## Youth Training Programme

### Qualifications

Applicants must be aged 16 years or over and must have completed a minimum of five years' secondary education and a week's work experience within the industry.

### Programme

Following an induction to Holiday Inn successful applicants train for a two year period leading towards a National Vocational Qualification (NVQ).

### First year

During this period trainees gain the basic skills within their chosen area. This will be achieved through a combination of on-the-job training, carried out in the workplace, and off-the-job training at the Hospitality Training Foundation or a local college, through day release. On completion of the first year, trainees will have achieved an NVQ Level 1.

### Second Year

Building on the skills acquired in the first year trainees now begin to specialize, developing their own initiative and taking on greater responsibility. On completion of the second year trainees will have acquired an NVQ Level 2.

### Opportunities

Upon successful completion of the programme trainees should be ready to take on positions such as:

- Commis chef
- Restaurant waiter/waitress
- Room service assistant
- Room attendant
- Receptionist

# Graduate Management Development Programme

### Qualifications

Applicants need to have achieved or be working towards an HND, BA or BSc qualification in Hotel and Catering or related subjects. Alternatively, they might have completed a postgraduate conversion course or obtained full HCIMA membership. They must also have gained six months' experience within a service environment. Management trainees must be willing to work in any location that the company thinks appropriate.

### Qualities

Management trainees need to be committed to developing a career in the hotel industry, be physically fit, self-motivated and willing to demonstrate service excellence. They should have excellent interpersonal skills, with an ability to make a positive impact and work effectively within a team. They have to be able to adapt quickly to changing situations and be able to cope effectively within time constraints.

### Programme

Successful applicants undergo 12 months' structured training. One month's training is completed within each of the five principal areas of the hotel, food and beverage, rooms, finance, human resources and sales. For the remaining seven months, applicants develop their supervisory/management skills within specialist areas. Throughout the 12 months' off-the-job training in areas such as interactive skills, finance and management skills is provided.

*Opportunities*

Upon successful completion of the programme management trainees should be ready to take on positions such as:

- Assistant restaurant manager
- Assistant guest services manager (food and beverage)
- Assistant financial controller
- Assistant guest services manager (front office)
- Assistant accommodation services manager (housekeeping)
- Assistant human resources manager
- Assistant conference and banqueting manager

Ability, the size of the hotel and availability of suitable vacancies would influence what kind of first appointment was offered.

# Skills

Apart from the qualities which a personnel Manager recruiting staff to a hotel would be looking for, there are also a number of key skills that need to be developed once people have started in their jobs. Most of these skills are either personal or technical. Some of them are needed in a range of jobs, while others are related to the specific requirements of a particular job.

# Personal skills

The Holiday Inn group assesses personal skills in terms of six critical practices. These are summarised below:

---

*Six critical practices*

**1 Outgoing**

Acting in a friendly, accepting and informal manner with our guests. Take every opportunity to make eye contact, smile and speak to guests and make an individual effort to find out the guest's name and use it.

**2 Customer focus**

Constantly strive to do your best for the customer. Always look for ways to improve your guest service delivery and the opportunity to sell the hotel's products.

**3 Using resources/team player**

Being prepared to ask for and offer assistance to others in similar circumstances in order that the situation is corrected and improve through your team contribution and effort.

**4 Follow through**

If you take on a great issue you should personally see it through to make sure the guest is satisfied in the time promised. If you have to pass it on, you should

---

give details and deadlines to the person concerned and check back, ideally with the guest, to ensure that action has been taken and the guest is satisfied.

**5 Tactical**

In identifying a risk to or opportunity for guest service do not hesitate to take action to resolve the situation – you have authority to do so, even if it is not in your job role.

**6 Structuring**

Demonstrating an organized approach to your work, following proven procedures and systems. Take time to identify and inticipate problems and opportunities before they arise in relation to your job role and take action to resolve them

When applicants are interviewed for jobs with the company they are judged against these critical practices. They are asked questions about how they would react and what they would do in a range of different circumstances. The interviewer is trying to find out things such as whether they are good team players.

# Technical skills

Technical skills can vary from relatively simple tasks, such as the best way to carry plates of food from the kitchen to the table, to much more complex ones, such as repairing the hotel central heating system.

All departments in the Maidenhead/Windsor Holiday Inn now use computers. Reception staff must have keyboard skills and have to be trained to use the computer reservations system. Staff working in sales and marketing departments would need some knowledge of word-processing use.

Some of the skills that relate to specific areas are most obviously needed in the kitchen. Chefs need appropriate technical qualifications, such as NVQs, as well as appropriate previous experience. Staff working in the leisure areas will be required to have some first aid knowledge, as well as qualifications indicating that they can plan and monitor individual fitness programmes.

# Language skills

Being able to speak another language is not a requirement for working in a Holiday Inn, but it is regarded as a useful asset. The demand for this skill will depend on the location of the hotel and the main originating countries of the visitors.

The Holiday Inn group operates in 60 countries and therefore produces marketing materials in a range of languages including English, German, French, Italian, Dutch, Spanish and Portuguese.

## Activity

Study the brochure coupon in Figure 13.6.

Holiday Inn wishes to use this coupon to find out more information about the travel and accommodation habits of the people applying for a brochure. However they wish to keep the size of the coupon as it is in Figure 13.6.

1 Suggest three questions they might wish to ask.

2 Design a way of using the limited space at the bottom of the coupon to find out information that could be of use to Holiday Inn's Marketing Department.

You will need to design your questions in English. Assume there is enough space on the magazine page on which the coupon appears for translations of your questions into the other six languages used.

*Note*
You will probably need to invent some kind of key so that you can collect a range of answers. For example, if your question is 'Is there usually somebody else in your party?' simple Yes or No answers would not be very useful. A key that said A = spouse; B = children under 12; C = children 13-16; D = no would provide more valuable marketing information while taking up no more space on the coupon than the number of the question, the four alternative letters and four boxes to tick.

| |
|---|
| First Name, *Vorname*, Prénom, *Nome*, Voornaam, *Primer*, Nombre: |
| _____ |
| Family Name, *Name*, Nom de Famille, *Cognome*, Familienaam, *Apellidos*, Apelidos: |
| _____ |
| Sex, *Geschlecht*, Sexe, *Sesso*, Geslacht, *Sexo*: <br> Male, *Männlich*, Masculin, *Maschio*, Man, *Varón*, Masculino ❏ <br> Female, *Weiblich*, Féminin, *Femmina*, Vrouw, *Mujer*, Feminino ❏ |
| Address, *Straße*, Adresse, *Indirizzo*, Adres, *Dirección*, Endereço: |
| _____ |
| _____ |
| Town, *Ort*, Ville, *Città*, Woonplaats, *Ciudad*, Cidade: |
| _____ |
| Postal Code, *Postleitzahl*, Code Postal, *Codice Postale*, Postcode, *Código Postal*: |
| _____ |
| Country, *Land*, Pays, *Paese*, Land, *País*: |
| _____ |
| Preferred language, *Bevorzugte Sprache*, Langue préférée, *Lingua preferita*, Voorkeurtaal, *Idioma preferido*, Língua que prefere: <br> English ❏  Français ❏  Deutsch ❏  Italiano ❏ <br> Nederlands ❏  Español ❏  Português ❏ <br> Age, *Alter*, Età, *Leeftijd*, Edad, *Idade*: <br> 18-25 ❏  26-34 ❏  35-44 ❏  45-54 ❏  55+ ❏ |

**Fig. 13.6  Coupon from a Holiday Inn brochure**

# Working conditions

## Hours

Employees at the Maidenhead/Windsor Holiday Inn do a basic 40-hour week, mostly completed in eight-hour shifts. Some parts of a hotel, particularly the kitchen, require staff to be working at busy times of the day and so split shifts are needed. If the staff who prepared breakfast worked a straight eight-hour shift they would be finished by early afternoon and there would not be enough staff to prepare evening meals. Some employees, especially in the Housekeeping Department are employed on a part-time basis.

Ensuring that there are always adequate numbers of staff available in each department can be a complicated task in a big hotel. It is not simply a matter of asking people to do more hours when the hotel is busy. The European Union Working Time Directive says that employees cannot work an average of more than 48 hours a week over any four month period and that there must be at least an 11-hour gap between consecutive working shifts.

## Benefits

Holiday Inns provides a number of benefits to employees. Some of these, such as holidays and pensions, are standard but others, such as discounts on stays in Holiday Inns and free weekends in company hotels for each five years' of service, are particular to the company. Employees are also provided with membership of the Hospital Saturday Fund which gives them a number of refunds for common medical bills such as eye tests and some dental treatment.

## Advantages and drawbacks of hotel work

### Advantages

Hotels are generally warm, comfortable environments to work in. Most hotel employees will meet different people during the course of the day. Many tasks, for example preparing bedrooms or serving food, involve a finished product so that employees can get satisfaction from seeing the results of their work. Generally the workforce is young. The average age of employees at the Maidenhead/Windsor Holiday Inn is about 22. Because of this it is often possible for those with the right qualities and skills to gain promotion quite rapidly.

### Drawbacks

The main drawbacks of hotel work are that it does generally involve some evening work. The work load is not always evenly distributed over a shift. There are likely to be times, such as after breakfast at reception, when things are busy and staff have to work under pressure. There may be other times of day when things are much quieter.

## Activities

If you applied for a job with Holiday Inn, you would first have to fill in an application form (Figure 13.7).

1 Choose a type of job from this case study and, using a photocopy of page 238, fill in the two sections of the application form.

2 Compare the different answers provided by your group and discuss how you think a Personnel Officer might choose which of you to interview.

# M A I D E N H E A D · W I N D S O R

MANOR LANE · MAIDENHEAD · BERKSHIRE · SL6 2RA · TEL 01628 23444 · FAX 01628 770035

## APPLICATION FORM

### PLEASE COMPLETE THIS APPLICATION IN INK

| Position applied for: | Date of application: |
|---|---|

Other positions you would consider:

Employment status: ☐ Full-Time ☐ Part-Time ☐ Temporary ☐ Casual Work

Source of application

### PERSONAL DETAILS

| Surname: | Forename(s): |
|---|---|

Address:

| Telephone no: Work: | Home: |
|---|---|
| National Insurance number: | Date of Birth: |

### GENERAL INFORMATION

| Minimum salary acceptable: | Date available to start: |
|---|---|
| Do you have a valid work permit? ☐ Yes ☐ No | Nationality: |

Have you been convicted of any criminal offences which are not yet spent under the Rehabilitation of Offenders Act 1974?

If yes, please explain: ☐ Yes ☐ No

| Do you hold a current driving licence? | ☐ Yes ☐ No |
|---|---|
| Do you write or speak any other languages? If so please explain: | ☐ Yes ☐ No |

Hobbies and interests:

Please give any other facts which you feel would be useful in considering this job application:

**Fig. 13.7 Application form**

# History and background

Lilleshall Hall (Figure 14.1) was was built and the grounds laid out for the Duke of Sutherland in 1831. It was purchased by Mr Herbert Ford in the early twentieth century and turned into a tourist attraction with pleasure gardens and a narrow gauge railway.

In 1951 the Hall was opened as a National Recreation Centre. Alterations were made to create accommodation for 100 residents, 10 acres (4 hectares) of the grounds were converted into playing fields and an indoor training area was created by roofing and re-flooring the former stable yard.

The England football team used the facility prior to winning the World Cup in 1966. After that a major rebuilding programme began and was finally completed in 1980. It included accommodation for 76 in Kent Hall and conference and seminar rooms, a lecture theatre, and leisure facilities in the Queen Elizabeth Hall. This building also housed the International Sports Medicine Institute and the Human Performance Centre. Further facilities added were:

- **King George VI Hall and Princess Royal Hall** – provide gymnastic training facilities used by national teams; also house weight training rooms.
- **Ford Hall** – is equipped for table tennis, archery, dance and martial arts; conference, seminar rooms and bar facilities enable functions to use the Hall.

*Fig. 14.1 Lilleshall Hall*

- **Wenlock Hall** – is specially for five-a-side, basketball, volleyball and indoor hockey; also extensively used by the local community for other sports e.g. tennis, badminton
- **Sutherland Hall** – has facilities for archery, cricket and indoor bowls; also has an associated conference room.

Nowadays 230 residents can be accommodated at Lilleshall. The centre is also fully equipped for conferences and presentations.

Not all the facilities at Lilleshall are indoors. Outdoor facilities include: extensive playing fields, part of which is lit for winter training, floodlit hard tennis courts, grass tennis courts, a flatgreen bowls lawn, an orienteering course and a floodlit Astroturf pitch for football and hockey.

## Activities

1 Choose *three* sports that as far as you know do not have a National Centre. This could be because they are minority sports or because they are new sports, because they have been introduced from another country. Discuss the ways in which the people who play and administer these sports might try to promote them more widely.

2 List what you think would be the essential requirements if the governing bodies of each of these sports decided to investigate the feasibility of setting up a National Centre.

3 Discuss the advantages and disadvantages for participants in a particular sport of having a National Centre.

# Setting objectives for employees

The management of Lilleshall is in the hands of Lilleshall Sports and Conference Centre Limited. This team, which included many staff originally employed by the Centre, made a successful bid to manage it when the contract was put out to tender for a five year period starting in 1991.

The objectives of the team were set out in a **mission statement**. This is an important statement for all employees at Lilleshall because it explains what everyone working there should be trying to achieve.

Lilleshall Sports and Conference Centre's mission statement is:

- To maintain Lilleshall's position as the 'flagship' of the Sports Council National Sports Centres in the most cost-effective way
- To develop the excellence partnerships with the Governing Bodies of sport and the Home Office by improving service levels
- To maintain and develop open regional and local use of the Centre
- To develop staff motivation and awareness at all levels by focusing attention on the customer needs and quality of service through incentives and training

- To develop jointly with the English Sports Council quality facilities, hotel accommodation and services throughout the Centre
- To provide a happy and safe working environment for visitors and staff
- To achieve an extension to the initial contract at the end of the five year period
- To provide a sound return on capital investment

## Activities

1 A 'flagship', just like the ship that carried the Admiral of the fleet and flew his flag, is something regarded as the leader of a group and one that should set an example to the others.

Discuss what advantages and disadvantages there might be for Lilleshall in being regarded as the 'flagship' of the various National Sports Centres.

2 Explain what is meant by 'the development of excellence'. What activities might this involve for the governing body of one of the sports that uses Lilleshall?

3 Discuss some of the factors that you think might decide whether or not Lilleshall Sports and Conference Centre Limited is awarded an extension of its five year management agreement.

Which of these factors do you think will be most important and why?

# Structure of the organization

Lilleshall Sports and Conference Centre Limited has a Chief Executive who is responsible to a Board of Directors for the overall management of the Centre. His duties include:

- Overall financial control
- Client liaison
- Implementing the marketing strategy

The company is divided into four units headed by: the Chief Executive, the Finance and Administration Manager, the Operations Manager, and the Hotel Manager. The main working roles within each of these units are shown on the staff structure chart in Figure 14.2.

Each unit within the company has a number of different tasks to perform. For example:

- The **Chief Executive's Office** takes care of marketing, taking bookings, programming the use of the Centre, and liaising with the governing body.
- The **Finance and Administration Unit** controls budgets, looks after computer systems, administers reception and security, oversees personnel matters and manages invoicing and credit control.

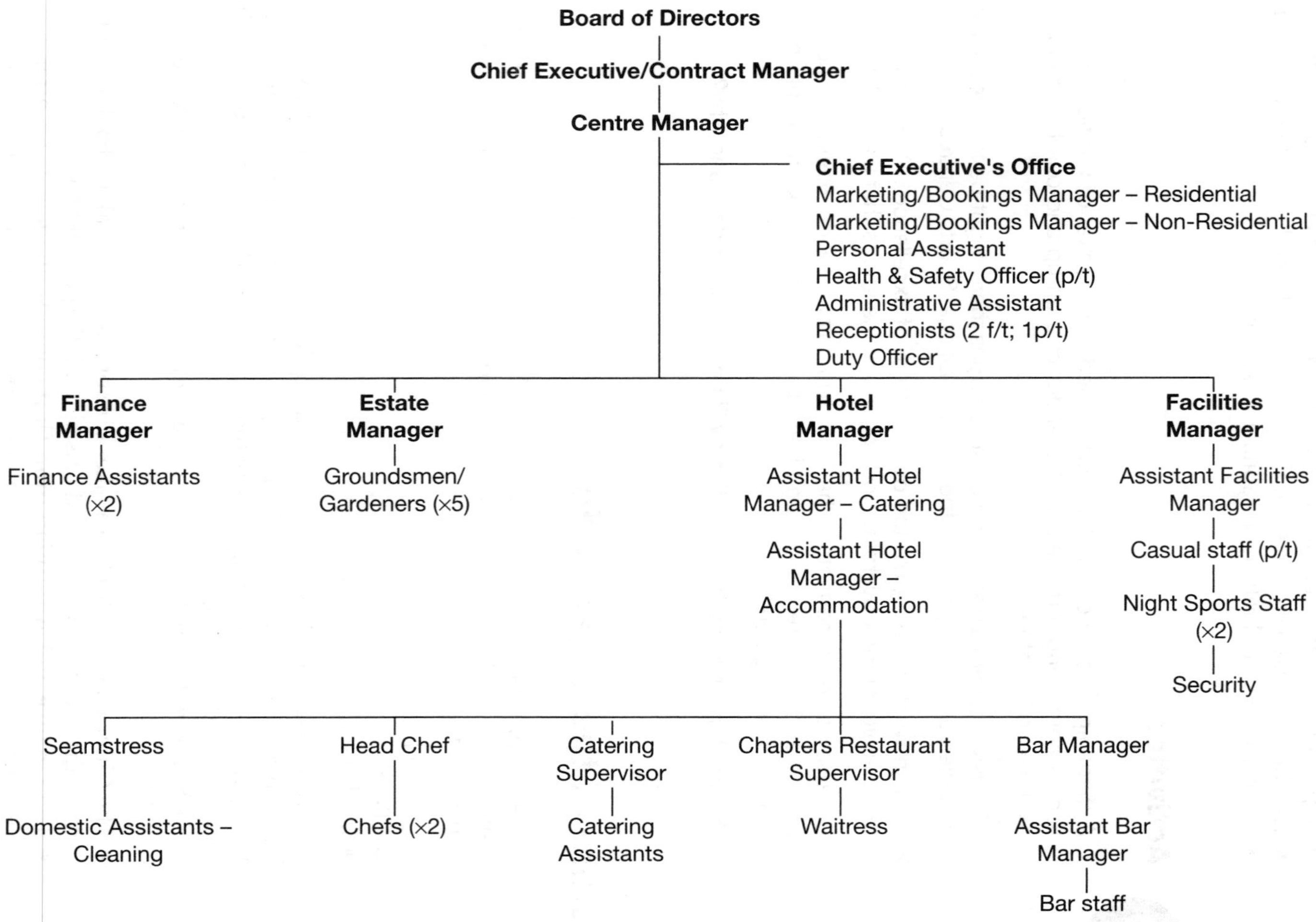

**Board of Directors**

**Chief Executive/Contract Manager**

**Centre Manager**

**Finance Manager**
- Finance Assistants (×2)

**Estate Manager**
- Groundsmen/Gardeners (×5)

**Chief Executive's Office**
- Marketing/Bookings Manager – Residential
- Marketing/Bookings Manager – Non-Residential
- Personal Assistant
- Health & Safety Officer (p/t)
- Administrative Assistant
- Receptionists (2 f/t; 1p/t)
- Duty Officer

**Hotel Manager**
- Assistant Hotel Manager – Catering
- Assistant Hotel Manager – Accommodation

**Facilities Manager**
- Assistant Facilities Manager
- Casual staff (p/t)
- Night Sports Staff (×2)
- Security

Seamstress

Head Chef
- Chefs (×2)

Domestic Assistants – Cleaning

Catering Supervisor
- Catering Assistants

Chapters Restaurant Supervisor
- Waitress

Bar Manager
- Assistant Bar Manager
- Bar staff

*Fig. 14.2  Lilleshall staff structure chart*

- The **Operations Unit** is responsible for maintenance of indoor facilities, health and safety procedures, maintenance of the gardens and outdoor sports facilities and the allocation of staffing in all these areas.
- The **Hotel Unit** looks after catering, bar services, shops and vending machines, and the provision of cleaning services.

# Selected working roles at Lilleshall

As a large indoor and outdoor centre catering for a wide range of sports, and with accommodation, catering and conference facilities on site, Lilleshall offers a wide range of employment opportunities. Some of these require very general skills, such as an ability to work in a team, but others, such as sports coaches (Figure 14.3), may require considerable experience and specialized skill. Some of the people working at Lilleshall will be employed by Lilleshall Sports and Conference Centre Limited but others, such as the sports coaches, may be employed by national and regional sports organizations that use the facilities.

Some of the responsibilities of individual staff at Lilleshall are as follows.

## Receptionists

There are always two receptionists on duty every day from 8 am to 9 pm. This means receptionists have to be willing to work late and at weekends.

The job requires them to work with customers, answer the telephone and operate the computer reservations system. They have to understand both accommodation and leisure facility booking systems. They may also be required to help with shop sales of sports goods.

Many receptionists at Lilleshall are school-leavers who are trained in-house alongside day-release NVQ training.

***Fig. 14.3 An indoor training session***

# Coaches

Lilleshall Sports and Conference Centre Limited does not employ coaches.

Organizations hiring facilities at Lilleshall must supply appropriately qualified coaches. Governing bodies of sports at a national level bring squads to Lilleshall with highly qualified and experienced top coaches.

Many coaching activities, for example step aerobics, are now subject to NVQ certification.

# 'Facilities men'

A range of staff are employed, sometimes on a part-time basis, to set up and service sports activities which require equipment and maintenance of playing areas. These include: badminton, table tennis, archery, indoor and outdoor hockey and five-a-side football. They are also responsible for the cleaning and maintainance of squash courts and snooker tables.

'Facilities men' are required to use the CRS system for bookings.

Cleaning after the facilities have been used in the evenings means some late working is required.

# Estates team

The Estates team has to keep the extensive grounds in good order. This involves tasks like mowing the grass, taking care of trees and shrubs and ensuring the estate looks clean and tidy.

They are also responsible for the preparation of pitches.

# Accommodation staff

The Hotel Manager and his/her assistant are responsible for 200 bed spaces on the site in several different accommodation blocks. This includes overseeing the work of 40 cleaners. Such things as tea and coffee-making facilities have to be checked before rooms are occupied.

Accommodation staff must be willing to work at weekends as these are the times of highest room occupancy because of coaching courses and conferences.

# Catering staff

Catering at Lilleshall is provided by Lilleshall Sports and Conference Centre Limited and managed by the Hotel Manager. The restaurant on site caters for residents, people attending conferences, community users of the Centre and for private parties and functions.

All food served in the dining room must conform to British Olympic Association healthy eating requirements.

Because some periods of the week are quieter than others, temporary and casual staff are employed to cover busier periods. All catering staff have to be willing to work some evenings.

Permanent staff receive in-house and NVQ training.

## Activities

1 What sort of job, if any, at Lilleshall do you think each of the following would be most suited to:

(a) Mike Asher, aged 23, fond of the open air, fit, plays in a band and so is not keen to work evenings.

(b) Eva Sharpe, aged 46, wants part-time job, willing to work weekends and evenings, only previous work experience serving in a department store.

(c) Carmen Gabriel, aged 30, History graduate, has worked and travelled in South America for past seven years, wants an active job that involves meeting people.

(d) Sanjay Joshi, aged 18, school leaver with Advanced GNVQ Leisure and Tourism, keen to acquire range of leisure experience, would eventually like a management role.

(e) Anita McMillan, aged 23, county hockey player, no coaching qualifications, currently working in local authority office in a clerical job, fancies a change.

(f) Don Buttivant, aged 59, retired accountant, looking for a part-time job that is not too strenuous, not keen to work at weekends

2 What reasons would you give for inviting them or turning them down for a job interview at Lilleshall?

# Skills

## Personal skills

Many jobs in leisure and tourism require well-developed personal skills. Talking to someone on the telephone, trying to teach someone to improve a sporting technique, or serving them a meal, requires the ability to make them feel they are being treated well. At a centre such as Lilleshall if the quality of service is not good, fewer people will use it and the task of meeting its financial objectives will become much more difficult.

Some of the most important personal qualities needed to work at Lilleshall are:

- **Reliability**, because the Centre is a seven-day-a-week operation
- **Flexibility**, because there is a significant amount of evening work and some staff are required to work different hours at different times of the year

- **Honesty**, because there are often personal belongings about in changing areas and bedrooms
- **Smartness**, because appearance and the wearing of uniforms and name badges helps to meet customer expectations about staff manner and efficiency

## Technological skills

Information technology is vital to the administration of Lilleshall. In addition to the **computer reservations system**, separate **databases** for residential and non-residential uses of the Centre are kept. Databases, with their accurate records of customers' use of the Centre, are an important marketing tool in encouraging more varied and extensive use by existing customers. **Spreadsheets** are used for accounts. Menus and publicity information are produced in-house using **desktop publishing** software (Figure 14.4).

The computerized booking system is used to provide regular reports for the Sports Council. These enable the performance of the Centre to be carefully monitored and give early indications of any trends that show changes in the patterns of use.

Clearly for some jobs at Lilleshall, some information technology experience is essential. It is a policy at the Centre to provide existing staff with opportunities to develop their IT skills as part of an Investors in People training programme.

## Job-specific skills

The kind of skills that relate to particular jobs at Lilleshall can be divided into three types:

- **Technical skills** are an essential part of facilities management. The maintenance of a range of equipment and systems on a large, complex site requires technical knowledge and expertise. Other roles, such as sports coaches or chefs, require technical qualifications and sufficient experience to be able to carry out the responsibilities effectively and safely.
- **Linguistic skills** are not required by all employees but because Lilleshall is a national centre it does receive frequent foreign visitors. Coaches and performers from overseas also attend courses and conferences at Lilleshall. In this environment people with foreign language skills can help to provide a more satisfactory experience for visitors from other countries.
- **Physical skills** are important in many job roles at Lilleshall, not just the coaching ones. Members of the estate team and the 'facilities men' need to be fit and to observe safe practices in carrying and moving heavy objects. The 'facilities men' in particular need to be observant and to have good co-ordination.

# Sporting Chance Cafe

## Menu

### Wednesday June 24th

Starters

Soup of the day
or
Prawn Cocktail

Main courses

Roast beef & Yorkshire pudding
or
Haddock and chips

Desserts

Ice Cream

*Fig. 14.4 Menu produced in-house using desk-top publishing software*

*A key role at Lilleshall is held by:*

**Lee Moore** – **Centre Manager** (new position from November 1996)

| | |
|---|---|
| *A Levels:* | Law, Economics and History |
| | County representation at football and athletics |
| *Degree:* | BA Combined Honours at University of Liverpool, Chester College |
| | MSc Sport and Recreational Management at Sheffield University |
| | Summer holiday jobs as Playleader and Lifeguard plus other 'business'-related work placements |
| *Previous employment:* | Deputy Manager – Much Wenlock Sports Centre (joint use with school) Shropshire County Council (commenced work June 1991) |
| | Acting Manager (April – November 1993) |
| | Manager from December 1993 to starting at Lilleshall |

'As Deputy Manager I was involved in the routine operations in the centre such as filling vending machines and setting up badminton nets as well as the strategic management of the centre.'

'The various holiday jobs I took on gave me valuable experience for the work I am involved with now.'

# Job description for the post of Centre Manager

An idea of the activities which the Centre Manager is required to carry out can be gained from the job description below:

---

*1. Description of the Post*

The person appointed will be employed in the service of Lilleshall Sports and Conference Centre Limited and will report directly to the Chief Executive/Contract Manager.

The postholder will be responsible for the operational management of the Centre, preparation of statistical information, personnel management and for the maintenance of the Quality Management System, in accordance with a contract specification.

The post is full time and a flexible approach to hours worked is essential to meet the demands of the Centre which is residential and open 52 weeks of the year.

The postholder will be required to deputize for the Chief Executive in his absence which will involve temporary residence on site.

*2. Duties*

- Operational control of Centre and internal communications
- To have a full working knowledge of the contract specification
- Responsible for the Company's information technology systems
- Preparation of statistical information
- Training/personnel management
- Maintenance of quality systems and records

*3. General*

The postholder will be required to enforce the Centre's Health and Safety Policy Statement as it affects the post and others and to report any defects, accidents, etc. to the Health and Safety Officer.

He/she will be expected to participate in training programmes as directed by the Chief Executive. All Staff are expected to assist and make welcome visitors and users of the Centre.

---

## Activities

1 Study the description of the post of Centre Manager and the duties it involves.

 Make a list of the skills that you think would be required in order to cope with all aspects of the job effectively.

2 If you were selecting suitable candidates for the post, which of these skills would you give most weight to and which would be less important?

3 Suggest ways of checking whether candidates possessed each of the skills you have identified.

# British Airways – working for an airline

## Company aims and objectives

British Airways is a very large company. It operates flights carrying more than 32 million passengers a year, visiting 174 destinations in 83 different countries. The company's mission statement, which expresses its main aim for the future, is:

To be the best and most successful company in the airline business.

In order to achieve, this British Airways has identified a number of separate goals. These cover all the areas in which the company thinks it needs to show excellence in order to maintain and improve on its present strong position in the highly competitive airline industry.

British Airways' seven main goals are:

- **Safe and secure** – to be a safe and secure airline
- **Financially strong** – to deliver a strong and consistent financial performance
- **Global leader** – to secure a leading share of air travel business world-wide with a significant presence in all major markets
- **Service and value** – to provide overall superior service and good value for money in every market segment in which BA competes
- **Customer driven** – to excel in anticipating and quickly responding to customer needs and competitor activity
- **Good employer** – to sustain a working environment that attracts, retains and develops committed employees who share in the success of the company
- **Good neighbour** – to be a good neighbour, concerned for the community and the environment

## A profile of British Airways employees

### Some key facts

- British Airways employed over 44,000 people in the UK and 7,000 overseas in the year ending in March 1996. Of these, 18,600 work in customer service areas, with air cabin crew accounting for 10,500 of them. Over 3,000 of British Airways' employees are pilots.
- Over 90% of those who work for the airline are on permanent full-time contracts, with approximately 3,000 people being on part-time contracts.
- Heathrow is the most important location for British Airways operations. Over 31,000 British Airways employees are based there. Approximately half of the

remainder work at Gatwick; the others are based either in other parts of the UK or else overseas.

- Half of British Airways UK employees have worked for the company for ten years or more. The airline employs very few people below the age of 20, but the age profile of its employees in the UK suggests a fairly even spread across all groups:

| Age range | 15–19 | 20–24 | 25–29 | 30–34 | 35–39 | 40–44 | 45–49 | 50–54 | 55-59 | 60+ |
|---|---|---|---|---|---|---|---|---|---|---|
| No of UK employees | 132 | 2,743 | 7,007 | 8,369 | 6,435 | 5,664 | 5,955 | 4,594 | 2,474 | 1,233 |

- The average age of the entire British Airways workforce in the UK works out at 42 for men and 35 for women.
- Of all British Airways employees in the UK 63% are male; 37% female. However these proportions vary considerably in different areas of the company's operations. For example, 98% of the pilots are male; 69% of the air cabin crew are female.

## Activities

Study the British Airways advertisement for permanent full-time telephone sales agents (Figure 15.1).

PERMANENT FULL-TIME
TELEPHONE SALES AGENTS

Even when their minds are concentrated on the Big Night, they still need their travel and accommodation arrangements to work in total harmony. Which is why the British Airways Telephone Sales Team is always here to help companies in the travel trade: ensuring the most comprehensive and efficient customer service is always provided.

That's the great thing about joining the British Airways team in Manchester. You're actually helping travel industry specialists and their customers by offering genuine customer care - using the industry's most advanced reservation system to provide a professional service, solve any queries and, in short, give customers the support and advice they need.

Not surprisingly, it's a very successful service, which is why we are now looking for more people, with or without experience, to join the team in our superb Manchester Telephone Sales Centre. It's a bright, lively environment, currently operating between 7.30am and 9.15pm, although you'll need to be willing and able to adapt to a flexible working pattern.

If you're 18+, enthusiastic - and dedicated to offering the very best customer service - this is the chance to make the most of your GCSE education and good telephone voice.

For an application form and more information, please call preferably between 5.00pm and 7.00pm on Thursday 15th and Friday 16th June.

They were demanding customers.
You performed brilliantly.

**BRITISH AIRWAYS**
The world's favourite airline

***Fig. 15.1 British Airways advertisement***

1 Discuss what impressions of British Airways as a company you get from this advertisement.

Some of the things you might consider are:

- What ideas and impressions you get from studying the photograph
- Why the advertisement places great emphasis on customer service
- What the key words are in the text of the advertisement
- What the advertisement suggests about working conditions for telephone sales agents

2 List the requirements applicants would probably have to meet before they would be considered for the position of telephone sales agent.

3 List the personal qualities that you think British Airways would expect to find in successful applicants for the advertised positions.

4 Suggest a range of ways in which British Airways could find out whether applicants possess the personal qualities you identified in (3).

## British Airways and equal opportunities

One of British Airways' main objectives is to be 'the first truly global airline'. Achieving this means the company will operate in many different countries and deal with people from many different cultures. This is one reason why British Airways places considerable emphasis on equal opportunities (Figure 15.2). What equal opportunities actually means is clearly set out for existing and potential employees:

*Fig. 15.2 Equal opportunities at British Airways*

Equality is about...

   ...showing the same respect to everyone we encounter in our work – whether customers, colleagues, job applicants, or people in the local community;
   ...accepting and valuing the contribution of individuals;
   ...enabling all employees to reach their full potential.

Equality is **not** about...

   ...giving any group more favourable treatment than others;
   ...reinforcing stereotypes;
   ...making token gestures.

## What can be done to achieve equality?

Most people agree that some sections of the population appear to do less well in applying for jobs, in levels of earnings and in achievement of promotion, than others. It is not difficult to write an equal opportunities policy that agrees this is unsatisfactory and that something should be done about it. What is harder to achieve is to set up activities that actually improve the opportunities for groups that often experience disadvantage in employment terms.

Here are some approaches introduced by British Airways:

- The establishment of the British Airways nursery
- The introduction of flexible working hours
- The support for job-share arrangements
- The inclusion of equal opportunities issues in training programmes
- The setting of targets for the percentages of all employees and of management who are women or ethnic groups
- The provision of work placements for students with disabilities

## Activities

1 Make a list of groups that you think may experience some disadvantages in employment terms.

2 Choose three different working environments from the leisure and tourism industries.

Suggest some appropriate activities that could be offered in each of these work-places that would improve the opportunities of the groups you listed in (1).

# The range of employment opportunities in an airline

Table 15.1 gives nine outlines of job descriptions. These represent just a small sample of the types of work carried out by British Airways employees:

**Table 15.1**

| | |
|---|---|
| ● **Dispatcher** | The person doing this job is often called a 'red cap' in British Airways because he or she wears a distinctive red hat. The role is very important since each flight has just one dispatcher who monitors every part of the loading and preparation of the aeroplane – cargo, food, passengers and crew. He or she keeps in touch with every team and gives the final approval for the aeroplane to leave. |
| ● **Apprentice Engineer** | While training to become a fully qualified engineer, an apprentice checks all the major moving parts on an aircraft, makes component changes and modifications on the ground and takes part in overhauling the components in the workshops. He/she may be part of the team that makes daily inspections and tests on aircraft to make sure they are safe to fly. There is a block release programme at college to provide the theoretical side of the training. |
| ● **Customer Service Agent** | Customer service agents represent the airline to the public. Their role involves looking after passengers at the airport terminals. They have to greet customers of many different nationalities, check them in by computer, make security checks, answer queries at the service desks, assist the boarding of flights and meeting arrivals. Shift work is required since the airport operates 24 hours a day. |
| ● **Field Sales Manager** | The manager of the field sales force is based in one of the British Airways regions and is responsible for managing, motivating and organizing the sales-force team. This team wins and retains corporate customers and builds long-term relationships with them. The job involves developing a strategy to meet sales targets for the whole team. |
| ● **Supervisor, Food Assembly** | This post involves ensuring that meal trays for airline passengers are available at the correct time and are supplied to the correct standard and quality. It means making checks on the quality of raw materials and of completed trays, and making sure that food trays are correctly labelled and that specially ordered food is available. It also involves preparing staff rosters and generally supervising staff. |
| ● **Pilot** | Pilots are members of the flight crew. These are the men and women who fly the aircraft and have to have the operational skill and the technical expertise necessary to take the aeroplane safely from take-off to landing. Flight crew also need the leadership qualities and concern for customer care required to make sure that customers will continue to choose to fly with British Airways. |
| | One way in which pilots are recruited is through the British Airways Cadet Pilot Scheme, which takes young men and women after 'A' levels and, subject to them proving themselves suitable, trains them in all the skills and knowledge required to earn a Commercial Pilot's Licence. |

*Table 15.1 Continued*

| | |
|---|---|
| ● **Ramp Agent** | This position involves a variety of tasks including loading cargo, mail and baggage and handling passenger baggage in the terminals used by British Airways. The baggage and freight have to be correctly and quickly loaded on to outgoing aircraft, and unloaded from arriving planes, to be delivered to the terminal buildings. Ramp agents also drive the specialized vehicles which push back the aircraft from the departure gates and they are responsible for de-icing the aeroplanes. |
| ● **Cabin Crew** | Members of the cabin crew look after customers in flight and their prime responsibility is for the safety of the passengers. As well as serving meals, duty-free goods and drinks, they are trained to deal with any circumstances, common or unexpected, that can arise. The post requires a working knowledge of a second language, self-confidence, an unflappable nature and a warm personality. Cabin crew recruited by British Airways must also have a minimum of six months' customer service experience. |
| ● **Telephone Sales Staff** | This post involves selling British Airways' services, either via travel agents or direct to the public, over the telephone. It is necessary for people doing this job to know everything about British Airways' products, to be familiar with airline geography and to have an excellent telephone manner. The calls are many and varied and each sales-person may have to handle up to 100 calls a day. |

# What does it take to become an airline employee?

There are some qualities that an airline would expect all its staff to possess – for example, honesty, enthusiasm, pride in appearance and good timekeeping. However, some job roles are much more specialized than others and require a high level of technical skill. Others are mainly concerned with dealing with the public, and so demand an ability to establish good relationships with people quickly. The four examples that follow – airline pilot, customer service agent, air cabin crew and telephone sales staff – show some of the skills and qualities that are expected in specific job roles.

# Airline pilots

Anyone wishing to join British Airways as a trainee pilot will have to apply for the British Airways **Cadet Pilot Scheme.** This is a very intensive programme which enables successful recruits to qualify for a Commercial Pilot's Licence in 70 weeks.

# The role of the pilot

The operation of modern aircraft is very dependent on computers. This means pilots spend far less time 'flying' their aircraft in the traditional sense. Instead they concentrate on managing flights in the most efficient way, using computers to control and monitor the aircraft's progress.

However this does not mean that the pilot has nothing to do! Captains and co-pilots still make the vital command decisions required to guarantee the most important part of their role – the safe operation of their arcraft. They must still be experts in flight planning and they must still have all the flying skills required to 'go manual' should the need arise (Figure 15.3).

The crew has many tasks to complete during the flight. Continual checks have to be made on the aircraft's technical performance, fuel load and position – as well as on outside factors such as weather conditions and air traffic. Contact with the ground must be maintained so that they can react appropriately to information about changing conditions or circumstances during the flight.

## The qualities needed

It is vital that pilots are able to keep a cool head under pressure. They must also be able to organize a complex workload with ever-changing priorities. Concentration has to be maintained, despite frequent interruptions and requests. Even during periods of a flight when things are fairly quiet it is vital that pilots are ready to react quickly and accurately.

The pilot also shares the responsibility for delivering a high standard of customer service during the flight. Competition means that it is essential for British Airways to provide first rate service at the lowest possible price. Customer safety is the first-priority but pilots also have a responsibility to see that their own flights run as efficiently as possible and do not waste fuel or time. When planes are not flying, pilots

*Fig. 15.3 Pilot at the controls of a modern passenger aircarft*

negotiate with engineering teams to make sure that all necessary work is done efficiently and safely without unnecessarily increasing the amount of time aircraft spend on the ground. During flights they keep passengers up to date with flight progress, pointing out places of interest and responding, where possible, to special requests such as flight deck visits.

These roles have a direct effect on the sort of qualities British Airways is looking for in future pilots. Communications skills, business awareness, team spirit and organizational ability are now just as important as the technical knowledge, physical fitness and leadership skills they have always looked for.

## Working conditions

Flying an aeroplane is a demanding job and pilots need both stamina and physical fitness. Different time zones, climates and cultures mean pilots have to be able to adapt well to different conditions. They have to be able to work in a cramped space and often have only 12 hours' rest between flight duties.

There are two basic working patterns open to British Airways pilots:

- **Short haul flights** (where most new pilots begin) entailing a number of round trips to domestic or European destinations. In some cases, this will mean returning to home base at the end of the working day. Each week-long block of work tends to be followed by two to three days off.
- **Long haul** provides an alternative for more experienced pilots – flying larger aircraft to destinations world-wide. These trips can last ten days or more and involve stopovers. These assignments may be followed by two to three days off.

## Pilot training

Not anyone can become a pilot. Even getting selected to train depends on a number of minimum requirements. British Airways insists all candidates must:

- Possess qualifications up to 'A' level
- Successfully complete a number of aptitude tests
- Undertake an interview and some group activities
- Pass medical examinations approved by the Civil Aviation Authority (CAA)

British Airways Cadet Pilots train full time over a 70-week period. The programme combines flight training with academic study, theoretical instruction and private study. Cadets have to sit tests and examinations at regular intervals throughout their training. Those who complete it successfully earn their Commercial Pilot's Licence – the basic qualification needed to transport passengers for gain.

During their training cadets first have to study basic aviation theory and practice. This covers a wide range of topics – from aerodynamics, meteorology and engineering principles to navigation, radio operation and the rules of the air. Only then does flight training begin.

Successful students are accompanied by an instructor on a light, single-engined, two-seat trainer, developing the skills needed to reach the first milestone: flying solo and attaining the CAA Private Pilot's Licence. During the weeks that follow, much time is spent flying on progressively longer trips and practising the many tasks involved in planning and managing flights, whatever the aircraft. Fellow cadets also fly together as Pilot and Co-pilot, learning how to cooperate as part of a flight deck crew.

Having mastered light aircraft, cadets then progress to much larger, twin engined aircraft, with their sophisticated systems and more demanding characteristics. Training in instrument flying begins, teaching cadets to fly without reference to the environment outside.

After much study and practice, cadets commence flying in controlled airspace, joining normal commercial air traffic and flying into major airports. It is then time to sit the CAA Instrument Rating exam which must be passed to earn a Commercial Pilot's Licence.

Finally flight simulators are used to practise on larger jet aircraft from the British Airways fleet. Training ends with final exams and general flying tests and the award of a Commercial Pilot's Licence.

However, training does not end here. British Airways pilots are also trained in team building, time management, customer service and general business awareness. Flight simulators continue to be used to refresh and develop pilots' skills and knowledge.

## Career development

Successful graduates of the British Airways Cadet Pilot Scheme normally begin as co-pilots, flying twin-engined aircraft such as the ATP, Boeing 737 or 757 to short haul destinations throughout the UK and Europe. This usually entails five or six round trips per week, enabling a rapid development of experience within some of the world's busiest air corridors and airports.

Later on, pilots may become eligible to fly long haul routes on larger aircraft, including the latest Boeing 777s and 747-400s. Some may choose to remain on smaller aircraft, flying short haul routes, if this is where the company needs them. Short haul involves much less time away from home, which may become particularly important if, for instance, a pilot has a young family.

Those with considerable experience may go on to achieve the rank of Captain, taking charge of their own aircraft.

## Activities

Read the article below about working as an airline pilot:

I enjoy my job but there is more stress than you'd think. You're responsible for the safety of a lot of people. The hours can mean that you don't get to see your family as much as you'd like. You have to be able to cope with constant changes of climate and time zones too. Every six months there are flying and medical tests and, if you don't pass those, you may be out of a job. Every time you fly a new type of aircraft you have to take more tests to prove your competence.

Now that I'm on long haul flights I do get a few days' break in some interesting places, but often you just want some rest. Sight-seeing opportunities are not as common as you'd think. We do get the benefit of discounted flights though.

I always wanted to learn to fly and was fortunate to be accepted onto a pilot sponsorship scheme. Acquiring a commercial pilot's licence is an expensive business. When I was a trainee we had to pay the initial costs of training, although the airline I then worked for allowed us to repay this from our first three years' salary.

I'm due to retire at 55. I'm not sure what I'll do then. I don't think I'll be happy just sitting at home so I'm looking into the possibility of doing some lecturing.

1 Outline what you think are the main advantages and disadvantages of being an airline pilot.

2 Consider whether *anyone* can become an airline pilot. Discuss which groups from the population in general you would say were unlikely to become airline pilots and suggest reasons why they will probably not do so.

3 One recent estimate suggested that fewer than 10% of cadets on commercial airline training courses were female.

What factors do you think have contributed to this low percentage? What could be done to try to increase the number of female recruits?

# Customer service agents

## The role of a customer service agent

Customer service agents are responsible for looking after British Airways customers while they are in the airport terminals. Their main duties include:

- Passenger handling
- Computerized check-in procedures
- Answering flight and general enquiries
- Helping passengers who need particular assistance through control points
- Checking boarding passes prior to embarkation

> Without customer satisfaction, we do not have a business. Service excellence must always be our goal.
>
> Robert Ayling, Chief Executive, British Airways – Company Report 1995-1996

## The qualities needed

This role necessitates meeting new people all the time. A customer service agent has to be able to establish a good rapport with passengers, make people feel well looked after and be diplomatic when the need arises. They have to be able to deal with information, enquiries, complaints and administering embarkation procedures. Some people find the prospect of air travel stressful and so they also have to be able to reassure people.

In order to become a customer service agent for British Airways applicants have to satisfy a number of criteria. They should:

- Be at least 18 years of age
- Have the equivalent of GCSE grade C in English, Maths and Geography
- Have 18 months' experience in a job involving direct contact with the public
- Be smart, willing to wear a uniform and not overweight in proportion to their height
- Speak clearly and be easily understood
- Be physically fit
- Be willing to work shifts

In addition to all these, the ability to speak an additional language is regarded as an advantage.

# Training

Applicants to become customer service agents receive six to eight weeks' initial training. Whether they are full- or part-time candidates they are required to attend a training and induction course on a full-time basis. The training includes classroom teaching and shadowing experienced customer service agents.

## Working conditions and benefits

Customer service agents are employed to work inside airport terminals, so the working environment is frequently busy. The job involves looking after passengers generally and so means carrying out a variety of tasks. These include using computer terminals, making security checks, providing flight information, and organizing flight boarding, arrival and transit arrangements (Figure 15.4).

*Fig. 15.4  Customer service agent at work*

Major airports have to remain open 24 hours a day. There are always some passengers in the terminals who may need the support of the customer service agent. This means that the job necessitates shift work.

British Airways full-time customer service agents work $8\frac{1}{2}$ hour shifts which start at varying times of day. Early shifts start at 5 in the morning and late shifts end shortly after midnight. The job involves working some night shifts. Part-time customer service agents work four, five or six hour shifts. There are various shift starting times throughout the day for part-time workers. For them, early shifts begin at 6 in the morning; late shifts end at 9 at night.

Full-time British Airways customer service agents are entitled to 22 days' holiday a year and they have an option to join the company's contributory pension scheme. They also have access to sports and social facilities, as well as subsidized catering. Airline travel concessions are available after customer service agents have served an agreed qualifying period.

# Air cabin crew

## The role of cabin crew

The main responsibilities of air cabin crew are the safety and comfort of the passengers. The attitude and levels of service offered by air cabin crew are often what passengers remember about a flight and so the role is very important in attracting and keeping customers. The job involves a range of activities, including demonstrating emergency procedures, serving meals and drinks, and selling duty-free goods – ranging from wines and spirits to perfume and jewellery (Figure 15.5).

Though many aspects of the job are routine, the air cabin crew have to be able to deal with the unexpected as well. They may have to provide help for passengers with special needs, such as nervous flyers or parents with very young children. They may have to deal with anti-social behaviour, such as passengers smoking in designated non-smoking areas or people who have over-indulged in alcohol.

*Fig. 15.5  Air cabin crew member at work*

# The qualities needed

Obviously personal qualities are particularly important in fulfilling the roles of air cabin crew successfully. The ideal recruits for this job would be:

- Friendly and caring
- Mature and organized
- Calm and efficient under pressure
- Self-reliant and independent
- Good team workers
- Good communicators with all types of people

## Other requirements

There are some basic requirements that every recruit to BA's air cabin crew has to meet. These cover such things as age, height and place of permanent residence. Though a foreign language qualification is not a compulsory requirement, British Airways does welcome applicants with conversational skills in a second language.

Good health is important in a job that is physically demanding, where space is constricted and where staff have to cope with different climates and time zones. Apart from a general clean bill of health and fitness, airlines will only appoint people to serve as air cabin crew who have good eyesight and who are able and willing to have vaccinations against such diseases as yellow fever, typhoid, hepatitis and polio.

## Selection process

Air cabin crew jobs attract a lot of applicants. British Airways uses a four-stage process in order to recruit air cabin crew. Each stage must be passed successfully and is designed to select the best possible candidates. The stages include written tests to assess aptitude for airline work, group assessments, in-depth interviews, a medical examination, and a language assessment.

## Training

British Airways has developed a study pack that can be used by successful applicants before they start work. Formal training includes group activities, videos, presentations with guest speakers and practical exercises. It covers all aspects of cabin crew duties such as delivering excellent customer service, passenger care, cultural awareness and special needs, safety and emergency procedures, first aid and currency exchange.

## Working conditions and benefits

International airlines operate throughout the 24 hour day, so that air cabin crew have to be willing to work unsocial hours. Uniforms, good hotel accommodation while away from home, and restaurant, sports and social facilities are all provided for BA's air cabin crews. As with other BA employees, once they have completed the required qualifying period, air cabin crew become eligible for reduced rate air travel.

## Activities

You are in charge of organizing the preparation of a study pack for air cabin crew to read prior to commencing their initial training.

1 Outline the main topics that you think the pack should cover.

2 How long before starting work do you think recruits should have the pack?

3 What methods of learning would you recommend to enable recruits to be well prepared when they actually begin work?

# Telephone sales staff

## The role of telephone sales staff

BA's telephone sales staff may have to answer up to 100 calls every day (Figure 15.6). Every call is different. They may involve:

- Selling airline flights
- Booking hotel accommodation
- Arranging car hire
- Quoting information about air fares

Sales staff are office-based and are organized into small work teams. They are set monthly sales targets and it is their responsibility to try to achieve these.

*Fig. 15.6  Telephone sales staff at work*

## The qualities needed

Confidence, a friendly telephone manner, good product knowledge and profession-alism are essential. All new British Airways sales agents attend a four week induction course. The course teaches:

- Effective telephone selling techniques
- Knowledge of British Airways products
- Airline geography
- Fares and ticketing
- How to use the British Airways business system

New recruits also learn about providing the high levels of customer service that British Airways expects its employees to deliver. During this induction course the performance of each potential employee is assessed continually and they qualify as a telephone sales agent only after passing the final assessment.

Good communication skills are essential in this job. Sales agents have to be alert to what customers want and good at persuading them of the value of the company's products.

## Working conditions

British Airways telephone sales staff are all based in offices in Manchester, Newcastle upon Tyne and Glasgow. Sales staff are available at weekends and during the evenings and flexible working hours are a necessary part of the job. The role obviously requires a lot of talking and the ability to maintain concentration over long periods of sitting at a desk.

## Activities

1 Photocopy the two grids on pages 265 and 266. Then complete them by writing a mark of 1, 2 or 3 in each space:

1 indicates the skill or personal quality is not vitally important for the role;

2 indicates the skill or personal quality is fairly important for the role;

3 indicates the skill or personal quality is extremely important for the role.

| Skills | Pilot | Customer service agent | Air cabin crew | Telephone sales staff |
|---|---|---|---|---|
| Verbal communication | | | | |
| Verbal presentation | | | | |
| Another European language | | | | |
| Driving licence | | | | |
| Report-writing ability | | | | |
| Computer literate | | | | |
| Fast, accurate typing skills | | | | |
| Numeracy | | | | |
| Telephone skills | | | | |
| Geographical awareness | | | | |
| Investigative skills | | | | |
| Interpersonal skills | | | | |
| Good clear English | | | | |
| Listening skills | | | | |

2 Compare your own estimates of the importance of different skills and qualities with the rest of your group and try to reach agreement on a single version of the two tables.

3 Assess the extent to which you think you possess each of these skills and qualities:

1 indicates not at all;

2 indicates to some extent;

3 indicates you think these are personal strengths.

4 What does your assessment of your own skills and qualities suggest about the kind of employment that would most suit you?

| Personal qualities | Pilot | Customer service agent | Air cabin crew | Telephone sales staff |
|---|---|---|---|---|
| Ability to work under pressure | | | | |
| Ability to manage stressful situations | | | | |
| Ability to make quick decisions | | | | |
| Self-motivated | | | | |
| Business-like appearance | | | | |
| Sense of humour | | | | |
| Warm manner | | | | |
| Attention to detail | | | | |
| Enthusiasm | | | | |
| Common sense | | | | |
| Ability to work as a team | | | | |
| Responsible attitude | | | | |
| Logical and enquiring mind | | | | |
| Ability to work to deadlines | | | | |
| Commitment and perseverance | | | | |
| Empathy | | | | |

# Case study 16 Chessington World of Adventures – working at a major tourist attraction

## Company aims and objectives

What do Madame Tussaud's, Warwick Castle, Rock Circus, the London Planetarium, Alton Towers and Chessington World of Adventures have in common? They are, of course, all tourist attractions, but they are also part of the same business organization. They belong to the Tussauds Group, which is in turn owned by a parent company, Pearson plc.

Each individual attraction within the Tussauds Group has its own **mission statement**. The mission of Chessington World of Adventures is to:

> build and maintain a position as the most profitable, highest quality theme park in the South of England – longer term in the UK, with an international reputation.

This suggests that the attraction is aiming to expand. In the short term it intends to improve its regional reputation; in the long term its policy is to look for ways of making itself better known outside the South East of England.

A mission statement is a very general view of what a company hopes to achieve. It is usually supported by a list of more specific, immediate aims. Chessington's policy makers have divided the aims of the attraction into two main areas – **strategy** and **values** – and these are shown in Table 16.1:

### Table 16.1

| | |
|---|---|
| **Strategy – financial** | • Grow profit in real terms |
| | • Achieve a satisfactory cash flow return on investment |
| **Strategy – non-financial** | • Provide daytime family entertainment of a very high quality, offering a unique blend of fun, thrills and excitement |
| | • Develop the potential the park offers for public and private entertainment in the evening |
| **Values – visitors** | • Exceed our visitors' expectations through a standard of excellence in all our operations with the emphasis on value for money and with the underlying reassurance of safety and security |
| **Values – employees** | • Develop and retain capable employees who are themselves committed to achieving our goals |
| | • Provide secure and fairly rewarded employment |
| | • Equip employees with the requisite skills to deliver a first-class service to their customers |
| | • Build on the reputation of being an excellent, equal opportunities employer |

*Table 16.1 Continued*

| Values – community | • Conduct our business affairs properly, honestly and honourably at all times |
| | • Promote a positive and responsible image as a valuable asset to the local community, economically and environmentally |
| | • Care for our animal collection with the emphasis on rare and endangered species |
| | • Participate in the International Breeding Programme and cooperate with other zoological establishments |

# History of Chessington

There has a building on the site of the modern Chessington for more than 600 years. The original mansion was used as an archery school. It became a Royalist stronghold in the Civil War but was captured and burned by Cromwell's forces. It was rebuilt but has been damaged by two major fires since, the last one destroying the east wing of the house in 1984.

The Goddard family opened a zoo on the site in 1931. In those days it provided a popular day trip for families from London. Some of the animals also performed at some times of year in circuses. By the 1970s the popularity of zoos in general was declining. At its peak Chessington Zoo attracted over 800,000 visitors a year but this figure began to fall and it became clear that there was a need for investment to improve the attraction's overall appeal.

The zoo had always included a variety of other types of entertainment, including a circus, a funfair and a miniature railway and this aspect of the attraction drew interest from other organizations involved in the leisure industry. In 1978 the Pearson Group bought Chessington and Madame Tussaud's and began to invest in the development of a major leisure attractions group.

It took six years of planning and £12 million in investment to transform the original attraction into Chessington World of Adventures. Opened by HRH Prince Edward in 1987, the new theme park contained a range of rides, attractions and activities. It included parts of the original zoo, with new enclosures for the animals and an extensive breeding programme.

# The theme park market

By 1993 there were ten theme parks in the UK. The number of people visiting these attractions rose from 5.4 million in 1985 to 10.8 million in 1994. Over the past five years the number of visitors to UK theme parks has increased at an annual rate of about 4%. Figure 16.1 shows the attendance figures at UK theme parks in 1994 and 1995.

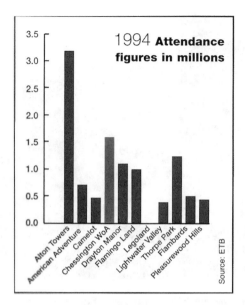
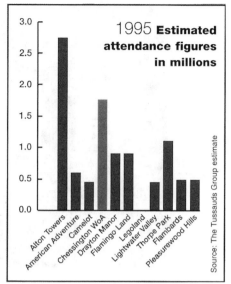

**Fig. 16.1  Attendance figures at UK theme parks**

With its control of Chessington, Alton Towers and Madame Tussaud's the Tussauds group now has some 44% of all the admissions to UK theme parks and somewhere in the region of half the total revenue earned by them.

The increases in visitor numbers also mean that more money is spent at theme parks. Revenue earned at UK theme parks increased from £29 million in 1985 to £130 million in 1994.  So what makes people want to visit theme parks? Research suggests there are five main reasons:

- People are taking more day trips, because they are less expensive and easier to organize than a holiday
- Investment in new and exciting rides makes theme parks a greater attraction than they used to be (Figure 16.2)
- Theme parks have advertised more widely and effectively in the 1990s
- Media coverage of Disney attractions has widened awareness and interest of British consumers in domestic theme parks
- Media coverage of theme parks in general has made them more socially acceptable to all sections of the population

# More visitors means more jobs

Visitor numbers and the amount that they spend are related to the number of employment opportunities in an attraction. A small number of visitors means limited revenue. Fewer staff are required to attend to the needs of visitors and there is less income available to pay employees. There are a number of ways in which theme parks seek to *increase* the number of visitors they receive. These include: investment in new rides, facilities and services; extending opening hours; marketing strategies; improving the service to customers; discounts and promotions. Chessington World of Adventures has employed all of these strategies (Table 16.2).

**Fig. 16.2 Dragon River in the Mystic East and The Vampire Ride in Transylvania**

*Table 16.2*

| | |
|---|---|
| ● **Investment in new rides, facilities and services** | Chessington has invested £11 million in two years, developing Sealion Bay, Terrortomb and Rameses Revenge ride. |
| ● **Extending opening hours** | Chessington runs special Summer Nights in July/August and Fright Nights in October where opening times are extended to 9.30 pm. |
| ● **Marketing strategies** | Advertising and other marketing initiatives have aimed to extend public awareness of the Chessington World of Adventures brand name. |
| ● **Improving the service to customers** | Chessington has conducted research into the expectations and satisfaction levels of visitors with regard to staff, catering, facilities and overall enjoyment. |
| ● **Promotions** | Chessington uses quality, branded promotions to try to fill the park at quieter times and to launch new attractions. |
| ● **Discounts** | These are rarely used at Chessington. More people paying less upsets those who have paid full price. There is a fear that discounts endanger the quality of the visitor experience. |

## Activities

A recent analysis of future trends for theme parks suggested the following were areas where further developments were likely to take place:

(a) working with companies and organizations from all sectors of industry to promote attractions and company products jointly (e.g. special admission offers available on sweet wrappers, launching new products in theme park setting);

(b) making greater use of theme parks as interesting venues for live entertainment, both indoor and outdoor (e.g. concerts, sports events);

(c) building on the secondary spend levels (e.g. catering, merchandising) which currently account for 40% of total theme park revenue;

(d) developing more sophisticated ways of marketing theme parks (e.g. targeted direct mail, using an external sales force).

1 Discuss which of these activities could lead to a possible increase in employment opportunities at a theme park.

2 What factors would have to be taken into consideration before a theme park decided to employ *extra* staff to handle these developments?

3 Choose one of the four developments and list the advantages and disadvantages for the managers of a theme park of hiring a different agency or company to carry out the development work for them.

# Working with people

## Who are the visitors?

Many of the jobs at Chessington involve direct contact with public. One of the first things that employees have to learn is that not every visitor is the same. There are some obvious differences: young and old, male and female, British and overseas visitors. Dividing visitors into these categories does not say very much about how they feel when they arrive and what they are hoping to get out of the visit. Recent research conducted at Chessington identified three different types of adult visitor and three different types of child visitors (Table 16.3).

## How should employees behave towards visitors?

> If you enjoy what you do your visitors will enjoy your company, and you theirs. So have fun and enjoy your work.
> *Source*: Chessington's *Seasonal Staff Handbook*

**Table 16.3**

| Adults | Children |
|---|---|
| ● Child appreciators – these people see children as having lives of their own. They like to see children enjoying themselves. | ● Daredevils – these children are independent and adventurous. They are always seeking to test their own limits. |
| ● Child dependants – these people tend to live their own lives through the experiences of their children. | ● Anxious triers – these children want more freedom to try new and adventurous things but often feel insecure when they have it. |
| ● Adult martyrs – these people want something to occupy their children and are irritated if the children are not satisfied. | ● Clingers – these children are always looking for parental support and guidance and need encouragement to do things on their own. |

All managers of visitor attractions will agree that good customer service is an essential ingredient of a good day out. It is a major factor in establishing the reputation of an attraction, because it makes visitors feel welcome and ensures that their expectations of a fun day out are not spoiled by lack of information or by problems not being quickly resolved.

New employees at Chessington are not simply told to be 'nice' to visitors. They are asked to believe that they are putting on a show for visitors and their performance has to be good enough to convince visitors that they are experiencing something special. Like all performances newcomers need to rehearse exactly what they should do. Chessington's *Seasonal Staff Handbook* provides clear instruction about what is needed from employees who are 'staging the show':

Smile and be friendly and courteous to visitors at all times and make sure you know who to call for assistance or additional information.

Swearing in front of a visitor is not acceptable.

Always say 'please' and 'thank you' when interaction with a visitor takes place, and especially where a monetary transaction has occurred.

Address visitors with 'sir' or 'madam' and ascertain names wherever possible. Once you have a name, use it.

Do not gossip on stage, or talk in groups around the Park. Look out for visitors who may require assistance.

Initiate eye contact with visitors, and welcome them.

Remember that you are 'on stage' and act appropriately. Look out for the safety of yourself and visitors and report spillages or dirty facilities to your supervisor.

Handle complaints with sensitivity and genuine care. Call for assistance or escort the visitor to Visitor Services. Aim to react quickly so that the visitor does not have to repeat the problem more than twice before the problem has been rectified.

## Activities

Suppose Chessington decides to produce a short video to show to its new employees. It is proposed to divide the film into five sections: First Impressions, A Warm Welcome, Talking to People, Special Needs, Team Work.

1 Suggest one scenario for each section of the film showing the behaviour and attitudes expected of new staff at Chessington.

2 Suggest one scenario for each section of the film showing the consequences of not achieving the standards of behaviour and attitudes illustrated in activity 1.

# Employment structure at Chessington

Chessington World of Adventures is only open to the public for seven months of the year. This has an important effect on the attraction's employment structure. Although there may be 1,000 people employed on the site at the height of summer, some 800 of these will be on seasonal contracts. In other words approximately 200 people work at Chessington as permanent employees.

Of the **seasonal workers**, the proportion involved in different activities can be broken down like this:

- 50% work in retail shops or catering outlets
- 20% work as ride attendants
- 10% work on site clearance and maintenance
- 10% work on games and entertainments
- 10% work in other areas such as administration

Seasonal employees tend to come from three main groups: students, mothers whose children are at school, and people who have taken early retirement from their previous employment.

The **permanent workers** are employed in finance and marketing and practical activities to do with maintenance, engineering and information technology (Figure 16.3). The structure of senior management at Chessington World of Adventures provides an overall picture of working roles within the attraction. The Operations Department is the area where the majority of seasonal workers are employed.

# Types of seasonal employment at Chessington

Some 1.77 million people visited Chessington in 1995. The task of looking after them was often the responsibility of seasonal workers. Some would work the whole season; some just during college or university vacations; some with home commitments worked part time.

The main job opportunities were as shown in Figure 16.4 (page 275).

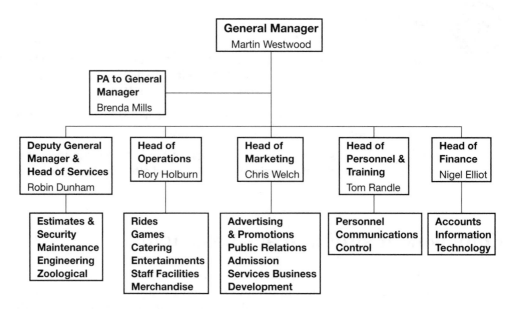

*Fig. 16.3 Chessington staff structure chart*

# Job descriptions for seasonal employees

A job description is a formal document explaining the specific duties and conditions of employment of an employee. Even those who only work for a short spell need a clear idea of what they are expected to do, what hours they will be expected to work, and what the company will provide for them in the way of training, clothing and equipment.

The Estates Department at Chessington World of Adventures employs a number of Seasonal Security Operatives. Below is a job description for this role:

---

**Job title:  Seasonal Security Operative Estates Department**

**Summary**

Chessington World of Adventures is a progressive company competing in the Leisure Industry. The Park itself is approximately 45 hectares, comprised of leisure rides, retail units, circus, zoo and parkland areas. Last year we were visited by over 1.7 million people, making us the number 1 theme park in the South of England. This success has been achieved by the very high standard of professionalism shown by staff employed by the Company. We require, and our customers expect, the highest level of safety and security within the Park. It is the Security Operative's responsibility to maintain a safe and friendly environment for our customers to enjoy.

**Main duties**
- Access control for staff and business visitors
- General park patrols

---

## Gift Shops

Working in one of our many themed gift shops, you could find yourself selling a variety of products from chocolate and candy in The Sweet Shop to fiendishly foul fare in Fangtasia. Duties will include operating tills, shelf filling and light cleaning duties in shops and kiosks.

## Admissions

Working here could involve either operating the tills at the entry gate and providing advice and guidance to our visitors, or working mainly with a PC helping to organise and arrange 'Group' visits for schools, clubs and corporate clients.

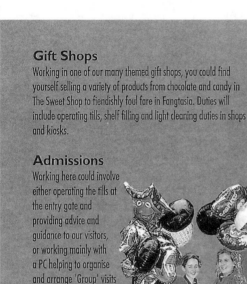

## Catering

With a variety of catering units, it's no surprise that we pride ourselves on the quality and variety of food available in the park. In this large department work could involve serving visitors, operating the tills and clearing tables, to kitchen portering and preparing and cooking meals.

## Games

Manning one of our side shows or working in the Cavalarcade amusement arcade, you will be involved in serving customers, handling cash and ensuring that all visitors enjoy participating in the game of their choice.

## Estates

Work here is essentially concerned with ensuring that the park is at all times clean, tidy and presentable and that all our visitors can be assured of a happy and trouble free day. Site cleaners are therefore required to keep the park and its grounds litter free and security staff are needed to patrol the park and ensure that Company property and visitors are protected. In addition car parking staff are needed to assist in directing the flow of cars and coaches into and out of the park to ensure easy access and exit.

## Rides

Here you will be assisting with the loading and unloading of visitors on our many varied rides from hanging roller coasters to more sedate children's roundabouts. You will ensure that all safety procedures are strictly followed in order that our visitors have a safe and enjoyable ride.

## Laundry

A free laundry service is provided for all uniformed staff and so this department gets very busy during our operating season. From washing to ironing and carrying out minor repairs you will come into contact with all levels of staff.

## Cashiers

To assist with the increase in staff over our operating season, we always require a number of numerate and well organised individuals to work in our Accounts Department. Work involves cash handling and operating a computerised system.

## Visitor Services

Office based, good customer service skills are a must for this position where you will be providing an advisory service to our visitors, both in person and on the telephone, on matters such as general enquiries, lost property, visitor problems etc.

*Fig. 16.4 The main job opportunities at Chessington*

- Cash escorts
- Monitoring and operating CCTV cameras
- Switchboard operating
- Retail security
- Assisting first aid staff when required

**Employment conditions**
- Aged 18 or over
- Ability to work a shift system any time between 7 am and 11 pm. End of shift will depend on park closing times which change throughout the season.
- Willingness to work five days out of seven, including Saturday and Sunday working.
- Readiness to work 8 or 9-hour day, with long-term seasonal staff working 40 to 45 hours per week.
- The Company will allocate two days off in lieu of weekend working for those working five days out of seven.
- Ability to operate a personal radio for which training is provided.
- Ability to patrol the park throughout the day, responding to any incidents that might occur.
- Willingness to wear the uniform provided by the Company and smart black shoes provided by the employee.
- A lunch break of 45 minutes and two 15-minute breaks are given during each full working day.

## Activities

Three candidates have applied for the post of Seasonal Security Operative. Only one vacancy remains in this area but the park is due to open in a few days' time so it is vital that a suitable person is appointed fairly quickly.

Completed application forms for the three applicants are given in Figure 16.5.

1 Divide into groups of three and study the job description for the post carefully.

Draw up a list of skills and personal qualities that you would expect good candidates to possess.

2 Discuss each of the applicants in turn, noting their strengths and weaknesses.

3 Assess each candidate against the list of skills and personal qualities that you drew up in activity 1.

4 As a group try to agree an order of preference for the three candidates, from the one you think would be most suited to the job to the one you think would be least suited.

5 Prepare a brief report explaining what part equal opportunities played in your selection process.

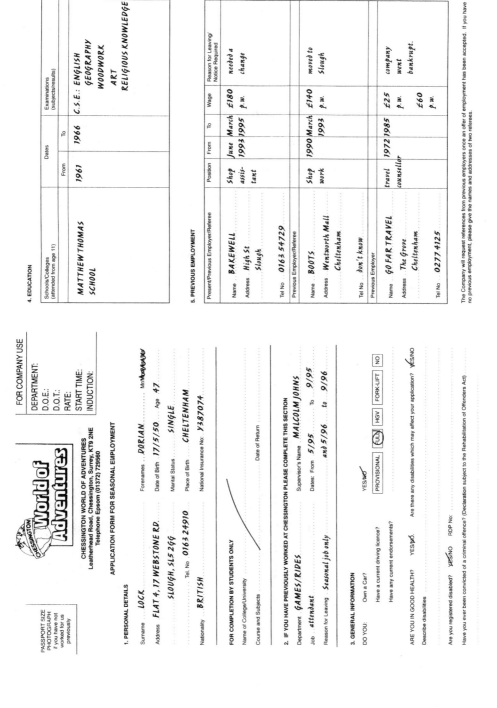

**Fig. 16.5 Completed application forms for three applicants**

CHESSINGTON WORLD OF ADVENTURES

## AVAILABILITY FORM 1997

INVESTOR IN PEOPLE

Name: D LOCK

Dept: ESTATES-SECURITY

Signature: D Lock

| | T | W | Th | F | S | S | M | T | W | Th | F | S | S | M | T | W | Th | F | S | S | M | T | W | Th | F | S | S | M | T | W | Th | F | S | S | M | T | W |
|---|---|---|---|---|---|---|---|---|---|---|---|---|---|---|---|---|---|---|---|---|---|---|---|---|---|---|---|---|---|---|---|---|---|---|---|---|---|
| March | | | | | 1st | 2 | 3 | 4 | 5 | 6 | 7 | 8 | 9 | 10 | 11 | 12 | 13 | 14 | 15 | 16 | 17 | 18 | 19 | 20 | 21 | 22 | 23 | 24 | 25 | 26 | 27 | 28 | 29 | 30 | 31 | | |
| April | 1st | 2 | 3 | 4 | 5 | 6 | 7 | 8 | 9 | 10 | 11 | 12 | 13 | 14 | 15 | 16 | 17 | 18 | 19 | 20 | 21 | 22 | 23 | 24 | 25 | 26 | 27 | 28 | 29 | 30 | | | | | | | |
| May | | 1st | 2 | 3 | 4 | 5 | 6 | 7 | 8 | 9 | 10 | 11 | 12 | 13 | 14 | 15 | 16 | 17 | 18 | 19 | 20 | 21 | 22 | 23 | 24 | 25 | 26 | 27 | 28 | 29 | 30 | 31 | | | | | |
| June | | | | 1st | 2 | 3 | 4 | 5 | 6 | 7 | 8 | 9 | 10 | 11 | 12 | 13 | 14 | 15 | 16 | 17 | 18 | 19 | 20 | 21 | 22 | 23 | 24 | 25 | 26 | 27 | 28 | 29 | 30 | | | | |
| July | 1st | 2 | 3 | 4 | 5 | 6 | 7 | 8 | 9 | 10 | 11 | 12 | 13 | 14 | 15 | 16 | 17 | 18 | 19 | 20 | 21 | 22 | 23 | 24 | 25 | 26 | 27 | 28 | 29 | 30 | 31 | | | | | | |
| August | 1 | 2 | 1st | 3 | 4 | 5 | 6 | 7 | 8 | 9 | 10 | 11 | 12 | 13 | 14 | 15 | 16 | 17 | 18 | 19 | 20 | 21 | 22 | 23 | 24 | 25 | 26 | 27 | 28 | 29 | 30 | 31 | | | | | |
| September | | | | 1st | 2 | 3 | 4 | 5 | 6 | 7 | 8 | 9 | 10 | 11 | 12 | 13 | 14 | 15 | 16 | 17 | 18 | 19 | 20 | 21 | 22 | 23 | 24 | 25 | 26 | 27 | 28 | 29 | 30 | | | | |
| October | 1st | 2 | 3 | 4 | 5 | 6 | 7 | 8 | 9 | 10 | 11 | 12 | 13 | 14 | 15 | 16 | 17 | 18 | 19 | 20 | 21 | 22 | 23 | 24 | 25 | 26 | 27 | 28 | 29 | 30 | 31 | | | | | | |
| November | | | | 1st | 2 | 3 | 4 | 5 | 6 | 7 | 8 | 9 | 10 | 11 | 12 | 13 | 14 | 15 | 16 | 17 | 18 | 19 | 20 | 21 | 22 | 23 | 24 | 25 | 26 | 27 | 28 | 29 | 30 | | | | |

Please tick precise dates when you will be available to work at Chessington World of Adventures - it is important that you understand that you are committed to work the dates you indicate and that this may include working on Sundays, Bank Holidays and Bank Holiday Weekends.

**Please fill in the following measurements as fully as possible to help us with uniform allocation:**

| Height: | 6'0" | Waist: | 34 | Trousers Size: | 30/32 |
|---|---|---|---|---|---|
| Shoe Size: | 9 | Chest: | 38 | Shirt Size: | Medium |
| Dress Size: | | | | | |

**6. PREFERRED DEPARTMENT**

Please indicate, in order of preference 1-9, in which department you would ideally like to work. (A brief description of the work involved is given in the seasonal staff leaflet posted with this form).

| RIDES | | GAMES | |
|---|---|---|---|
| ADMISSIONS | | GIFT SHOPS | |
| CATERING | | ESTATES (i) SITE CLEANING | |
| | | (ii) SECURITY | |
| | | (iii) CAR PARKING | |
| CASHIERS | | LAUNDRY | |
| VISITOR SERVICES | | | |

You will understand that it is not always possible to offer each individual their selected first choice.

**7. PLEASE GIVE DETAILS OF INTERESTS/HOBBIES AND ANY OTHER FURTHER INFORMATION IN SUPPORT OF YOUR APPLICATION**

My main interest is acting. I've appeared in a number of productions in Cheltenham and London. I like working with people. I've worked a lot in retail but I'm interested in doing something different now.

**8. ADDITIONAL PERSONAL DETAILS**

Applicants are requested to tick the relevant boxes below to enable the Company to monitor its equal opportunity policy. Monitoring is recommended by the Codes of Practice for the elimination of racial discrimination and for the elimination of discrimination on the grounds of sex and marital status.
This information is used for no other purpose and will be treated as confidential.

Male ☐    Female ☑

Ethnic Group:

White ☑   Black-Caribbean ☐   Black African ☐   Black other ☐ (please specify)

Indian ☐   Pakistani ☐   Bangladesh ☐   Chinese ☐   Other ☐ (please specify)

I confirm that the information given on this form is, to the best of my knowledge, true and complete. Any false statement may be sufficient cause for rejection or, if employed, dismissal.

Signature: D Lock    Date: 12/4/97

(N.B. Please remember to complete and sign the availability chart overleaf).

**Fig. 16.5**

FOR COMPANY USE
DEPARTMENT:
D.O.E.:
D.O.T.:
RATE:
START TIME:
INDUCTION:

**CHESSINGTON WORLD OF ADVENTURES**
Leatherhead Road, Chessington, Surrey, KT9 2NE
Telephone Epsom (01372) 729560

## APPLICATION FORM FOR SEASONAL EMPLOYMENT

PASSPORT SIZE PHOTOGRAPH if you have not worked for us previously

### 1. PERSONAL DETAILS

Surname ... O'HOULE ......... Forenames ..... SEAN .......... Mr/Mrs/Miss/Ms

Address ... 17 RYLE ST. ..... Date of Birth . 25/2/37 ... Age .60.

CHESSINGTON KT8 4QQ ....... Marital Status ..... MARRIED

Tel. No. 0163 24910 ...... Place of Birth ..... DUBLIN

Nationality ..... BRITISH ...... National Insurance No: XS37416

**FOR COMPLETION BY STUDENTS ONLY**

Name of College/University

Course and Subjects ............ Date of Return

### 2. IF YOU HAVE PREVIOUSLY WORKED AT CHESSINGTON PLEASE COMPLETE THIS SECTION

Department ..................... Supervisor's Name

Job ........... Dates: From ............ To

Reason for Leaving

### 3. GENERAL INFORMATION

DO YOU:     Own a Car?                                          YES/NO

Have a current driving licence?     PROVISIONAL  FULL  HGV  FORK-LIFT  YES/NO

Have any current endorsements?                                 YES/NO

ARE YOU IN GOOD HEALTH?   YES/NO   Are there any disabilities which may affect your application?   YES/NO

Describe disabilities

Are you registered disabled?   YES/NO   RDP No:

Have you ever been convicted of a criminal offence? (Declaration subject to the Rehabilitation of Offenders Act)

### 4. EDUCATION

| Schools/Colleges (attended from age 11) | Dates From | To | Examinations (subjects/results) |
|---|---|---|---|
| St. Josephs RC School | 1943 | 1952 | |

### 5. PREVIOUS EMPLOYMENT

| Present/Previous Employer/Referee | Position | Dates From | To | Wage | Reason for Leaving/ Notice Required |
|---|---|---|---|---|---|
| Name .. HARDWICKS Address Downham Way Epsom Tel No. 0111 3537 | night watchman | 17.4.89 | present | £225 p.w. | factory is closing down |
| Name .. BARTON + LOWNDES Address Dock St Liverpool Tel No N/A | (Ware)house man | Summer 1981 | Sept. 1988 | about £170 p.w. | made redundant |
| Previous Employer Name .. MR K. ROBINS FIELD END FARM Tarporley Cheshire Tel No | farm labourer | 1976 | 1980 | £80 a week | offered job with more money |

The Company will request references from previous employers once an offer of employment has been accepted. If you have no previous employment, please give the names and addresses of two referees.

*Fig. 16.5*

CHESSINGTON WORLD OF ADVENTURES

AVAILABILITY FORM 1997

INVESTOR IN PEOPLE

Name: .. *Sean O'Howe* ...........................

Dept: ..... *Security* ...........................

Signature: ...................

| | T | W | Th | F | S | S | M | T | W | Th | F | S | S | M | T | W | Th | F | S | S | M | T | W | Th | F | S | S | M | T | W | Th | F | S | S | M | T | W |
|---|---|---|---|---|---|---|---|---|---|---|---|---|---|---|---|---|---|---|---|---|---|---|---|---|---|---|---|---|---|---|---|---|---|---|---|---|---|
| March | | | | 1st | 2 | 3 | 4 | 5 | 6 | 7 | 8 | 9 | 10 | 11 | 12 | 13 | 14 | 15 | 16 | 17 | 18 | 19 | 20 | 21 | 22 | 23 | 24 | 25 | 26 | 27 | 28 | 29 | 30 | 31 | | |
| April | 1st | 2 | 3 | 4 | 5 | 6 | 7 | 8 | 9 | 10 | 11 | 12 | 13 | 14 | 15 | 16 | 17 | 18 | 19 | 20 | 21 | 22 | 23 | 24 | 25 | 26 | 27 | 28 | 29 | 30 | | | | | | |
| May | | 1st | 2 | 3 | 4 | 5 | 6 | 7 | 8 | 9 | 10 | 11 | 12 | 13 | 14 | 15 | 16 | 17 | 18 | 19 | 20 | 21 | 22 | 23 | 24 | 25 | 26 | 27 | 28 | 29 | 30 | 31 | | | | |
| June | | | | 1st | 2 | 3 | 4 | 5 | 6 | 7 | 8 | 9 | 10 | 11 | 12 | 13 | 14 | 15 | 16 | 17 | 18 | 19 | 20 | 21 | 22 | 23 | 24 | 25 | 26 | 27 | 28 | 29 | 30 | | | |
| July | 1st | 2 | 3 | 4 | 5 | 6 | 7 | 8 | 9 | 10 | 11 | 12 | 13 | 14 | 15 | 16 | 17 | 18 | 19 | 20 | 21 | 22 | 23 | 24 | 25 | 26 | 27 | 28 | 29 | 30 | 31 | | | | | |
| August | ✓ | ✓ | 1st | 2 | 3 | 4 | 5 | 6 | 7 | 8 | 9 | 10 | 11 | 12 | 13 | 14 | 15 | 16 | 17 | 18 | 19 | 20 | 21 | 22 | 23 | 24 | 25 | 26 | 27 | 28 | 29 | 30 | 31 | | | |
| September | | | | 1st | 2 | 3 | 4 | 5 | 6 | 7 | 8 | 9 | 10 | 11 | 12 | 13 | 14 | 15 | 16 | 17 | 18 | 19 | 20 | 21 | 22 | 23 | 24 | 25 | 26 | 27 | 28 | 29 | 30 | | | |
| October | 1st | 2 | 3 | 4 | 5 | 6 | 7 | 8 | 9 | 10 | 11 | 12 | 13 | 14 | 15 | 16 | 17 | 18 | 19 | 20 | 21 | 22 | 23 | 24 | 25 | 26 | 27 | 28 | 29 | 30 | 31 | | | | | | |
| November | | | | 1st | 2 | 3 | 4 | 5 | 6 | 7 | 8 | 9 | 10 | 11 | 12 | 13 | 14 | 15 | 16 | 17 | 18 | 19 | 20 | 21 | 22 | 23 | 24 | 25 | 26 | 27 | 28 | 29 | 30 | | | |

Please tick precise dates when you will be available to work at Chessington World of Adventures - it is important that you understand that you are committed to work the dates you indicate and that this may include working on Sundays, Bank Holidays and Bank Holiday Weekends.

**Please fill in the following measurements as fully as possible to help us with uniform allocation:**

| Height: | *5 feet 8 ins* | Waist: | *40* | Trousers Size: *28* |
|---|---|---|---|---|
| Shoe Size: | *8* | Chest: | *42* | Shirt Size: *Large* |
| Dress Size: | | | | |

**6. PREFERRED DEPARTMENT**

Please indicate, in order of preference 1-9, in which department you would ideally like to work. (A brief description of the work involved is given in the seasonal staff leaflet posted with this form).

| RIDES | |
|---|---|
| ADMISSIONS | |
| GAMES | |
| GIFT SHOPS | |
| CATERING | |
| ESTATES (i) SITE CLEANING | |
| (ii) SECURITY | ✓ |
| (iii) CAR PARKING | |
| CASHIERS | |
| LAUNDRY | |
| VISITOR SERVICES | |

You will understand that it is not always possible to offer each individual their selected first choice.

**7. PLEASE GIVE DETAILS OF INTERESTS/HOBBIES AND ANY OTHER FURTHER INFORMATION IN SUPPORT OF YOUR APPLICATION**

*Gardening, darts, snooker.*

*I have worked as a night watchman so I have some experience of security*

*work.*

**8. ADDITIONAL PERSONAL DETAILS**

Applicants are requested to tick the relevant boxes below to enable the Company to monitor its equal opportunity policy. Monitoring is recommended by the Codes of Practice for the elimination of racial discrimination and for the elimination of discrimination on the grounds of sex and marital status. This information is used for no other purpose and will be treated as confidential.

Male ✓          Female

Ethnic Group:

White ✓   Black-Caribbean ☐   Black African ☐   Black other ☐   (please specify)

Indian ☐   Pakistani ☐   Bangladesh ☐   Chinese ☐   Other ☐   (please specify)

I confirm that the information given on this form is, to the best of my knowledge, true and complete. Any false statement may be sufficient cause for rejection or, if employed, dismissal.

Signature .................... Date *13/4/96*

(N.B. Please remember to complete and sign the availability chart overleaf).

**Fig. 16.5**

**CHESSINGTON WORLD OF ADVENTURES**
Leatherhead Road, Chessington, Surrey, KT9 2NE
Telephone Epsom (01372) 729560

PASSPORT SIZE PHOTOGRAPH if you have not worked for us previously

## APPLICATION FORM FOR SEASONAL EMPLOYMENT

### 1. PERSONAL DETAILS

Surname ... MISTRY   Forenames ... BINA ... Mr/Mrs/Miss/Ms

Address ... 8 MADELY RD   Date of Birth 8/8/65   Age 32

EALING, LONDON W5   Marital Status ... SINGLE

Place of Birth ... LONDON

Tel. No. 0167 2492

National Insurance No: X297724

Nationality ... BRITISH

### FOR COMPLETION BY STUDENTS ONLY

Name of College/University

Course and Subjects ...   Date of Return

### 2. IF YOU HAVE PREVIOUSLY WORKED AT CHESSINGTON PLEASE COMPLETE THIS SECTION

Department ... CATERING   Supervisor's Name ... MRS WATSON

Job ... WAITRESS   Dates: From 7/87 To 9/87

Reason for Leaving ... STUDENT AT COLLEGE

### 3. GENERAL INFORMATION

DO YOU:   Own a Car? YES/**NO**

Have a current driving licence? PROVISIONAL **FULL** HGV FORK-LIFT NO

Have any current endorsements? NO

ARE YOU IN GOOD HEALTH? **YES**/NO   Are there any disabilities which may affect your application? YES/**NO**

Describe disabilities

Are you registered disabled? YES/**NO**   RDP No:

Have you ever been convicted of a criminal offence? (Declaration subject to the Rehabilitation of Offenders Act) YES/**NO**

### 4. EDUCATION

| Schools/Colleges (attended from age 11) | Dates From | To | Examinations (subjects/results) |
|---|---|---|---|
| Ealing High School | 1976 | 1983 | O level: English B, Maths C, History B, Geog B, RE B; A level English Lit. C, History E |
| Ealing College of FE | 1983 | 1985 | BTEC Nat Dip. Business Studies |

### 5. PREVIOUS EMPLOYMENT

| Present/Previous Employer/Referee | Position | From | To | Wage | Reason for Leaving/Notice Required |
|---|---|---|---|---|---|
| Name London Borough of Ealing  Address Town Hall, London W5  Tel No 0167 28333 | Admin Assistant | 1986 | 1995 | up to £14,000 p.a. | left to travel in India and Far East. |
| Previous Employer/Referee  Name  Address  Tel No | | | | | |
| Previous Employer  Name  Address  Tel No | | | | | |

The Company will request references from previous employers once an offer of employment has been accepted. If you have no previous employment, please give the names and addresses of two referees.

**Fig. 16.5**

CHESSINGTON WORLD OF ADVENTURES

## AVAILABILITY FORM 1997

INVESTOR IN PEOPLE

Name: ..B.Mistry................................

Dept: ......Security................................

Signature: *B.Mistry*

| | T | W | Th | F | S | S | M | T | W | Th | F | S | S | M | T | W | Th | F | S | S | M | T | W | Th | F | S | S | M | T | W | Th | F | S | S | M | T | W |
|---|---|---|---|---|---|---|---|---|---|---|---|---|---|---|---|---|---|---|---|---|---|---|---|---|---|---|---|---|---|---|---|---|---|---|---|---|---|
| March | | | | | 1st | 2 | 3 | 4 | 5 | 6 | 7 | 8 | 9 | 10 | 11 | 12 | 13 | 14 | 15 | 16 | 17 | 18 | 19 | 20 | 21 | 22 | 23 | 24 | 25 | 26 | 27 | 28 | 29 | 30 | 31 | | |
| April | 1st | 2 | 3 | 4 | 5 | 6 | 7 | 8 | 9 | 10 | 11 | 12 | 13 | 14 | 15 | 16 | 17 | 18 | 19 | 20 | 21 | 22 | 23 | 24 | 25 | 26 | 27 | 28 | 29 | 30 | | | | | | | |
| May | | | 1st | 2 | 3 | 4 | 5 | 6 | 7 | 8 | 9 | 10 | 11 | 12 | 13 | 14 | 15 | 16 | 17 | 18 | 19 | 20 | 21 | 22 | 23 | 24 | 25 | 26 | 27 | 28 | 29 | 30 | 31 | | | | |
| June | | | | | | 1st | 2 | 3 | 4 | 5 | 6 | 7 | 8 | 9 | 10 | 11 | 12 | 13 | 14 | 15 | 16 | 17 | 18 | 19 | 20 | 21 | 22 | 23 | 24 | 25 | 26 | 27 | 28 | 29 | 30 | | |
| July | 1st | 2 | 3 | 4 | 5 | 6 | 7 | 8 | 9 | 10 | 11 | 12 | 13 | 14 | 15 | 16 | 17 | 18 | 19 | 20 | 21 | 22 | 23 | 24 | 25 | 26 | 27 | 28 | 29 | 30 | 31 | | | | | | |
| August | | | 1st | 2 | 3 | 4 | 5 | 6 | 7 | 8 | 9 | 10 | 11 | 12 | 13 | 14 | 15 | 16 | 17 | 18 | 19 | 20 | 21 | 22 | 23 | 24 | 25 | 26 | 27 | 28 | 29 | 30 | 31 | | | | |
| September | | | | | | 1st | 2 | 3 | 4 | 5 | 6 | 7 | 8 | 9 | 10 | 11 | 12 | 13 | 14 | 15 | 16 | 17 | 18 | 19 | 20 | 21 | 22 | 23 | 24 | 25 | 26 | 27 | 28 | 29 | 30 | | |
| October | 1st | 2 | 3 | 4 | 5 | 6 | 7 | 8 | 9 | 10 | 11 | 12 | 13 | 14 | 15 | 16 | 17 | 18 | 19 | 20 | 21 | 22 | 23 | 24 | 25 | 26 | 27 | 28 | 29 | 30 | 31 | | | | | | |
| November | | | | 1st | 2 | 3 | 4 | 5 | 6 | 7 | 8 | 9 | 10 | 11 | 12 | 13 | 14 | 15 | 16 | 17 | 18 | 19 | 20 | 21 | 22 | 23 | 24 | 25 | 26 | 27 | 28 | 29 | 30 | | | | |

ALL * dates until end of September

Please tick precise dates when you will be available to work at Chessington World of Adventures - it is important that you understand that you are committed to work the dates you indicate and that this may include working on Sundays, Bank Holidays and Bank Holiday Weekends.

**Please fill in the following measurements as fully as possible to help us with uniform allocation:**

| Height: | 5' 4" | Waist: | | Trousers Size: | |
|---|---|---|---|---|---|
| Shoe Size: | 3 | Chest: | | Shirt Size: | |
| Dress Size: | 12 | | | | |

**6. PREFERRED DEPARTMENT**

Please indicate, in order of preference 1-9, in which department you would ideally like to work. (A brief description of the work involved is given in the seasonal staff leaflet posted with this form).

| RIDES | | GAMES | |
|---|---|---|---|
| ADMISSIONS | | GIFT SHOPS | |
| CATERING | | ESTATES (i) SITE CLEANING | |
| | | (ii) SECURITY | ✓ |
| | | (iii) CAR PARKING | |
| CASHIERS | | LAUNDRY | |
| VISITOR SERVICES | | | |

You will understand that it is not always possible to offer each individual their selected first choice.

**7. PLEASE GIVE DETAILS OF INTERESTS/HOBBIES AND ANY OTHER FURTHER INFORMATION IN SUPPORT OF YOUR APPLICATION**

My main interests are cooking, travel and yoga. Going to India and the Far East as an independent traveller enabled me to meet a lot of people and deal with many sticky situations. I am fit and would like to get some experience of working in tourism prior to applying to a degree course.

**8. ADDITIONAL PERSONAL DETAILS**

Applicants are requested to tick the relevant boxes below to enable the Company to monitor its equal opportunity policy. Monitoring is recommended by the Codes of Practice for the elimination of racial discrimination and for the elimination of discrimination on the grounds of sex and marital status. This information is used for no other purpose and will be treated as confidential.

Male ☐   Female ☐

Ethnic Group:

White ☐   Black-Caribbean ☐   Black African ☐   Black other ☐ (please specify)

Indian ☑   Pakistani ☐   Bangladesh ☐   Chinese ☐   Other ☐ (please specify)

I confirm that the information given on this form is, to the best of my knowledge, true and complete. Any false statement may be sufficient cause for rejection or, if employed, dismissal.

Signature *B.Mistry*   Date 12/4/97

(N.B. Please remember to complete and sign the availability chart overleaf).

**Fig. 16.5**

# Job descriptions for permanent employees

There are approximately 200 people working all year round at Chessington. Because of the high number of seasonal workers who have to be recruited each year, the role of the Personnel Department is particularly important. This department oversees the recruitment of all staff, as well as being responsible for the administration of all records and information relating to employment. The job description below, for a Personnel Administrator, gives an idea of the range of responsibilities involved in this kind of work:

---

**JOB TITLE:** Personnel Administrator

**OVERALL PURPOSE:** to provide timely and effective administrative and secretarial support to the Personnel Department.

**MAIN DUTIES**

1. Recruitment

(i) To type internal vacancy notices and external advertisements and place with appropriate advertising agency/local media.
(ii) To carry out all administration with regard to inviting/rejecting candidates for interview and liaising with line managers concerned to set up interview dates.
(iii) To issue job offers/terms and conditions of employment for both permanent and seasonal members of staff and liaise closely with wages to ensure passage of correct documentation/information.
(iv) To obtain references for all permanent employees (and a percentage of seasonal employees).

2. General
(i) To maintain accurate information on starters and leavers and respond quickly to mortgage, tenancy and reference letters received.
(ii) To administer sickness records for both permanent and seasonal members of staff.
(iii) To produce on a monthly basis the pension documentation to be submitted to Maple House via Accounts.
(iv) To operate the Personnel Computer System to issue standard letters, access information and run ad hoc reports as and when required.
(v) To liaise closely with wages to ensure that salary reviews, secondments and transfers are all actioned and all relevant parties informed.
(vi) Secretarial duties including word processing, typing, filing and dealing with complimentary ticket requests.
(vii) To assist in Communication Control/Reception as and when required.

---

As this job description shows, while the skills required by seasonal workers are mainly concerned with personal qualities, there are areas of work in a tourist attraction that require more specific knowledge. This role particularly requires a good educational background, previous experience and a high level of initiative.

# Working conditions

Working conditions for employees at Chessington will vary depending on which department they are in and whether they are seasonal or permanent staff. The Chessington *Seasonal Staff Handbook* outlines what employees should know about the terms of their employment. The aspects covered include: use of the staff canteen, wages, complimentary tickets, personal finances, costumes and appearance. Some of the key points are as follows

## Use of the staff canteen

Meals are available to staff at cost price. Passes must be shown. All food and drink must be consumed on the premises. Staff are responsible for leaving areas of the canteen they have eaten in clean and tidy.

## Wages

Wages are paid directly into staff bank accounts. Payment is one week in arrears. Students working only in holidays do not have to pay income tax. Supervisors will deal with any queries over wages. Anyone working the full season will receive a 2.5% bonus.

## Complimentary tickets

Ten complimentary tickets for attractions in the Tussauds Group are available to staff who have worked four weeks or more. They cannot be used on event days or during August.

## Costumes

Trousers or skirts are provided as uniform items. Shirts and blouses should be tucked inside trousers or skirts and sleeves should not be rolled up. Socks, stockings and shoes should be black or near black, clean, in a good state of repair and sensible in style. Staff name badges must be worn at all times.

## Appearance

Hair should be neat and clean. Outlandish hair styles or colours are not acceptable. Long hair must be tied back.

Jewellery should be limited to engagement and wedding rings, plain watches, and, for female staff, single, discreet stud earrings.

Female staff may use moderate, subtle make-up but not nail varnish. Nails should be clean and short.

Sunglasses may only be worn in bright sunlight. They must be removed when speaking to visitors. Mirrored sunglasses are not permitted.

No visible tattoos are permitted.

Personal belongings such as coats, bags and cigarette packets may not be taken into any of the areas used by visitors.

## Activities

Chessington is involved with many international breeding and conservation programmes. The experience gained from these is put to good use during school visits. Chessington Education Service provides talks on many subjects, including:

- Birds – flight, beaks, claws, habitat, feeding, species

- Cats – different species, habitats, feeding, endangered species

- Camouflage – slides illustrating camouflage developed by living creatures

- Movement – slides showing development of bird and animal movement

- Primates – how they move, different species, habitat, endangered species (Figure 16.6)

- Reptiles – how they move, habitat, feeding, different types

- Ungulates – hoofed animals, different species, habitat, food

1 List the skills and qualities you would look for in recruiting a member of staff to join Chessington's Education Service with the main responsibility of planning and delivering talks and presentations to school and other visiting groups.

2 Discuss the level of qualifications you would expect applicants for this position to have and explain why you think this level would be appropriate.

3 What kind of previous experience would you regard as an advantage in selecting candidates to be interviewed for this post?

*Fig. 16.6 Breeding programme –
gorilla and baby at Chessington*

4 If the responsibilities of the person appointed were also to include working with animals, suggest some additional aspects of their working conditions that would need to be set out and agreed before they commenced work.

# Glossary

**attractions** – the elements of a destination which encourage people to choose to visit it, e.g beaches, views, historic buildings, entertainment facilities, festivals, events etc.

**brand** – a name or trade mark used to make a particular product easy for potential purchaser to identify.

**Computer reservations system (CRS)** – a means of using computer links to read information about and make bookings of holidays, accommodation, vehicle hire and entertainments.

**conservation** – protecting from damage and managing buildings, artefacts and landscape in such a way that they can be enjoyed by future generations.

**culture** – all the things learned and attitudes shared by a distinctive group of people e.g. language, religion, art, values, sense of humour etc.

**customer service** – all elements of a company's business which relate to the way in which they meet the needs of all their customers e.g. efficiency, price, communications, handling complaints.

**database** – computer software enabling extensive records of information about, for example, a company's clients to be stored and retrieved.

**demonstration effect** – imitation of the behaviour and customs of others, especially the tendency of host communities to copy dress and consumption patterns of tourists.

**diversification** – the practice of broadening a range of products or services which a business depends on, or of introducing products into new markets.

**desktop publishing** – using computer software packages to design documents such as flyers, brochures and newsletters.

**facility** – something specially arranged or constructed in order to provide either recreation or a service e.g. a restaurant.

**job description** – a statement describing the responsibilities, duties and standards expected from the holder of a specific post.

**local authority** – bodies responsible for local government decisions e.g. county, borough, district and parish councils.

**marketing** – the process of finding out what customers want and then developing, promoting and distributing goods and services to them which meet their needs.

**mission statement** – a brief description of a company's present position and future objectives, intended to create a united purpose among employees.

**multiplier effect** – the principle that expenditure on one economic activity, such as tourism, has an effect on the turnover of other businesses in the same location.

**occupancy rates** – a means of measuring how successfully hotels are performing by calculating the percentage of rooms occupied and whether each of these is a single or double occupancy

**park and ride schemes** – schemes encouraging visitors to park on the outskirts of cities and continue their journeys into the centre by bus services aimed at reducing traffic congestion

**person specification** – a description of the skills and qualities expected in the ideal candidate for a specific job role

**preservation** – maintaining items such as buildings and artefacts in their present form

**promotion** – methods and techniques used to advertise and sell goods and services e.g. advertising, discounts, trade exhibitions, brochures, promotional events.

**sampling** – methods of collecting information from a selected group in order to make predictions about the behaviour and habits of the population in general.

**secondary spend** – money spent by visitors on items other than admission to a facility or attraction e.g. on food or on souvenirs.

**service** – actions provided on a commercial basis which meet someone else's needs e.g. home delivery pizzas.

**spreadsheet** – computer software used to store, calculate and display financial accounts and information.

**Tourist Information Centre (TIC)** – an office providing tourists with information about local attractions, facilities, services and accommodation.

# Index